BARRON'S BUSINESS LIBRARY

Financial and Business Statements

George T. Friedlob
Clemson University

Franklin J. Plewa, Jr.
Idaho State University

New York • London • Toronto • Sydney

All inquiries should be addressed to:
Barron's Educational Series, Inc.
250 Wireless Boulevard
Hauppauge, NY 11788

Library of Congress Catalog Card Number 90–27730

International Standard Book Number 0-8120-4183-6

Library of Congress Cataloging-in-Publication Data

Friedlob, G. Thomas.
    Financial and business statements / George T. Friedlob, Franklin J.
Plewa, Jr.
      p.   cm. – (Barron's business library)
    Includes index.
    ISBN 0-8120-4183-6
    1. Financial statements.   I. Plewa, Franklin James.   II. Series.
HF5681. B2F7725   1991
657'.3–dc20   90-27730
                                           CIP

PRINTED IN ITALY

1234   9929   987654321

Contents

Introduction to Reports and Basic Accounting

INTRODUCTION AND MAIN POINTS

Almost all measures of business activity involve numbers and are presented in accounting reports. Dollars earned last quarter, labor variances at a new plant, production scheduled for next month—all sorts of reports are prepared and presented to managers, owners, regulatory agencies, and other interested parties on a regular basis. Other reports, such as those analyzing capital acquisitions or reporting the results of special management studies, are prepared on an as-needed basis. Regularly prepared reports help the reader make routine decisions; they might be consulted by stockholders considering whether to buy or sell stock, managers adjusting production techniques, and purchasing agents ordering raw materials, for instance. Other reports provide information for nonroutine decisions, helping managers select a merger candidate or react to a change in market conditions, for example.

After studying the material in this chapter:

▬ You will appreciate the many forms accounting reports can take.

▬ You will realize that all accounting reports are created for a particular end use and that understanding that use can help you begin to understand the report.

▬ You will understand the basic mechanics of the double-entry system of accounting.

▬ You will understand the principles that underlie all accounting reports.

HOW THIS BOOK IS ARRANGED

Learning to understand accounting reports is a formidable objective. Accountants produce reports for many different end uses; some reports go to stockholders, creditors, and others outside the company, while others are targeted for managers and employees inside. The Securities and Exchange Commission

(SEC), the Financial Accounting Standards Board, and various committees of the American Institute of Certified Public Accountants have promulgated volumes of formal principles, standards, and rules to organize and regiment reporting to individuals outside the company. Reporting inside the company is less structured but is often confusing to the uninitiated.

Regardless of their appearance, accountants' reports are created to meet an objective and to satisfy a need. If you understand the objective and know what is necessary to satisfy the need, you can learn to understand the report. This book contains nineteen chapters, each of which offers a practical guide to understanding some aspect of a particular report and is designed to be read either straight through or in random order. If you are puzzled, for example, over the significance of earnings per share, you can consult the chapter on earnings and read the section that discusses that topic. Similarly, if you do not understand the mechanics of budgeting or performance reporting, you can turn directly to those particular chapters for help.

Financial and Business Statements is divided into seven sections, each focusing on one type of report—the annual report, other public reports, financial-statement analysis, budgeted reports, performance reports, government reports, and inflation-adjusted reports.

Section One introduces the reader to the contents of an annual report; each of its seven chapters covers one component of a typical statement. Management's presentation, financial statements, notes, supplementary schedules—all are discussed in practical, down-to-earth language so you can begin to understand and interpret published annual reports. Section Two covers other public reports, including quarterly reports, compilations and reviews, and filings with the SEC. Section Three consists of two chapters on financial-statement analysis. These chapters contain the ratios, techniques, and tips needed to analyze and understand the content of the reports discussed in the first twelve chapters.

Section Four covers budgeted reports, including standard costs and variances for control, and the business plans required by many bankers. The use of budgets (and other tools) for performance appraisal and the reports of company internal auditors are discussed in Section Five. The material in these two sections should arm you with the basics necessary for understanding the ways accounting reports are used to evaluate and control performance. Whether you are an employee evaluated by a system of accounting reports or a manager using reports to assess and control the behavior of others, a knowledge of the process and games involved is invaluable.

Finally, there are sections on government reports and inflation-adjusted reports. The discussion of government reports includes governmental budgets and encumbrances (quite different from profit-oriented budgeting), funds, and the comprehensive annual financial report. The section on inflation-adjusted reports covers company and personal financial statements, including a how-to discussion on preparing the type of personal financial statement required by lenders.

ACCOUNTING STRUCTURE AND PRINCIPLES

In order to understand many accounting reports, you must have at least a rudimentary understanding of basic accounting. This is particularly true for understanding annual reports or budget schedules that culminate in forecasted statements. The accounting you will need is not that difficult. We will introduce you first to the basic structure of accounting and then to the accounting principles that govern annual reports, the subject of the next seven chapters.

The Basic Structure of Accounting

Accounting is based on a simple relationship that explains both the different types of accounts and the way events are recorded and that can be understood by thinking of a business or government entity in terms of resources and sources.

All the economic resources that a company owns came from somewhere—their source. The dollar amount of resources must equal the dollar amount of sources. The basic accounting relationship (called the accounting equation) can be stated as:

$$\text{Resources Owned} = \text{Sources of the Resources}$$

The accounting term for the resources owned by the company is *assets*. The two sources of a company's assets are borrowing (debt) and owner investment. The dollar amount of assets must equal the dollar amount of debts and owners' investment.

$$\text{Assets} = \text{Debts} + \text{Owners' Investment}$$

The accounting term for debts is *liabilities;* another name for owners' investment is *owners' equity*. Owners' equity includes both the owners' initial investment and reinvestment of company earnings not distributed to owners. In its final form, the *accounting equation*, sometimes called the *balance-sheet equation*, is as follows:

$$\text{Assets} = \text{Liabilities} + \text{Owners' Equity}$$

Understanding the balance-sheet equation is fundamental to understanding accounting. The construction of the balance sheet provides a system of checks on the accuracy of the accounting system. This system of checks is called the *double-entry system,* so called because each economic event must affect the balance-sheet equation in two ways in order to keep the equation in balance. For instance, if a company is formed by an investment in stock of $5,000, two components of the equation must be increased to show the effect of this transaction: assets (cash) and owners' equity (owners' investment). If either assets or owners' equity is not increased, the equation will not balance.

$$
\begin{array}{lcl}
\text{Assets} & = & \text{Liabilities} + \text{Owners' Equity} \\
+\$5,000 & = & 0 \qquad\qquad + \$5,000
\end{array}
$$

If the company then borrows another $15,000, two more effects must be recorded: Assets are increased by the cash received, and the property rights of the bank are recorded.

	Assets	=	Liabilities	+	Owners' Equity
	+$5,000	=	0	+	$5,000
	+15,000	=	+15,000	+	0
Total	$20,000	=	$15,000	+	$5,000

If the company buys a building for $4,000, the asset "cash" must be decreased and the asset "building" increased. In this example, one asset is traded for another of equal value, and the equation still balances. When a loan is repaid, cash (an asset) is decreased and a liability is decreased. When one account is increased, another must be decreased to keep the equation in balance.

Revenues are increases in owners' equity produced by inflows of assets as a result of doing business. As cash or accounts receivable increase, owners' equity also increases. *Expenses* are decreases in owners' equity produced by outflows of assets (or inflows of liabilities) from doing business. Expenses result when the company consumes the benefit of its assets. The assets are decreased, and the owners' equity is also decreased.

Revenues and expenses, like assets, liabilities, and owners' equity, are types of accounts. The accounting equation, expanded to include revenues and expenses, is as follows:

$$\text{Assets} = \text{Liabilities} + \text{Owners' Equity} + \text{Revenues} - \text{Expenses}$$

This equation contains all the types of accounts that accountants use; there are no others.

Basic Accounting Principles

Basic accounting principles are the rules and assumptions that underlie financial reporting in published annual reports, quarterly reports, and reports to the SEC. The same principles also guide accountants in the preparation of budgets and other reports for use inside the organization. These principles tell accountants what items to measure and when and how to measure them. Basic accounting principles include:

1. the accounting entity
2. measurement of resources and obligations
3. periodicity
4. going concern
5. historical cost and unit of measure
6. accrual accounting
7. substance versus form
8. conservatism
9. materiality

Each of these concepts is defined and discussed in the remaining sections of this chapter.

Accounting Entity. The *accounting entity* is the business unit for which financial statements are being prepared. Legal form does not determine the accounting entity. For example, only corporations and trusts are granted legal existence separate from their owners; a proprietor's business is legally an extension of his personal affairs. Accountants do, however, account for the personal affairs of the proprietor as separate from the business affairs of the proprietorship. Unless the proprietorship affairs are accounted for separately, it is not possible to determine if the business activity has been profitable. An accounting entity may also be composed of a parent company and its majority-owned subsidiaries—legally separate entities but in substance a single economic entity.

Measurement of Resources and Obligations. *Business resources* (assets) are those items of value that the business possesses and can use to produce a profit. *Obligations (liabilities) are amounts owed to nonowners of the business. The difference between assets and liabilities is the owners' interest (equity)* in the business, including personal investment *(contributed capital)* plus any profits earned by the business and not paid out to the owners *(retained earnings).* A set of financial statements contains measures of assets, liabilities, and owners' equity at the end of the fiscal period (in the balance sheet), as well as changes that have occurred in assets, liabilities, and owners' equity during the period (in the income statement, statement of retained earnings, and statement of cash flows).

Periodicity. *Periodicity* is the assumption that a company's life must be divided into periods of time in order to measure profit or loss. Ultimately, profitability can be determined only by comparing the owners' interest at the time the business began to interest at the time of dissolution. However, viewing profit or loss at the end of the business's life does not provide timely information for management, investment, and credit decisions. Therefore, accountants divide a company's life into fiscal periods—for example, a year (fiscal year) or a quarter (fiscal quarter).

Going Concern. A measurement concept, the principle of *going concern* assumes that, in the absence of contrary evidence, the company will continue to operate indefinitely. From a valuation standpoint, this allows for carryover of previous values placed on assets, liabilities, and owners' equity. It also requires that measurement techniques be consistent from one fiscal period to another.

Historical Cost and Unit of Measure. Assets and liabilities are recorded in the accounting records at their original or *historical cost.* For example, if we purchase land for $1 million with a $1 million mortgage, the asset land is entered at $1 million and the liability mortgage note payable is also entered at $1 million. These values continue in the accounting records until another business event indicates the need for changing them. Examples of such events are the sale of assets, payment of liabilities, and the ability to repurchase an asset at less than its historical cost.

The *unit of measure* employed in financial statements of U.S.-based entities is the *nominal dollar,* or the dollar arising from the exchange transaction unadjusted for inflation or deflation. As a result, one company may have land acquired in 1930 recorded on its books at $100,000 while another company has a similar piece of property, acquired in 1988, recorded on its books at $1 million.

Accrual Accounting. The *accrual principle* attempts to translate into dollars of profit or loss the actual activities of the fiscal period. It combines two ideas—revenue recognition and matching.

The *revenue-recognition* principle requires that revenue (sales price) be recorded when the necessary activities to sell a good or provide a service have been completed. Revenue is recorded at the point of sale regardless of whether cash is collected or a receivable from the customer is created at that time.

The *matching* principle tells the accountant when to record a production cost as expense. It has three parts: cause and effect, systematic and rational allocation, and immediate recognition.

Cause and effect means that the costs directly associated with producing a certain revenue are expensed in the same period that the revenue is recorded. Sales commissions are an example of cause and effect; there is a direct association between the sale and the effort of the salesperson that can be measured by the salesperson's salary and commission.

Systematic and rational allocation is used for other costs—those for plant and equipment, for example—that are long-lived and that help produce revenue for several accounting periods. While there is not a direct causal link between plant occupancy and the sale of a unit of product, occupancy benefits the company for more than one fiscal period. The accountant expenses the cost of these types of assets over their expected lives. If a piece of equipment is expected to be used for ten years (the activity measure), its historical cost should be expensed as a cost of revenue production over that same period (i.e., depreciation).

Other costs that are not long-lived and do not have a causal relationship to revenue are recognized immediately—that is, when they arise. Management salaries are an example of this type of cost. It cannot be said that the company president's salary directly produces sales or that the cost of his or her services is long-lived; a president who is not paid stops working. Therefore, the cost is an expense in the period in which it arises.

Under the matching principle, an expense can be recorded before, after, or at the time a cost is actually paid. From the accountant's point of view, it is the earnings activity that gives rise to the conversion of cost to expense. It does not matter whether that cost has been paid or a liability created.

Substance Versus Form. The accountant attempts to report the economic *substance* of the transaction without regard to its *form*. Although a business pledge to a charity is not a binding obligation upon a company, an accountant still records it as a liability. The company has made a promise; it cannot avoid honoring that promise without damaging its reputation. Therefore, the company is likely to pay the pledge.

Another example of substance versus form is the capital lease, a long-term lease that transfers the basic rights of ownership and that is treated as an alternative way to purchase an asset. The business that leases the asset records an asset and a liability, just as it would have if it had financed the purchase of the asset by borrowing on a long-term note from a bank.

Conservatism. *Conservatism*, a downward measurement bias, means preferring undervaluation to overvaluation, understatement of income to overstatement of income. The accounting practice of conservatism favors valuing assets at their historical cost even though the asset, such as land, may have increased in value each year since its acquisition. Conservatism favors recording losses even before they actually occur if they are considered likely to occur; however, the recording of a gain is postponed until the gain actually occurs even when the gain is considered likely to occur.

Materiality. *Materiality* refers to relative importance of accounting information to the user of the financial statements. A transaction must be accounted for within the measurement and reporting principles known as Generally Accepted Accounting Principles (GAAP) when the amounts involved are judged to be material.

Materiality of a transaction must be determined by its effect on the financial statement. When pooled in the financial statement, similar transactions, each involving immaterial amounts, may together have a material effect. For instance, a single purchase of a microcomputer costing $1,500 may not be material; readers of the financial statement may not care if it is expensed or recorded as an asset. But what about 500 microcomputers, purchased at different times during the year? It would be misleading to treat this $750,000 purchase of office equipment as expense in the year of purchase, because the computers have a useful life of more than one year and will benefit the company over their useful life. The combined amount of the purchases is material.

CHAPTER PERSPECTIVE

In this chapter, we have discussed the forms accounting reports can take—routine and nonroutine, and the various audiences for which they are prepared—among them stockholders, managers, and government agencies. There is a purpose for each report; understanding that purpose is essential to beginning to understand the report.

Accountants use a double-entry system to record events in the accounting system according to the nine basic principles underlying all accounting reports: the accounting entity, measurement of resources and obligations, periodicity, going concern, historical cost and unit of measurement, accrual accounting, substance versus form, conservatism, and materiality.

The next section of this book focuses on annual reports; the sections that follow discuss other types of reports.

Management's Presentation, Statement Notes, and the Audit Opinion

INTRODUCTION AND MAIN POINTS

A company's annual report is produced only in part by accountants; only the financial statements included as part of the annual report are wholly the numbers and schedules one expects accountants to produce. Much of an annual report is produced by the company's nonaccounting managers and discusses a variety of topics, some based on accounting figures, some not. (A second group of accountants, the company's independent external auditors, evaluates the financial information provided in the annual report and provides an expert opinion on its accuracy and completeness; this opinion is an important part of the report.)

This chapter focuses on the contents of the annual report; later chapters cover the accounting requirements of the financial statements.

After studying the material in this chapter:

■ You will understand the purpose of an annual report.

■ You will know the sources of the accounting principles governing financial reporting.

■ You will know which components of the annual report are produced by management and which are produced by accountants.

■ You will realize the importance of the notes to the financial statements.

■ You will understand the importance of the auditor's opinion and the types of opinions auditors can render.

■ You will be familiar with the structure of consolidated financial statements, the form of financial statements used by most companies.

THE ANNUAL REPORT

An annual report is designed to satisfy the information requirements of many different people with many different needs. Stockholders, creditors, economists, financial analysts, suppliers, and customers all look to annual reports to satisfy their information needs. Because they must satisfy such a diverse audience, annual reports are rigidly structured by both convention and legal requirements.

The heart of an annual report is the financial statement, which must conform to accounting and reporting standards established by the Financial Accounting Standards Board (FASB), the Securities and Exchange Commission (SEC), and various committees of the American Institute of Certified Public Accountants (AICPA). The requirements of these different groups are a mixed blessing. Because financial statements are very structured, they are not tailored to meet the needs of any one group precisely, and each group of users may find something lacking. But because of the high degree of structure and the involvement of the CPA, users of financial statements can be sure that the information they receive adheres to the principle of fair presentation; they can review the financial statement of a company in New York or California and decide to buy stock, lend money, or in some other way become involved with the company, solely on the basis of its audited financial statements.

REPORT HIGHLIGHTS, LETTER TO SHAREHOLDERS, AND REVIEW OF OPERATIONS

Management's part of the annual report usually consists of three sections: the annual report highlights, the letter to shareholders, and the review of operations.

1. *Annual Report Highlights.* The highlights section focuses on the bright spots in the company's operations, financial statements, stock performance, or whatever management wishes to present. Frequently, graphs or tables that display the favorable trends management wishes to emphasize are included. This section also contains the company's sales, profits, and earnings per share for several years.

2. *Letter to Shareholders.* The letter to shareholders commonly begins with a statement such as "I am pleased to report . . ." and is signed by the president alone or with the chairman of the board. The key to understanding the letter to shareholders is to ask "What do I expect them to say?" and "What did they really say?" The answer to the first question is usually obvious: The letter will contain a predictably self-congratulatory, optimistic message. But the second question is harder to answer. Vague wording, colorful adjectives, and mean-

ingless euphemisms are commonplace, and messages may be obscure.

3. *Review of Operations.* The review of operations, a public relations presentation, usually consumes the largest part of the annual report and is designed to impress the reader. The company may dwell on its products or its many locations in beautiful settings—whatever management and the public relations department decide is effective. Most of the photographs and artwork are in this section. You may enjoy it—but interpret it with caution!

THE NOTES TO THE STATEMENTS

Financial statements provide the substance of the annual report. At a minimum, they consist of a balance sheet, income statement, statement of cash flows, and the accompanying notes and auditor's opinion. The notes to the financial statements are as important, if not more important, than the statements themselves. Many times, numbers by themselves do not adequately express material information (that which would make a difference to a financial statement user; see Chapter 1); notes to the financial statements are largely descriptive and include information on such things as accounting methods, commitments, lease obligations, contingencies, and significant events affecting the company between the end of the fiscal year and the issuance of the annual report. Note disclosures relating to the following areas are discussed in this chapter:

1. Accounting methods
2. Commitments
3. Leases
4. Contingencies
5. Pensions

1. *Accounting Methods.* Accountants use many methods to summarize business transactions in financial statements. In many instances, several acceptable methods of reporting a transaction have evolved and are in current use. Because different methods exist for recording the same transaction, accountants have had a hard time standardizing financial reporting.

Accounting principles require that if a company has a choice of valuation methods, it must disclose the method used; traditionally, this is done in Note One. For example, different accounting methods exist for valuing inventories and computing depreciation. Acceptable inventory methods include specific identification, FIFO, LIFO, average cost, and lower of cost or market. Acceptable depreciation methods include straight-line, units of production, sum of the years' digits, and double declining balance. Note One specifies which inventory and depreciation methods have been used by a particular company.

Note One is important because the choice of accounting methods directly affects balance-sheet valuation and the computation of net income. For example, some methods of depreciation allow higher expense deductions than do other methods. Depending on the method of depreciation that is selected, net income will vary, as will the value carried in the balance sheet.

Financial statements of a company are not directly comparable from year to year unless the company consistently uses the same valuation methods. Companies are required to disclose a change in accounting methods (Chapter 9 discusses disclosures relating to a company's change in accounting principle). Similarly, direct comparison of financial statements of two different companies is not possible unless they are based on the same accounting methods. Note One is very important because it tells us the methods used by the company to prepare its financial 9tatements and therefore whether two reports are or are not comparable.

Figure 2-1 is an example of the disclosure of accounting methods in a typical Note One.

2. *Note Disclosure of Commitments.* A commitment is a contractual agreement to do something. Some of the more common types of commitments disclosed in financial statements involve long-term purchase arrangements, the terms of outstanding loans, agreements to refinance existing debt, lines of credit, lease arrangements, and employee pension plans (discussed later in this chapter). You should pay close attention to these arrangements. Many commitments affect the company in the future by adding to its debt structure and increasing the amount of cash necessary to meet current obligations.

Different types of commitments are entered into by a company. Some commitments directly affect the balance sheet at the time they occur. For example, borrowing $1 million increases assets by $1 million and liabilities by $1 million. Commitments that are unexecuted affect the company's future operations and may not be recorded on the balance sheet. An example is a commitment to purchase 5 million parts from a supplier over the next five years. Regardless of whether accounting principles require the commitment to be recorded on the balance sheet, the principle of materiality requires that the details of significant

Notes to Consolidated Financial Statements

Note 1—Summary of Significant Accounting Policies:
Principles of Consolidation: The consolidated financial statements include the accounts of all significant wholly owned and majority-owned subsidiaries. Intercompany transactions and balances have been eliminated. Investments in partially-owned equity companies are accounted for under the equity method.
Inventories: Inventories are generally stated at cost which is not in excess of market. Domestic manufactured inventories of standard products are valued on the last-in, first-out (LIFO) method and all other inventories are valued using the first-in, first-out (FIFO) method.
Property and Depreciation: The company principally uses accelerated depreciation methods for both tax and financial reporting.

FIG. 2-1 *A Note One fragment showing the disclosure of accounting principles.*

commitments be disclosed in the notes to the financial statements.

3. *Notes Relating to Leases.* Leases are a type of commitment. Some noncancellable long-term leasing arrangements, known as capital leases, are viewed as alternative purchase and mortgage arrangements and transfer the risks of ownership to the lessee (the party leasing the asset). Capital leases are essentially purchases of capital assets. A typical note disclosure of lease commitments is shown in Figure 2-2.

The lessee of a capital lease records an asset "Property Subject to Capital Leases" and a liability "Obligations Under Capital Leases." The amount recorded as the "historical cost" of the leased asset is treated as if it were the purchase price of the asset. Since this is a long-term arrangement, the lease payments must allow the lessor to recover not only the original investment in the leased property but also a reasonable return—"interest."

The lessee expenses the leased asset's historical cost over the term of the lease (or the asset's economic life if the lessee will obtain ownership of the asset at the end of the lease term). Lease payments are divided between principle payments on the

Note 7 Lease Commitments

The present value of net minimum lease payments, net of the current portion and unamortized discount, totaled $64 million and $71 million at December 31, 1989 and 1988, respectively.

At December 31, 1989, future net minimum lease payments for capital and operating leases (excluding oil and gas, coal and other mineral leases) were the following (in millions):

	Capital	Operating
1990	$ 14	$ 149
1991	11	133
1992	10	115
1993	9	103
1994	9	97
Thereafter	116	690
Total minimum lease payments	$ 169	$ 1,287
Less—executory costs	(7)	
imputed interest	(92)	
current portion	(6)	
Present value of net minimum lease payments, net of current portion and unamortized discount	$ 64	

Rental expense for operating lease, net of immaterial sublease rentals, was $206 million in 1989, $172 million in 1988 and $142 million in 1987.

Included in the 1989 and 1988 property, plant and equipment accounts were $243 million of property leased under capital leases and $124 million and $108 million, respectively, of related accumulated amortization.

FIG. 2-2 *Note showing the disclosure of lease commitments.*

recorded lease obligation and interest expense, just as loan payments are divided between payments of principle and interest expense.

Short-term leases and leases that do not transfer the risks of ownership are called operating leases. In such an arrangement, the lessee does not record the leased asset or obligation on the balance sheet; all lease payments are recorded as rent expense.

Care should be taken when comparing financial statements of companies that lease to the financial statements of companies that do not lease. All leases give the lessee the benefit of using an asset in exchange for payments at specified intervals. Regardless of whether accounting principles require the lease to be recorded on the balance sheet, the company has a resource to use and an obligation that must be met by cash payments. The financial statement note on leases provides you with the significant details of the lease arrangement and the lease payment schedule.

4. *Note Disclosure of Contingencies.* A contingency exists when, because of a past transaction or event, a company stands to gain or lose. The amount of gain or loss is "contingent"— that is, dependent—on another transaction or event. For example, suppose a customer who falls and is injured at your place of business then files a lawsuit. You are now in a contingency situation: The event giving rise to possible loss is the injury of the customer. The amount of loss, if any, will be determined in the future by settlement or court verdict.

All contingencies may be classified by likelihood of outcome: remote, possible, or likely. Contingencies that managers, their lawyers, and their accountants believe have only a remote chance of gain or loss are usually not disclosed. In situations in which a gain or loss is possible, the contingency must be disclosed, along with management's estimate of the range of possible gain or loss.

If a contingency is viewed as likely to result in a loss, it must be accrued (a loss recorded along with an estimated liability). The amount that must be accrued is the most reasonable estimate of loss. If a single estimate of loss cannot be determined, the smallest amount in management's estimated loss range will be accrued. The nature of the contingency and the estimated range of loss are described in footnote disclosures.

Contingencies that are likely to result in gain are not accrued, only disclosed. This is the principle of conservatism (see Chapter 1) at work. Conservatism favors recording losses before they are realized if they are considered likely to occur, but postpones recording a gain until it occurs. The nature of the gain contingency is described in the notes to the financial statements.

Notes on contingencies should be evaluated with care. Contingency losses may be time bombs waiting to wreck a profitable company. Ask yourself these questions: What will be the cash-flow impact on the company if the possible or likely contingency loss comes to pass? Is the company's debt and liquidity structure capable of handling the loss?

5. *Notes Relating to Pensions.* The key to understanding the cost of providing employee pension benefits is to realize that the accounting records reflect management's best guess as to what the actual cost will be, rather than fixed, predictable costs. Employees earn pension rights through service to the company. Accountants attempt to measure the cost of these retirement benefits at the time the employee earns them, rather than when the employee actually receives them. Pension expense represents the amount of money that management should invest at the end of the year to cover future pension payments owed to employees for this additional year's service; the investment plus the interest it will earn must provide for these payments when they are made in the future.

Why is pension cost only a best guess? All kinds of assumptions about unknowable factors must be made to calculate the required annual investment. Some of these assumptions are the average years of company service of an employee at retirement, the salary level of the employee at retirement, the number of years an employee is expected to live after retirement, and the rate of interest the invested funds are expected to earn. As these estimated values change, revisions are made to pension cost. Rather than adjusting the current period's pension expense for the total change in estimate, these revisions are spread over the current and future accounting periods.

When employers adopt an employee pension plan, they usually grant employees credit for their years of service prior to the adoption of the plan. The cost of the investment to cover future pension payments for these years of service credit (prior service cost) is also spread over current and future accounting periods.

Management may choose to invest more or less than the current year's pension expense. If more than the current year's pension expense is funded, the excess funding is recorded in an asset account called "Prepaid Pension Cost." If less than the current year's pension expense is funded, the difference is recorded in a liability account called "Unfunded Accrued Pension Cost."

Most invested pension funds are handled by a trustee. The trustee, typically a financial institution that specializes in pension investments, maintains separate accounting records for the invested funds. The investment is not reported on the balance sheet of the employer company.

Notes to the financial statements disclose the following:

1. A description of the pension plan, including the employee groups covered
2. The type of benefit formula used to calculate the employees' retirement benefits
3. Management's funding policy
4. The current period's pension expense, with prior service cost and other costs that are being spread over the current and future periods backed out
5. A schedule that reconciles management's funding policy with the current value of the invested funds, indicating the amount of prior service cost and cost arising from changes in estimates that have not yet been expensed

Don't get carried away trying to analyze these data. Remember, they are only best-guess information. It is questionable whether companies even realize the magnitude of the obligation they create every time they agree to increase employee benefits.

Like pension benefits, retirement health care benefits granted to employees can be a substantial future obligation. Presently, companies show expense for the health-care benefits actually paid rather than the health-care benefits earned by the employees. If a company's work force is young or a company does not yet have a large number of retirees, a report of health-care benefits paid does not provide good information about the company's future obligation.

If you ever encounter a liability account called "Unfunded Projected Benefit Obligation," beware. This means that, given the current rate of earnings, the company's pension fund investments are not enough to cover the future benefits management expects to pay their employees. Similarly, a company whose policy is to fund less than its current year's pension expense may find itself in a tight spot down the road.

OTHER DISCLOSURES
Supplementary Tables

A number of supplementary tables may accompany an annual report. Some of the most frequently encountered are reporting by segments, financial reporting and changing prices, five-year summary of operations, and two-year quarterly data. Figure 2-3 shows a typical supplementary table containing a five-year summary of selected financial data.

FIVE-YEAR SUMMARY OF SELECTED FINANCIAL DATA
(Dollar amounts in millions, except per-share amounts)

For the years ended December 31,	1989	1988	1987	1986	1985
RESULTS OF OPERATIONS:					
Net sales and operating revenues	$ 20,068	$ 19,417	$ 17,096	$ 15,344	$ 14,534
Income before extraordinary gain (loss)	256	313	184	172	455
Net income	285	302	240	181	696
Preferred dividend requirements	7	7	27	74	224
Earnings per common share before extraordinary gain (loss)	.92	1.26	.78	.66	2.21
FINANCIAL POSITION:					
Total assets	20,741	20,747	16,739	17,467	11,586
Senior funded debt, net	6,872	6,179	4,739	5,613	1,955
Subordinated debt, net	1,281	1,438	1,600	1,832	1,796
Redeemable preferred stocks	13	13	13	13	337
Stockholders' equity	5,899	6,224	5,164	4,308	3,281
Common dividends declared per share	2.50	2.50	2.50	2.50	2.50
Average shares outstanding (thousands)	269,486	243,120	200,986	149,730	103,843

See Management's Discussion and Analysis and the Notes to the Consolidated Financial Statements for information regarding business acquisitions, asset dispositions, the issuance of stock of subsidiaries and other items affecting comparability.

FIG. 2-3 *A supplementary schedule showing selected financial data.*

Management's Discussion and Analysis

Management's Discussion and Analysis, an objective presentation required by the Securities and Exchange Commission, covers all developments affecting three areas of the company's business: results of operations, capital resources, and liquidity.

The management discussion and analysis section, unlike the report highlights, letter to shareholders, and review of operations, is not produced by the public relations department. It is supposed to contain a discussion of all past and future conditions and uncertainties that may materially affect the business. You may find this section quite informative.

THE AUDITOR'S OPINION

The independent auditor's opinion, a short report addressed to the shareholders of the company, gives an opinion on the financial statements prepared by management. An unqualified opinion is good; any other opinion is less than good. Qualified opinions, most of which contain the phrase "except for," should put you on guard.

The standard report form, which was adopted in 1988, is designed to increase public awareness of the nature and the limitations of the audit. As stated in the first paragraph of the report, management—not the auditors—is primarily responsible for the financial statements; the statements are prepared under management's direction.

The second paragraph of the audit report describes just what an audit is. The auditor tests the accounting records and supporting documents to form an opinion on the reasonableness of the financial statements. Standards developed by the American Association of Certified Public Accountants offer guidance and define the auditor's responsibilities in various situations. For instance, the standards require that an auditor confirm receivables and payables; however, because auditors draw test samples, only a sample of receivables and payables is confirmed. Testing all accounting records would be too time-consuming and expensive; remember, it took a year to accumulate the data. Based on the outcome of the test samples, the auditor forms an opinion on the reasonableness of financial statement presentation.

The third paragraph of the audit report contains the auditor's opinion. An auditor may express a "clean," "qualified," or "adverse" opinion or "disclaim" and express no opinion at all.

The auditor also states that the financial statements are "in conformity with generally accepted accounting principles" (GAAP). GAAP, the accounting profession's collection of rules governing financial statement presentation and measurement, includes the basic accounting principles discussed in Chapter 5. The accounting profession and auditors view financial statements that follow GAAP as fair presentation.

Qualified Opinion

A qualified opinion points out to the financial-statement user the particular area the auditor believes is not fair presentation. The auditor believes that the remainder of the statements are fairly presented.

Adverse Opinion

An adverse opinion states that the auditor does not believe the financial statements are fairly presented and lists the factors that lead an auditor to that opinion.

Auditors base their opinions of financial statements on evidence gathered from the test samples. Because they do not do a test of the complete accounting records, material misstatement may exist without the auditor's being aware of it. As pointed out above, a qualified or adverse opinion raises the question of fair presentation. When a qualified or adverse opinion is given, the financial-statement user should read carefully and seek to understand the auditor's objections to the presentation.

Exhibit 1 shows the standard audit report form for an audit of the Cleveland Can Company by Dalton, Hammond, and Barkley, CPAs.

EXHIBIT 1
Standard Audit Report Form
(Unqualified Opinion)

We have audited the accompanying balance sheet of Cleveland Can Company as of December 31, 1990, and the related statements of income, retained earnings, and cash flows for the year then ended. These financial statements are the responsibility of the Company's management. Our responsibility is to express an opinion on these financial statements based on our audit.

We conducted our audit in accordance with generally accepted auditing standards. Those standards require that we plan and perform the audit to obtain reasonable assurance about whether the financial statements are free of material misstatement. An audit includes examining, on a test basis, evidence supporting the amounts and disclosures in the financial statements. An audit also includes as-

---

sessing the accounting principles used and significant estimates made by management, as well as evaluating the overall financial statement presentation. We believe that our audit provides a reasonable basis for our opinion.

In our opinion, the financial statements referred to above present fairly, in all material respects, the financial position of Cleveland Can Company at December 31, 1990, and the results of its operations and its cash flows for the year then ended in conformity with generally accepted accounting principles.

Dalton, Hammond, and Barkley, CPAs

January 17, 1991
Cleveland, Ohio

CHAPTER PERSPECTIVE

In this chapter, we have discussed the components of the annual report produced by a company's management and accountants. We discussed the purpose of the annual report, the source of the accounting principles that govern financial reporting, and the notes to the financial statements, emphasizing the importance and meaning of notes on accounting principles, commitments, leases, contingencies, and pensions. Finally, we explained the involvement of the independent auditor and discussed the standard audit report and the types of opinions an auditor might render.

The Balance Sheet: Classification and Current Assets

INTRODUCTION AND MAIN POINTS

Annual reports must contain three financial statements: the balance sheet, the income statement, and the statement of cash flows. The income statement and the statement of cash flows both show business activity (earning and spending) over a period of time—usually a quarter of a year. The balance sheet, in contrast, is a report of resources owned and debts owed at a particular point in time. In this chapter, the first of three on the balance sheet, we talk about the structure of the balance sheet and the formal classification of accounts within it. We then begin our discussion of the classified accounts by examining current assets, comprising primarily cash, receivables, and inventories.

After studying the material in this chapter:

■ You will know what a balance sheet is and how it differs from the other statements in the annual report.

■ You will understand how accountants classify accounts within the balance sheet to assist readers of financial statements.

■ You will know what current assets are and how accountants decide which assets belong in this group.

■ You will know which items are included as cash on the balance sheet.

■ You will know which items are included as receivables on the balance sheet.

■ You will understand how the statements are affected by the allowance for uncollectible accounts.

■ You will know what components may comprise total inventory and why they are carried at the lower of cost or market.

THE STRUCTURE OF THE BALANCE SHEET

As we explained in Chapter 1, accountants use a system of recordkeeping, called double-entry bookkeeping, which is based on the relationship between business resources and the source of those resources. Business resources, or assets, may be obtained using funds obtained either by borrowing (creating a liability) or from the investment of the owners (creating owner's equity or property rights in the business). The relationship between assets, liabilities, and owners' equity is expressed as:

$$\text{Assets} = \text{Liabilities} + \text{Owners' Equity}$$

A balance sheet, or statement of financial position, is a report that displays the business's assets, liabilities, and owners' equity at a specific date. The recorded value of the assets always equals the recorded value of the liabilities plus owners' equity. In Chapter 1, we gave a simple definition of assets, liabilities, and owner's equity. In this chapter, we will expand those definitions.

ASSETS

Assets are those items of value that a business possesses and can use as it attempts to produce a profit. In order for a company to record an asset on its balance sheet, the resource must possess three characteristics: (1) the potential to generate positive cash flow, (2) the ability to be controlled, and (3) the right of use or control, granted in a past transaction or event.

The first characteristic, positive potential cash flow, means that management believes the resource is capable of bringing cash into the business. Controllability indicates that the resource provides an advantage that can be used as the company sees fit. The third characteristic, the right of use, results from the historical, backward-looking nature of accounting. Financial statements report only the results of past transactions or events.

To be listed as an asset on a balance sheet, a resource must also be capable of being valued. Because valuing assets can be difficult or impossible, significant resources often go unrecorded. Employees, probably the most important resource a business has, are an example. You would not hire someone unless you believed the person could contribute positively to your operations. The right to control or assign the employee job tasks belongs to management and arises out of the employment contract. But how do you measure and objectively value an employee? Obviously, you can't. Even though an employee can be considered an asset, valuation problems prevent employees from being listed as assets on a balance sheet.

Legal ownership is not a required characteristic of an asset. Equipment leased long-term that transfers the basic rights and risks of ownership is recorded as an asset on the books of the lessee.

LIABILITIES

Liabilities—the debts of the business—are the amounts owed to nonowners. Liabilities possess three characteristics: (1) they represent the possibility of a future payment of cash to settle the obligation, (2) they are obligations that management has little chance of avoiding, and (3) they are the result of a past transaction or event.

Obligations do not have to be legally binding before they are recorded as a liability on the balance sheet. A business pledge to a charity is not legally binding on management, but it is recorded as a liability, because the obligation can be valued and all three characteristics of a liability are present: an obligation exists as a result of management's signing a pledge card at some time in the past; there exists the possibility of a future payment of cash to settle the pledge; and management cannot honorably avoid payment of the pledge.

OWNERS' EQUITY

Owners' (or shareholders') equity is the difference between the recorded value of a business's assets and its liabilities. It includes amounts directly invested by the owners (contributed capital) plus any profits earned by the business that have not been paid out to the owners or shareholders (retained earnings).

When the corporation sells shares of stock, it creates ownership. The cash received increases assets and equity (contributed capital) equally. For a company to realize net income, the inflow of assets from earnings (as measured by revenues) must exceed the outflow of assets to produce those earnings (as measured by expenses). Assets increase, and liabilities are not affected; therefore, ownership (retained earnings) must be increased. A simple example will illustrate:

John invests $100,000 to begin a business. Immediately after his investment, John draws up the following balance sheet.

Assets		**Liabilities**	
Cash	$100,000		$ 0
		OWNERS' EQUITY	
	———	Contributed Capital	100,000
	$100,000		$100,000

John pays $10,000 to buy inventory (an asset until it is resold). His balance sheet now appears as follows:

Assets		Liabilities	
Cash	$ 90,000*		$ 0
Inventory	10,000	**OWNERS' EQUITY**	
		Contributed Capital	100,000
	$100,000		$100,000

*$100,000 − $10,000

John eventually sells merchandise that originally cost him $4,500 (expense) for $6,500 (revenue) for a net income of $2,000. His balance sheet then appears as follows:

Assets		Liabilities	
Cash	$ 96,500*		$ 0
Inventory	5,500**	**OWNERS' EQUITY**	
		Contributed Capital	100,000
		Retained Earnings	2,000***
	$102,000		$102,000

*$90,000 + $6,500
**$10,000 − $4,500
***$ 6,500 − $4,500

CLASSIFIED BALANCE SHEET

To assist readers of financial statements, the accounts on a balance sheet are usually grouped according to length of life, liquidity (ease of conversion to cash), or another characteristic. A balance sheet with accounts grouped this way is called a *classified balance sheet*. Most classified balance sheets contain the following asset, liability, and owner's equity categories:

Assets
  Current Assets
  Long-term investments
  Property, Plant and Equipment
  Intangibles
  Other Assets

Liabilities
  Current Liabilities
  Long-term Liabilities

Shareholders' Equity
  Capital Stock
  Additional Paid-in Capital
  Retained Earnings

Each of these categories contains many individual accounts; for example, "Current Assets" may include cash, short-term investments, and inventories. "Capital Stock" and "Additional Paid-in Capital" together are called contributed capital. These categories and the individual accounts that are included in them will be discussed in Chapters 4 and 5.

An actual balance sheet from a published annual report is shown in Figure 3-1.

A caution is in order: The balance sheet is a still picture. It presents resources, obligations, and equity at only one point in time, typically the fiscal year-end. As you can see from the simple example above, each transaction affects the balance sheet, causing it to change immediately; in addition, some assets and liabilities go unrecorded because of measurement problems. To detect such cases, you should pay close attention to the notes to the financial statements. Material information that cannot be quantified is reported in a note to the financial statements, as discussed in Chapter 1.

CURRENT ASSETS

Current assets, the first category listed in the balance sheet, for the most part are short-term assets. Current assets include cash, items that provide cash, and certain items that prevent the outflow of cash in the short term. The key to understanding the current assets category of the balance sheet is to examine the accountant's definition of current assets phrase by phrase.

Accountants define *short term* as one year or one company operating cycle, whichever is greater. The meaning of short term may be different for different companies, depending on operating cycle, or the length of time required to go from cash to cash in operations. For example, suppose cash is first invested in inventory, either by manufacturing or purchasing inventory for resale. Next, inventory is sold, creating an account receivable. Finally, the receivable is collected and cash is collected; the cycle is now complete. (The length of time a company's cash is tied up in accounts receivable and inventory can be estimated using a technique explained for activity ratios in Chapter 11.)

Usually, cash is tied up for from thirty to sixty days in both accounts receivable and in inventories; a company's operating cycle is usually sixty to 180 days. As a result, the time span for defining current assets is usually one year, since it is greater than the operating cycle. But some companies leave cash in inventories for very long times. For instance, a whiskey distiller who

CONSOLIDATED BALANCE SHEET

ASSETS

Current assets:

Cash, including short-term cash investments of $18,038,000 and $6,157,000	$20,017,000
Accounts receivable, less allowance for doubtful accounts of	
$546,000 and $268,000	24,606,000
Other notes and accounts receivable	815,000
Inventories	14,412,000
Prepaid expenses	382,000
Total current assets	60,232,000
Property and equipment, net	9,312,000
Goodwill and other intangible assets, less amortization of	
$1,186,000 and $1,006,000	258,000
Other assets	211,000
Total	$70,013,000

LIABILITIES AND STOCKHOLDERS' EQUITY

Current Liabilities:

Capital lease obligations due within one year	$ 135,000
Notes payable	1,555,000
Accounts payable	5,072,000
Accrued payroll and other employee compensation	3,816,000
Income taxes payable	1,897,000
Accrued taxes, other than payroll and income taxes	782,000
Deferred income taxes	82,000
Other accrued liabilities	1,041,000
Total current liabilities	14,380,000
Capital lease obligations	344,000
Deferred income taxes	616,000
Stockholders' equity, as restated to give effect to the stock split discussed in Note 8:	
Preferred Stock, $1.00 par value per share; 500,000 shares authorized, none outstanding	—
Common Stock, $.01 par value per share; 20,000,000 shares authorized, 12,683,385 and 10,675,926 shares outstanding	127,000
Additional paid-in capital	37,247,000
Retained earnings	17,445,000
Equity adjustment for foreign currency translation	(146,000)
Total stockholders' equity	54,673,000
Total	$70,013,000

See accompanying notes to consolidated financial statements

FIG. 3-1 *Example of a classified balance sheet from a published annual report.*

ages inventory for twelve years during the manufacturing process may have an operating cycle that is the total of the twelve years cash invested in inventory plus the thirty days cash invested in receivables. In this case, the time span for current assets is twelve years, thirty days. Current assets are listed on the balance sheet in order of liquidity, or the ease with which the asset can be converted to cash. Cash is always listed first since it is already cash, then accounts receivable (one step—collection—from cash), then inventories (two steps—sale and collection—from cash), and so on. There are three general types of current assets, listed here in the same order they appear on the balance sheet:

1. Cash
2. Items that provide cash in one year or one operating cycle, whichever is greater—primarily accounts and short-term notes receivable, inventories of raw materials, supplies, and finished goods.
3. Items that prevent the outflow of cash in one year or one operating cycle, whichever is greater—primarily prepaid items such as prepaid insurance, prepaid rent, and salary advances to employees.

An example of the current assets section of a balance sheet is shown in Figure 3-2.

Sometimes the term "working capital" is used to refer to current assets. But you must be alert: Working capital is also used to refer to *net* current assets, or current assets net of (less) current liabilities. Long ago, the term *net working capital* was used to refer to current assets minus current liabilities and *working capital* referred to current assets, but this distinction is now seldom made.

Cash

Cash is the most active asset in a company's balance sheet. There are few business transactions that do not affect cash in some

Assets		
Cash and marketable securities	$ 186,992	$ 163,854
Receivables	192,485	176,219
Inventories	187,643	197,330
Prepaid expenses	21,636	14,200
Current assets	588,756	551,603

FIG. 3-2 *Current assets section of a balance sheet.*

way, by either providing cash or requiring it. Cash is an unproductive asset (earning at best a nominal interest rate on time deposits), but it is vitally important to have adequate cash on hand if the business is to operate: Payrolls must be met, suppliers must be paid, overhead must be covered. Cash is also the most universally desirable asset that a company possesses: It is easily transported, hard to recognize once off the company premises, and easily convertible into other goods. Cash is subject to more accounting and management controls than any other asset.

Cash is the most liquid current asset. To be reported as "cash," an item must be readily available and not restricted for use in payment of current obligations. Items classified as cash include coin and currency on hand, petty cash funds, demand deposits (basically checking accounts, which are unrestricted funds available on deposit in a bank), change funds, and negotiable instruments (such as personal checks, traveler's checks, cashier's checks, bank drafts, and money orders).

Cash balances to be used for some special purpose are not reported as cash but are listed instead as restricted funds. An example of such a fund is an employee travel fund. This fund is not readily available to meet current obligations. Special-purpose cash balances are reported in the balance sheet as "restricted funds." Similarly, certificates of deposit, money market funds, treasury bills, and commercial paper are not readily available to meet current obligations and are generally classified as temporary investments.

Receivables

Receivables represent all claims expected to be settled in cash. The chief source of receivables is the company's trade or business. All receivables can be classified as either trade receivables (usually either accounts or notes receivable) or nontrade receivables (accounts or notes receivable arising from claims for losses or damages, claims for tax refunds, dividends or interest receivable, advances to employees, sales of property other than inventory, or deposits held by creditors or utilities).

Trade receivables are the most common type of receivable reported in the balance sheet and usually represent the largest dollar amount. All trade receivables are current assets by definition. On the other hand, nontrade receivables can be either current or noncurrent.

Receivables may appear in the current assets section of the balance sheet as illustrated below.

	Year 2	Year 1
Receivables:		
Trade	80,000	74,000
Other	20,000	25,000

Certain credit transactions may require the borrower to pledge or assign receivables as security for a loan. Assignment may be general or specific, depending on whether all accounts receivable or specific accounts receivable are pledged as collateral.

Notes receivable may be "discounted" to a bank. When notes receivable are discounted, the company receives immediate cash and the bank receives repayment, with interest, when the note is collected. When notes receivable are discounted with recourse, the company will disclose any obligations on the discounted notes.

Uncollectible Accounts. Accounts receivable are always shown on the balance sheet net of (that is, minus) any uncollectible accounts, also known as doubtful accounts or bad debts. Details related to allowances for uncollectible accounts, when not shown on the face of the balance sheet, are found in Note One, Significant Accounting Policies.

When a company accounts for uncollectibles, both the income statement and the balance sheet are affected: The estimated bad-debt expense is shown in the income statement, and the estimate of uncollectible accounts is shown as a subtraction from total accounts receivable in the current assets section of the balance sheet. A financial statement note showing the allowance for doubtful accounts is shown in Figure 3-3.

NOTE 4: RECEIVABLES

Receivables at December 31 are summarized as follows:

(Dollars in thousands)	1989	1988
Trade	$156,456	$150,991
Other	9,926	15,043
Allowance for doubtful amounts....	(1,616)	(1,782)
	$164,766	$164,252

FIG. 3-3 *Financial statement note showing allowance for bad debts (doubtful accounts).*

To understand the accounting treatment of bad debts, it is important to remember that the amounts involved are estimates of amounts that *may* become uncollectible. There are two goals for such accounting. One is to match the cost of bad debts to the sales revenue produced in the period. This means that, of necessity, some estimation must take place. At the end of the year, some credit sales will have been collected and others will have already proven to be uncollectible. The collectibility of the remaining receivables will not be known. Therefore, it becomes necessary to estimate the uncollectible amount that will result from these as yet uncollected accounts and to include that estimate in this year's bad-debt expense in order for the company to charge this year's profits with the bad-debt expense that resulted from this year's sales. If the company were to wait until each account proved to be uncollectible (or collectible), the costs of bad debts in one year would have to be charged against the next year. But accounting principles require that bad-debt expense be matched to the year benefited by the original sale. (The accounting concept of matching is explained in Chapter 1.)

The second goal in accounting for bad debts is to value correctly the amount of accounts receivable shown in the current assets section of the balance sheet. These accounts are all uncollected, but the company has not yet decided that any are definitely bad debts. (If the company judges an account to be uncollectible, it must be removed from the balance of accounts receivable.) As a result, the allowance for bad debts shown as a deduction from accounts receivable in the balance sheet is wholly an estimate.

There is some conflict between the two goals in accounting for bad debts—maximizing the accuracy of the income statement versus maximizing the accuracy of the balance sheet. Bad debt estimates are occasionally high or low, particularly on interim (monthly or quarterly) statements; bad debt estimates for annual statements are, by and large, not materially misstated. To prevent misstatement, a company that does not relate the amount of bad debts expensed to sales activity will be required to examine periodically the outstanding accounts receivable in detail and justify the amounts of the estimates that appear in the financial statements.

Inventories

Depending on the kind of business, a company may have one or more types of inventory. A retailer may have an inventory of purchased finished goods available for sale, while a manufacturer may have inventories of raw materials, inventories of partially completed work in process, and inventories of supplies used in operations, in addition to an inventory of manufactured finished goods available for sale.

Inventories are current assets, carried in the balance sheet at original, historical cost or at the lower cost or market value. The cost of purchased goods in a retailer's inventory includes the cost of transportation or freight-in but is reduced by any purchase discounts taken by the buyer or any returns made or allowances received. A schedule of ending inventories for a retailer is illustrated below.

Schedule of Ending Inventories

Beginning Inventory		75,000
Purchases	250,000	
Plus: Freight-in	10,000	
Less: Purchase Discounts	(5,000)	
Returns and Allowances	(15,000)	
Net delivered cost of purchases		240,000
Total goods available for sale		315,000
Less: Cost of goods sold		255,000
Ending inventory		60,000

The components of a manufacturer's inventories are shown either in the body of the financial statements or in the statement notes. A schedule of inventory components for a manufacturer is illustrated below.

Schedule of Manufacturer's Inventory

	12/31 Year 2	12/31 Year 1
Raw materials	$ 53,000	$ 60,000
Operating Supplies	18,000	27,000
Work-in-Process	95,000	87,000
Finished Goods	107,000	123,000
Ending inventory	$273,000	$297,000

Inventories are usually shown on the balance sheet at the lower of historical cost or current market value. This prevents a company from carrying inventories at an inflated asset amount and forces a company to expense any loss in value in the period the loss occurred. Without the lower-of-cost-or-market rule, inventories could be carried as current assets with an inflated value and any loss in value would not be charged against earnings until the goods were sold, possibly in the year following the actual decline in inventory replacement prices; therefore, managers would have an incentive to delay expensing the lost inventory value in the hope that market prices would rise again in the next year.

CHAPTER PERSPECTIVE

The balance sheet is a report of assets, liabilities, and owners' equity at a particular point in time. In this chapter, we introduced the structure of the balance sheet and explained the formal classification of accounts within the balance sheet, beginning our discussion of the classified accounts by examining current assets. The current assets classification is composed primarily of cash, receivables (reduced by the allowance for doubtful accounts), and inventories. In the next two chapters we will discuss non-current assets, liabilities, and owner's equity to complete our coverage of the balance sheet.

The Balance Sheet: Noncurrent Assets

INTRODUCTION AND MAIN POINTS

Noncurrent assets consist of (1) plant, property, and equipment, (2) intangibles, (3) investments, and (4) other assets. To understand the valuation of these long-lived assets, you must understand the accounting methods used to expense them. Long-lived, tangible, productive assets are depreciated; intangible assets are amortized; and natural resources are depleted. In this chapter, we discuss each kind of noncurrent asset, the way it is valued for inclusion on the balance sheet, and the way it is expensed.

After studying the material in this chapter:

▬ You will know what a noncurrent asset is.

▬ You will know how the different noncurrent assets are valued at acquisition.

▬ You will understand the need for different methods of depreciation for different assets.

▬ You will understand the weaknesses of historical-cost depreciation and amortization.

▬ You will understand the difficulties of accounting for different kinds of investments and why different accounting treatments exist.

▬ You will understand each type of noncurrent asset as it is presented in the balance sheet.

PROPERTY, PLANT, AND EQUIPMENT

The company's long-lived productive assets (such as land, buildings, machinery, furniture, and fixtures) make up the asset category "Property, Plant, and Equipment." These assets are carried at their historical cost less any depreciation—that is, any amount already charged off as an operating expense. The historical cost of a productive asset is the total cost of acquiring the asset and readying it for use; for example, the historical cost of a piece of machinery includes its invoice price, delivery charges, installation costs, and the cost of trial production runs to adjust the machine to the desired product quality. In other words, all costs incurred until the time production begins are considered part of the machine's historical cost.

Historical cost may also include interest cost. Many companies borrow funds to finance the construction of plant and equipment. These companies record this additional interest cost as part of the historical cost of their plant and equipment. Accountants call this type of interest avoidable interest, payments the company makes only because it is building.

"Property, Plant, and Equipment" also includes the assets "Leasehold Improvements" and "Property Subject to Capital Leases." Leasehold improvements are the cost of improvements made to leased property that will revert to its owner at the end of the lease term; property subject to capital leases is property that has been acquired through a long-term leasing arrangement that is essentially an alternative purchase and mortgage arrangement.

Valuing an asset at historical cost causes problems for the reader of financial statements, because, while historical cost is an objective measure, it may not be relevant. For instance, a piece of land valued at its 1940 historical cost of $1 million on a balance sheet tells us little about its current sales value or loan value. Comparisons between entities are also hampered by the use of historical cost: comparing the cost of property purchased in 1940 to the cost of similar property in 1988 is misleading. Although the property purchased in 1988 has a higher historical cost, it may not be more productive than the property purchased in 1940.

DEPRECIATION

In ordinary usage, depreciation means a decline in value; to an accountant, however, depreciation is the assignment of historical cost of a long-lived productive asset to production periods—the matching of costs of production (expenses) with the results of production (revenues). Rather than recording decline in value as depreciation, the accountant records the using-up of original cost of the asset over its productive life.

The exception to the concept of depreciation is land. Land is a renewable resource, and therefore is not used up. It cannot be depreciated and is valued on the balance sheet at its historical cost.

Depreciation expense reduces earnings in the income statement. In the balance sheet, the asset being depreciated is shown at its original historical purchase price less the total of all depreciation expensed to the balance sheet date. The total of depreciation expensed is maintained in an account called "Accumulated Depreciation." If a company has a $100,000 machine and has depreciated it $10,000 a year for four years, it appears in the balance sheet as:

Machine	$100,000	
Less Accumulated Depreciation	40,000	$60,000

or simply as:

Machine (net of depreciation)	$60,000

Figure 4-1 shows how one company disclosed the depreciation taken on fixed assets.

Methods of Depreciation

Most companies use one (or several) of four primary depreciation methods in preparing their annual reports. These methods are straight-line, units of production, sum of the years' digits, and double declining balance.

Straight-line. Straight-line depreciation assumes that equal benefit is derived from using the productive asset each year of its useful life. The formula for straight-line depreciation is:

$$[(\text{cost} - \text{salvage value}) \div \text{years of useful life}] = 1 \text{ year's depreciation}$$

For example, if a company purchases a machine for $10,000 and at the time of purchase estimates its productive life to be three years, after which time it will have a salvage value of $1,000, depreciation expense is $3,000 a year [($10,000 − $1,000) ÷ 3].

Units of Production. Units of production depreciation assumes that revenue produced parallels units of product produced. In other words, in years in which more product is produced, the company has greater revenue-producing ability and, hence, should incur more depreciation expense. The formula for units of production depreciation is:

In the Balance Sheet:
Property, Plant and Equipment (Note 6).   494,290   533,427

In the Statement Notes:
NOTE 6: PROPERTY, PLANT AND EQUIPMENT

Plant assets represent the original cost of land, buildings and equipment less depreciation computed under the straight-line method over the estimated useful life of the asset. Equipment lives range from 5 to 15 years, buildings from 10 to 30 years.

Timber resources are stated at cost. Depletion is charged to operations based on the number of units of timber cut during the year.

Depreciation and depletion expense amounted to $62,979,000 in 1989; $66,542,000 in 1988; and $54,897,000 in 1987. Details of property, plant and equipment at December 31 are as follows:

(Dollars in thousands)	1989	1988
Land	$ 15,178	$ 18,646
Timber resources	13,955	14,637
Buildings	154,026	143,230
Machinery & equipment	634,712	628,181
Construction in progress	38,781	72,882
	856,652	877,576
Accumulated depreciation and depletion	(362,362)	(344,149)
	$494,290	$533,427

FIG. 4-1 *Balance sheet and note disclosure of fixed assets showing depreciation.*

[(cost − salvage value) ÷ estimated units of product that will be produced over the life of the asset] = per unit depreciation.

To find a year's depreciation expense, multiply the number of units produced during the year by the per-unit depreciation rate. For example, assuming a cost of $10,000, a salvage value of $1,000, a useful life of three years, and an estimated production of 4,000,000 units of product over the three-year period, the depreciation rate per unit of product produced is:

[$10,000 − 1,000] ÷ 4,000,000 = $ .00225 per unit.

If a million units are produced during the year, depreciation expense of $2,250 is recorded for the year (1,000,000 × .00225).

Declining Balance Methods. Two declining balance methods of depreciation are the sum of the years' digits and the double declining balance method. Both of these methods take more depreciation in the earlier years of an asset's life than in the later years, on the assumption that an asset is most productive (and therefore has the most revenue-producing ability) in the early years of the asset's life before wear and tear begin to take their toll.

1. *Sum of the year's digits.* The formula for this declining balance method of depreciation is:

[cost − salvage value] ×
[years in reverse order ÷ sum of the year's digits].

For a machine that has a $10,000 cost, $1,000 salvage value, and a three-year life expectancy, the first year's depreciation expense is calculated as follows:

[$10,000 − $1,000] × [3 ÷ (1 + 2 + 3)] =
$9,000 × ⅙ = $4,500.

The second year's depreciation expense is ($9,000 × ⅔) = $3,000; the final year's depreciation is ($9,000 × ⅙) = $1,500. Notice that the rate of depreciation declines every year (½—⅓—⅙)—the depreciation base ($9,000) remains constant.

2. *Double declining balance.* The formula for double declining balance depreciation is:

net book value of the depreciable asset ×
(2 ÷ number of years estimated life).

Net book value of the depreciable asset is its original cost minus all depreciation taken to date (accumulated depreciation). Using our example of an asset that cost $10,000, with $1,000 salvage value and a three-year estimated life, the first year's depreciation expense is calculated as:

[($10,000 − $0) × ⅔] = $6,667.

The second year's depreciation expense is [($10,000 − $6,667) × ⅔] = $2,222. While calculating depreciation expense by this formula gives us [($10,000 − $8,889) × ⅔] = $741 of depreciation in the third and final year of the asset's life, the company actually records only $111 of depreciation. This is the difference between net book value at the beginning of the third year and the estimated salvage value at the end of the third year [($10,000 − $8,889) − $1,000]. Double declining balance is the only one of the four primary depreciation methods that ignores estimated salvage value in its formula. Therefore, in the final year of the asset's life, the asset must be depreciated only to a net book value equal to its expected salvage value.

The Weaknesses of Historical-Cost Depreciation

The basis for long-lived asset valuation is historical cost. Because depreciation does not measure actual decline in value, the net book value of a long-lived asset (historical cost − accumulated depreciation) is not a good measure of the cost of replacing the asset; neither is it a good measure of what the asset would bring if sold. Long-lived assets with net book value equal to their estimated salvage value or zero (if there is no salvage value) may continue to be used by the company to earn revenue while they are minimally valued on the balance sheet.

Depreciation computations are based largely on estimates of useful life and salvage value. Should either of these estimated figures change during the life of the depreciable asset, the company recomputes depreciation from that point forward. This computation uses the net book value as the historical cost and the new estimates of salvage and remaining years of useful life. For example, suppose management decides at the beginning of the third year that an asset—which cost $10,000 and has a $1,000 salvage value and a three-year estimated useful life—has in fact a remaining useful life of three years with a new estimated salvage value of $1,500. Straight-line depreciation expense for that third year is computed as follows: [$10,000 − $6,000] = $3,000, the net book value after two years straight-line depreciation; depreciation for succeeding years is calculated at [($3,000 − $1,500) ÷ 3 years remaining life] = $500 depreciation expense per year.

Comparability is hindered by using different depreciation methods. In our examples, the first year's depreciation expense varied according to the method used: straight-line—$3,000, units of production—$2,250, sum of the years' digits—$4,500, and double declining balance—$6,667. If four identical companies each uses a different method to compute depreciation for an identical asset, their net book values of the asset and their net incomes will be different. In other words, choice of depreciation methods can create artificial differences between companies in terms of asset valuation and net income.

INTANGIBLE ASSETS

Intangible assets are long-lived productive assets that do not have a physical existence. For the most part, they are legal rights given to the company that give it a competitive edge and aid the company in producing revenue. Examples of intangible assets are: patents, copyrights, trademarks and trade names, franchises, organization costs, and purchased goodwill.

Initially, intangible assets are recorded at historical cost. As an intangible's historical cost is expensed against production periods, the recorded value of the intangible declines. Unlike a depreciable asset whose historical cost is maintained in the asset account and reduced to net book value for the depreciation taken to date (recorded in a separate accumulated depreciation account), amortization taken to date on an intangible may be expensed directly against the asset account. If the balance sheet does not show an accumulated amortization account used to reduce the historical cost of the intangibles to their net book value, the amortization has been written off directly against the assets, and the values as shown for the intangibles are their net book values.

A company may become involved in defending its intangible in an infringement suit. If the company loses the suit, the intangible is worthless and its remaining net book value (along with legal fees) is written off (expensed). If the company wins the suit, its legal fees are added to the intangible's historical cost and expensed over the remainder of the original amortization period.

DEPLETION AND AMORTIZATION

Depletion (for natural resources) and amortization (for intangible assets), like depreciation, specify the assignment of the historical cost of a long-lived asset to operating periods; that is, they match costs of operation (expenses) with operation's results (revenues).

The method of depletion most often used is a units-of-production formula:

costs of the natural resource ÷ estimated recoverable (removable) units of the resource = per unit depletion rate

If a stand of timber costs $2 million and will produce 4 million cords, the depletion rate is $.50 per cord ($2,000,000 ÷ 4,000,000). If 500,000 cords are removed in one year, the depletion expense for that year is (500,000 × $.50) = $250,000.

Amortization is recorded on a straight-line basis (cost ÷ number of amortization periods). The amortization period is the lesser of the intangible's economic life, legal life, or forty years. Suppose we develop a patented process to use in the production of our product. The research-and-development costs were $15 million and were expensed throughout the research-and-development phase. However, attorneys' fees and patent application fees totaled $500,000 (the amount recorded as the historical cost of the patent). We estimate that the patented process will have an economic life of twelve years; therefore, we will expense this patent over the twelve-year period rather than over its legal life of seventeen years. At the end of twelve years, we do not expect the process to aid us in the production of revenues. Amortization expense will be ($500,000 ÷ 12) = $41,667 per year.

Amortization is also taken on "Leasehold Improvements" and "Property Subject to Capital Leases." If leased property will be returned to the lessor at the end of the lease term, the recorded cost of improvements and the leased property is expensed over the term of the lease. If the company will keep the property after the expiration of the lease, it should expense the improvements and property over their economic lives. In this case, the method of computing amortization should be the method we would use to depreciate similar assets that we own.

As with depreciation, the net book values of natural resources and intangibles are not good measures of either the cost of replacing these assets or the amount that could be realized if they were sold. Depletion and amortization computations are based on estimates that are subject to change. When an estimate changes, the net book value of the asset at that time becomes the basis for depletion or amortization over the remaining units of natural resource or amortization period. Management's ability to choose an arbitrary amortization period for certain intangibles such as purchased goodwill (as long as they do not exceed forty years) may create artificial differences between companies and lessen comparability.

TYPES OF INTANGIBLES
Patents

A patent—an exclusive right to use, manufacture, or sell a product or process—is granted for seventeen years. The patent's historical cost is expensed against the revenues that the patent helps produce over the lesser of its legal life (seventeen years) or its estimated economic life. In fields in which technology is rapidly changing, such as computer hardware and software, the economic life of a patent (the estimated period during which the patent will produce revenue) may be less than the patent's legal life.

Copyrights

A copyright gives exclusive control to the creator of a literary, musical, or artistic work, and may be assigned or sold. Currently, copyrights are granted for the life of the creator plus fifty years; however, a copyright's historical cost is expensed over the lesser of its estimated economic life or forty years (accounting principles require that intangibles be expensed over a period that may not exceed forty years). The historical cost of literary and musical copyrights is frequently expensed over the estimated life of the first printing (estimated economic life at the time of printing), since no one can reliably predict a best seller or other highly successful work that will enjoy a long economic life.

Trademarks and Trade Names

Trademarks and trade names are symbols or words that identify a product or company. They are granted for twenty years and are subject to indefinite renewals. Their historical cost is expensed over the lesser of their estimated economic life or forty years.

Franchises

A franchise is the right to sell a product or service under a trade name. The cost of the franchise is expensed over the life of the franchise (forty years in the event that the franchise's life exceeds forty years).

Organizational Costs

Organizational costs are the initial costs of creating a business entity and include attorneys' fees and state fees for incorporation. Organizational costs enable a business to produce revenue over its whole life. These costs are expensed over a period of not more than forty years.

Purchased Goodwill

To an accountant, goodwill is the "excess of cost over the market value" of net assets purchased by a company. In other words, "net assets" is the difference between the value of a company's total assets and its total liabilities. When one business purchases another, it may be willing to pay more for that business than the market value of the individual assets minus any liabilities. This is referred to in accounting as *goodwill*.

Why might a company be willing to pay more than market value for the net assets of another company? Because the purchaser is also acquiring intangibles—the reputation of the products or service of the purchased company, the quality of its personnel, brand-name recognition, and so on.

Accounting principles allow only purchased goodwill to be recorded in the accounts; internal development of a business reputation may not be assigned a value and recorded. Goodwill may have an indefinite economic life, but it must be amortized over a period not to exceed forty years.

Research-and-Development Costs

Research-and-development costs are the costs of discovering new technology and applying it to products, processes, and services. Occasionally, research-and-development costs are recorded as assets and amortized over the lesser of their economic life or forty years. However, accounting principles require that the majority of research-and-development costs be expensed as they arise because of the uncertainty of future benefits. The majority of research-and-development projects do not result in a marketable product, process, or service.

The total amount of research-and-development cost for the fiscal period must be disclosed. While the majority of projects may not succeed, the research they require helps keep a company competitive. The proportion of dollars spent on research and development to a company's sales is one measure of that company's investment in the future and its vitality.

INVESTMENTS

A company may invest its idle funds in many ways; for example, it can choose to leave them in a savings account, put them in certificates of deposit, or invest them in stock or bonds of other companies. This portion of the chapter discusses how a company reports its investments in stocks and bonds in the balance sheet.

Short-term investments, those expected to be held for less than one year, are current assets. Long-term investments are generally reported in their own section of the balance sheet between Current Assets and Property, Plant, and Equipment.

Four different methods exist for reporting the value of an investment in the balance sheet: cost, lower-of-cost-or-market, the equity method, and present value of the investment. Figure 4-2 shows the methods used to value each type of investment.

Investment	*Valuation Method*
Short-term investments	
Common Stock	Lower-of-cost-or-market
Preferred Stock	Cost
Bonds	Cost
Long-term investments	
Common Stock	(If company owns < 20% of outstanding shares)
	Lower-of-cost-or-Market
	(If company owns ≥ 20% but ≤ 50% of outstanding shares)
	Equity method
	(If company owns > 50% of outstanding shares, has entered into a parent-subsidiary relationship, and will prepare consolidated financial statements.)
Preferred Stock	Cost
Bonds	Present Value

FIG. 4-2 *Type of investment and balance sheet valuation method.*

Methods of Valuation

Cost. When an accountant uses the cost method of valuation, the investment is recorded on the balance sheet value at its historical cost. Income from the investment is recorded when dividends are declared or interest is due.

Lower-of-Cost-or-Market. When an accountant uses the lower-of-cost-or-market method, the investment is recorded on the balance sheet at its historical cost unless its current market value is less. Income from the investment is recorded when dividends are declared.

For example, suppose you own two stocks—UVW, Inc. and XYZ, Ltd. The cost of UVW was $100 per share; the cost of XYZ was $200 per share. At the end of the fiscal year, UVW is selling for $110 per share, and XYZ is selling for $160 per share. You should group these stocks together into a portfolio (all short-term investments in common stock or all long-term investments in common stock in which the company owns less than 20 percent of the outstanding shares). You then compare the cost of these portfolios to their current market values. The cost of your portfolio is $300 ($100 + $200), while the stock's current market value is $270 ($110 + $160).

Because the current market value of the portfolio is $30 less than its historical cost ($300 − $270), write it down in value $30 and report it on the balance sheet at $270. The write-down is called an unrealized loss—unrealized because the stock has not yet been sold. If it were sold today, you would incur a loss of $30.

If the investments are short term, the unrealized loss is recorded in the income statement as expense or loss. This is the conservative approach. Because these investments are being held only a short time (less than a year) and because the market value of these investments is less than their cost, a loss at the time of sale is likely. The best estimate of that loss is the difference between the investments' current market value and their historical cost.

If the investments are long term, the unrealized loss is no longer likely to occur. You then reduce the investment portfolio to its current market value and from owners' equity the "Net Unrealized Loss on Noncurrent Marketable Equity Securities."

When you prepare your next balance sheet, if the investments' current market value equals or exceeds their cost, they will be written back up to cost. If the portfolio is short term, you will record the difference on the income statement as revenue or gain; if the portfolio is long term, you will increase the investment account back to cost and remove the negative owners' equity account "Net Unrealized Loss on Noncurrent Marketable Equity Securities."

Equity Method. If the investor exercises significant influence over the affairs of the investee, the method of choice for accounting for the investment is the equity method. The investor gains such influence by buying common stock (the company's voting stock) and holding it as a long-term investment. An investor who owns 20 percent of the outstanding shares of common stock can elect one-fifth of the board of directors. Accountants assume that significant influence exists once an investor has acquired 20 percent or more of a company's common stock.

An accountant using the equity method initially records the investment at historical cost. As the investee earns income from the company, the investor records his or her share as income from investment. Income increases the value of the investee company and the value of the investment. As dividends are paid, the investor reduces the value of the investment. Dividends, paid in cash, are assumed to be a withdrawal of investment. Dividends are cash; income is only an increase in value. Recording income and dividends in this manner causes the investment account to mirror the changes that are occurring in the investee's stockholder's equity.

For example, suppose that we buy 10,000 of the outstanding shares of CDE Corp. for $2 million. This investment represents one-third of the outstanding shares. CDE's owners' equity has a recorded value of $6 million. Our investment account reflects a third of CDE's owners' equity, or:

Investor's Accounts	*Investee's Accounts*
Investment $2,000,000	CDE's Owners' Equity $6,000,000

If CDE has net income of $900,000 for the year, our investment will increase by $300,000, or:

Beginning Investment	$2,000,000	CDE's Beginning Owners' Equity	$6,000,000
+ Income	300,000	+ Income	900,000
	$2,300,000		$6,900,000

Next, suppose CDE pays $450,000 in dividends. We will receive $150,000 in dividends. The dividends are a withdrawal of investment and reduce our investment account:

		CDE's Beginning	
Beginning Investment	$2,000,000	Owners' Equity	$6,000,000
+ Income	300,000	+ Income	900,000
Dividends	(150,000)	− Dividends	(450,000)
	$2,150,000		$6,450,000

Notice that each time CDE's equity increases or decreases, our investment increases or decreases proportionately. CDE's owners' equity is $6,450,000. Because we own one-third of CDE, our investment is recorded at one-third of the value of CDE's owners' equity.

If we had paid more than $2 million for our investment in CDE, the excess amount paid would have been considered goodwill (see page 48 of this chapter). Accounting rules require that goodwill be expensed over a period of forty years or less. As the goodwill is expensed, the value of our investment decreases. After all the goodwill has been expensed, our investment account reflects our portion of the investee's recorded owner's equity.

Present Value. Long-term investments in bonds are recorded at present value. The present value of a bond is its cash value at a point in time.

Suppose we are willing to pay $1,100 for a 10-year, $1,000 bond that pays 10 percent interest annually. If we hold this bond to maturity, we will receive only $900 more than we originally invested. (We receive $1,000 in interest over the 10-year period plus the principle of $1,000 at maturity, but we invested $1,100—a $100 premium.) In this case, writing off $10 of the premium each year causes the investment to decrease $10 a year and $90 ($100 less the $10 write-off) to be recorded as interest income. At maturity, the bond will be valued at $1,000, its cash value.

Some industries have their own valuation methods for investments. For instance, insurance companies and brokerage firms value their short-term investments at current market value even if that value is greater than historical cost.

OTHER ASSETS

"Other assets" is a catch-all category that includes business resources that cannot be classified as current assets, investments, property, plant, and equipment, or intangibles—for example, long-lived assets that are awaiting sale and that are no longer being used in production. (Classifying them as property, plant, and equipment would imply that they are currently in use.) Long-term prepayments of expenses (such as a three-year insurance policy) may also be classified as "other."

CHAPTER PERSPECTIVE

Continuing our discussion of the balance sheet, this chapter discussed noncurrent assets. Noncurrent assets consist of (1) plant, property and equipment, (2) intangibles, (3) investments, and (4) other assets. We discussed each kind of noncurrent asset and the way it is valued for inclusion on the balance sheet. Long-lived, tangible, productive assets are depreciated; intangible assets are amortized; and natural resources are depleted. The chapter discussed the weakneses of historical-cost accounting, including the weaknesses of depreciation accounting and of valuing certain kinds of investments.

The Balance Sheet: Liabilities and Stockholders' Equity

INTRODUCTION AND MAIN POINTS

As we stated in Chapter 1, all assets are acquired with funds generated from borrowing or from stockholders' investment or, in the case of retained earnings, reinvestment. Hence, assets equal liabilities plus owners' equity. But there are many different kinds of liabilities and owners' equity accounts. Therefore, balance sheets display liabilities and owners' equity amounts separated into categories and subcategories that provide information to readers of financial statements and make analysis easier.

In this chapter, we discuss the types of liabilities and owners' equity accounts that you might find on the balance sheet omitting coverage of readily understood terms such as mortgage payable and concentrating on less widely understood concepts. After studying the material in this chapter:

■ You will understand how total equities are separated into useful categories and subcategories.

■ You will know the meanings of the different equity classifications.

■ You will know the accounts generally included in the balance-sheet equity categories.

■ You will understand the way accountants treat several nonroutine debt transactions, such as retirement before maturity and troubled-debt restructuring.

■ You will understand how accountants account for bonds.

■ You will understand the different sources of invested capital and be able to identify the features of the different classes of stock.

■ You will know what retained earnings are and will understand the significance of retained-earnings appropriations.

EQUITIES

Equities are property rights. The equity of creditors is called liability and is a liability, or debt, of the company. The equity of owners is called stockholders' equity or owners' equity. Equities are shown on the balance sheet in the general order of preference on liquidation. For example, the liabilities or equities of creditors are shown before the equities of owners because creditors would be paid before owners if the company were liquidated. Within owners' equity, common stock and retained earnings are listed after preferred stock issues because common stockholders would be the last persons paid at liquidation. This is not a hard-and-fast rule, but it does represent the general order in which accountants arrange groups of equities and individual equities within each group.

The equities side of the balance sheet usually appears in the following general order:

LIABILITIES
Current Liabilities
    Trade Payables
    Notes Payable
    Unearned Revenues
    Short-term Contingencies
Noncurrent Liabilities
    Mortgages Payable
    Notes and Bonds Payable
    Other Long-term Payables
SHAREHOLDERS' OR OWNERS' EQUITY
    Preferred Stock
    Common Stock
    Retained Earnings

Figure 5-1 shows the equities side of an actual balance sheet and portions of two financial statement notes that supplement the balance sheet and provide full disclosure of debt and capital structure.

CURRENT LIABILITIES

Current liabilities are obligations of the company that are expected to be paid, from current assets, within one year of the date on the balance sheet. The types of current liabilities shown on the balance sheet include:

■ Trade Accounts Payable: Amounts owed to supplies for merchandise or services, such as an unpaid invoice for merchandise purchases or the utility bill.

■ Short-term Notes Payable: Short-term interest-bearing debt. Notes are formal documents showing the amount borrowed (principal) and stating as an annual rate the percentage interest

Liabilities and Shareholders' Equity

Current Liabilities

Payable to suppliers and others........	$ 151,726	$ 154,013
Notes payable and current portion of long-term debt....................	29,046	22,465
Taxes on income	2,347	13,284
	183,119	189,762
Long-Term Debt (Note 12).............	226,240	275,535
Deferred Income Taxes...............	74,199	57,676
Shareholders' Equity		
Serial preferred stock, no par value Authorized 30,000,000 shares None issued (Note 7)		
Common shares, no par value Authorized 150,000,000 shares Issued 45,920,440 shares (Note 7)...	7,175	7,175
Capital in excess of stated value.......	48,319	45,982
Translation of foreign currencies	(8,238)	(3,516)
Retained earnings	485,093	417,115
Treasury shares at cost (1989–2,193,910; 1988–2,059,607	(20,775)	(12,270)
	511,574	454,486
	$ 995,132	$ 977,459

FIG. 5-1 *Liabilities and Shareholders' Equity Section of Balance Sheet*

that must be paid. Only the principal is recorded on the balance sheet under the title "notes payable." Any interest the company owes is called interest payable.

■ Current Portion of Long-term Debt: The portion of principal on long-term debt that will be paid within the year. Long-term debt is usually payable in installments (for example, mortgage payments). Any unpaid interest on long-term debt is recorded as interest payable.

■ Interest Payable: The unpaid interest on short-term and long-term debt. This is the interest charge for the days from the last payments to the balance sheet date.

■ Unearned Revenues: Payments made in advance by customers for product or services. Revenue is not recorded until the product is delivered to the customer or the service is completed.

■ Tax and Other Withholdings: Income taxes and social security taxes (FICA taxes) withheld from employees' paychecks.

NOTE 7: CHANGES IN AUTHORIZED CAPITAL

In April 1989, the shareholders approved an increase in the total number of authorized no par common shres from 75,000,000 to 150,000,000. In addition, the shareholders approved the authorization of 30,000,000 shares of Preferred Stock, no par value, which may consist of one or more series that the Board of Directors may, from time to time, establish and designate.

NOTE 12: DEBT

Debt at December 31 was as follows:

(Dollars in thousands)	1989	1988
Commercial paper, average rate of 8.8%–1989 and 9.4%–1988	$132,310	$169,590
Private placement notes payable, interest at 9.3%, due 1992 through 1998............	50,000	50,000
Notes payable through 1992 with variable interest rates (average rate of 9.8% at December 31, 1988)		31,000
Foreign denominated debt, average rate of 13.8% at December 31, 1989, and 15.3% at December 13, 1988	50,959	26,686
Industrial revenue bonds payable through 2007, average rate of 8.3% at December 31, 1989 and 1988	10,151	11,147
Other notes............................	11,866	9,577
Total debt	255,286	298,000
Less current portion.....................	29,046	22,465
Long-term debt	$226,240	$275,535

The Company maintains fully committed bank lines of credit to support its $200 million commercial paper program. One-half of these lines expires in 1993 with the remaining one-half expiring in 1994. Accordingly, commerical paper borrowings are classified as long-term debt on the balance sheet.

The Company has two interest-rate-swap agreements with banks: $25 million due 1992 at 9.8%, and $50 million due 1994 at 10.5%. The purpose of these agreements is to reduce the Company's exposure to floating interest rates on a portion of its commercial paper borrowings.

Certain of the Company's debt agreements impose restrictions with respect to the maintenance of financial ratios and the disposition of assets. The most restrictive covenant requires that long-term debt shall not exceed 90% of net tangible assets.

FIG. 5-2 *Supporting notes for Figure 5-1*

These withholdings plus additional FICA taxes and unemployment taxes must be paid quarterly by the employer to federal and state governments.

▬ Income Taxes Payable: The portion of income taxes the business has not yet paid. These are taxes due on the company's earnings (not withholdings as above).

▬ Contingencies: A number of "likely to occur" contingencies are recorded as liabilities (see Chapter 7). Examples are "Vacation Wages Payable" and "Estimated Liabilities Under Warranties." "Vacation Wages Payable" is the company's estimate of vacation pay that has been earned by employees but that has not been paid because the employees have not yet taken their vacations. "Estimated Liabilities Under Warranties" is the estimated repair cost of items manufactured and sold under warranty. Only the portion of the contingencies expected to be paid in the coming year are classified as current liabilities. Be sure to read the notes to the financial statements to get a feel for possible contingency.

NONCURRENT LIABILITIES

Noncurrent (or long-term) liabilities are obligations that are not expected to be paid for at least one year from the date on the balance sheet or are not expected to be paid from current assets. Noncurrent liabilities are carried at their present values, the amount of money the company would have to pay to settle the debt at the balance-sheet date and excluding any future interest that is not yet due. Most noncurrent liabilities call for periodic payments of principal and interest. The portion of principal that will be due within the year is classified as a current liability (see page 56).

Examples of noncurrent liabilities include long-term notes and mortgages payable, bonds payable, obligations under capital leases, unfunded accrued pension cost and unfunded projected benefit obligation, and deferred tax liability.

Unless you read carefully the notes to the financial statements, you will not understand noncurrent liabilities. Many long-term debt covenants place restrictions on the borrower. For instance, a debt covenant may require a company to maintain a 2:1 current ratio of current assets to current liabilities. What if the current ratio is only 1.9:1? Then the company is technically in default on its long-term obligation and the debt can be called due at any time. Unless management believes it can correct the current ratio deficiency within the specified grace period, it must reclassify the debt as current.

Settling Debt Before Maturity

Sometimes a company pays off debt before it is due. Any settlement of debt before its due date causes the company to report a gain or loss—a gain if the cost of settling the debt is less than the debt's recorded value on the balance sheet (including any interest) or a loss if the cost of settling the debt is greater than the debt's recorded value on the balance sheet (including any interest due). These gains and losses must be reported on the income statement as extraordinary items (see Chapter 7). Why might a company take a loss to settle a debt before it is due? The loss may be less than the future interest payments, or the company may now be able to borrow money at lower interest rates.

Restructuring of Troubled Debt

Sometimes a company experiences problems repaying its debts. A troubled-debt restructuring is an agreement by which the creditor grants the debtor concessions to help the debtor avoid defaulting. The concessions may take the form of transferring assets to the creditor, transferring the debtor's own stock to the creditor, or modifying the terms of debt.

The creditor may agree to settle the debt for noncash assets whose market value is less than the recorded value of the debt (including any interest due). The debtor reports a gain on the restructuring equal to the amount by which the debt exceeds the market value of the assets being given to the creditor. The gain is usually reported on the income statement as an extraordinary item.

Alternatively, the creditor may agree to settle the debt for shares of the debtor's stock. In other words, the creditor becomes an owner. The debtor reports a gain on the restructuring equal to the amount by which the debt exceeds the market value of the stock being given to the creditor. The gain is usually reported on the income statement as an extraordinary item.

When the creditor agrees to modify the terms of debt (principal, interest rate, or length of time), the debtor may have to pay more or less than the recorded value of the debt plus any interest due. If all of the new payments called for by the modified terms of debt are less than the recorded value of the debt (including any interest due), the debtor records a gain, usually as an extraordinary item on the income statement. Payments made by the debtor after restructuring are considered to be payments of principal. The debtor, who could not pay even the debt owed, let alone additional interest, does not recognize interest expense.

On the other hand, what if modifying the terms of debt results in total payments that exceed the recorded value of the debt (including any interest due)? In this case, the debtor recognizes the recorded value of the debt as the principal of the restructured debt. The amount by which the new payments exceed this principal is the debtor's interest expense over the remaining term of the debt.

BONDS

Bonds are a form of long-term debt, usually repaid in ten to twenty years. When a company needs to borrow a large amount of money—say, $20 million—it has two basic choices. The company can seek to find one lender who will supply the entire $20 million, or it can find several smaller lenders, each of whom contributes part of the total amount needed. When a company issues bonds, it is taking the second option. Each bond is a debt agreement for $1,000; a $20 million debt is divided into 20,000 bonds, each carrying a debt of $1,000.

When bonds are issued, the company can obtain its $20 million from any number of lenders (up to 20,000). When an investor (lender) "buys" $50,000 in bonds, the investor has, in essence, agreed to lend the company $50,000. The debt is supported by fifty bonds of $1,000 each. Each bond is a debt agreement, with the interest rate, interest payment schedule (usually semiannually), and bond maturity date (when the principal amount is returned) all contained in the bond.

The bond debt may be secured or unsecured; unsecured bonds are called debentures. All the bonds may be retired (repaid) at the same time, or they may be structured to mature (come due) in increments. Bonds that mature in increments are called serial bonds.

Amortization of Bonds

Amortization is the accounting method that causes the bond interest expense recorded by a company to be different from the cash paid as interest on the money borrowed. For example, a typical bond might be for a debt of $1,000 for ten years, with interest at 10 percent per year, paid semiannually. The company is, in essence, making two promises: to pay the lender $1,000 in ten years, and to pay interest of $100 (1,000 × .10) each year. As long as the market rate of interest is 10 percent for bonds of that particular type (secured or unsecured), for the same term and for companies in the same risk class, the company can issue the bond without a problem, receiving $1,000 and paying the principal and interest as agreed.

But suppose that the interest rate rises before the bond is issued. A lender will no longer purchase a $1,000 bond (and agree to lend $1,000) for 10 percent interest; the lender will either demand a higher return or insist on investing less than $1,000 in order to receive the payments (principal and interest) described in the bond agreement. Perhaps, at the higher market rate of interest, the lender might agree to lend only $900 in exchange for the payments described in the bond. The following would then be true:

The company would pay:

1. At the end of ten years	$1,000
2. In equal semiannual payments each year	
($100 × 10)	$1,000
Total amount paid	$2,000
Less amount received from lender	900
Excess paid over amount received	$1,100

The excess paid over the amount received is the true interest cost of the funds. The company pays $100 cash in interest per year, but the true average annual cost of the money borrowed is $110 (1,100 ÷ 10) per year. The company records the $100 cash outflow each year and the $110 average annual expense. The extra $10 interest expense ($110 − 100) in excess of the actual cash paid is the amortization of the excess paid over the amount received.

When bonds are presented in an annual report, details of the security agreement (if any), maturity dates, and interest rates can be found in the notes to the financial statements. The bonds are shown in the long-term liabilities section of the financial statements. When a bond is issued at face (for $1,000), the bond is presented in the balance sheet as follows:

Bond payable $1,000

If the market interest rate is more or less than the interest in the bond agreement, the bonds are sold at a discount or premium from face, and their presentation in the balance sheet is different. If a bond is issued for $900 (as described above) it appears in the financial statement as follows:

Bond payable	$1,000	
Less discount on bonds payable	100	900

Bonds sold for more than the face amount are accounted for in a similar fashion. A bond issued for $1,100 appears in the financial statements with a premium rather than a discount:

Bonds payable	$1,000	
Plus premium on bonds payable	100	1,100

STOCKHOLDERS' EQUITY

The amount of owners' equity can be calculated by subtracting the equity of creditors (liabilities) from the total assets of the company: $A - L = OE$. Expressed in this form, owners' equity is sometimes called "net assets," meaning "assets net of (less) liabilities." When creditors have transactions with a company, the transactions are at arm's length; when owners have transactions with their own company, it is as related parties, not at arm's length. Since owners can legally remove capital as dividends only under certain conditions and only from certain sources, the focus in accounting for owners' equity is on the *detailed sources of capital.*

A complex owners' equity presentation may have capital that comes from many sources, such as donations, treasury stock transactions, preferred stock, subscribed stock, common stock, appropriated retained earnings, and unappropriated retained earning. Each element or source of capital is fully described in a company's annual report. Some information about owners' equity is included in the body of the financial statements, and additional information is disclosed in the notes to the financial statements.

CLASSES OF STOCK

All stock issued by a company is either preferred stock or common stock, regardless of what name the issue of stock may be given. There is (except in very rare cases) only one class of common stock; all other classes of stock, regardless of name, are preferred in some way over the one class of common stock.

If a company is liquidated, creditors are paid proceeds of the liquidation before the claims of stockholders are considered. In addition, the different classes of stock are ranked in the order in which their holders will receive the proceeds of the liquidation.

The stock with the least claim to assets on liquidation is common stock. All other classes of stock are classes of preferred stock, since those stockholders have preference over common stockholders in liquidation, and perhaps in other ways.

Common Stock

Because of their bottom ranking as claimants on corporate assets at liquidation, holders of common stock are said to be residual equity holders; they receive the residual left after all creditors and all holders of other classes of stock have been paid. Holders of common stock may receive nothing or they may receive a great deal when a company is liquidated. While all creditors and preferred shareholders have a contractually stated amount that they will receive if the company is liquidated and funds are available, holders of common stock have no such contractually stated amount; they are last in line and, as such, receive whatever is left, large or small. They take the greatest risk but may also receive the greatest reward.

Holders of common stock have three rights that result from their stock ownership:

1. the right to share in assets on liquidation (as residual equity holders);
2. the right to receive distributions of earnings as dividends;
3. the right to maintain proportionate share of ownership when new common shares are issued (called the preemptive right) and to vote their opinion on company management.

Par Value. Par value (or stated value) is an arbitrary amount assigned to shares of stock, both common and preferred. Par or stated value had real meaning decades ago when securities regulations were different, but these terms have little significance now. Originally, par or stated value referred to the legal minimum capital to be furnished by the stockholder and not removed from the corporation except by a liquidating dividend. The regulators' concern was that owners and stockholders who believed the company to be in financial trouble would remove their investment and leave creditors without recourse. Securities regulations now prevent this action, but the terms still exist and stock is shown in the balance sheet with the stockholder's investment divided into par (or stated) value and Premium, "Paid in Capital in Excess of Par (or Stated) Value," or simply "Additional Paid in Capital."

Suppose stockholders paid $110,000 for shares of common

stock with a total par value of $90,000. The owners' equity section of the balance sheet would disclose the following:

Common Stock (at par)	$90,000
Additional Paid in Capital	20,000

Shares Authorized and Issued. For common stock and each class of preferred stock, the number of shares authorized by the charter and the board of directors, and the number of shares issued and outstanding are disclosed in the balance sheet. Occasionally, when there is treasury stock (explained later in this chapter), the number of shares outstanding will be less than the number issued because some shares are held in the treasury.

Preferred Stock

Holders of common stock may vote to create a class of stock—preferred stock—that has first claim on assets at liquidation. In addition, the class of stock is given preference in the distribution of dividends; preferred stock dividends usually must be paid before common stock dividends are paid. If the company does not create enough earnings to declare dividends for both common and preferred shareholders, holders of common stock may receive no dividends at all.

Why would holders of common stock permit (much less vote for) the creation of a stock that receives preference with regard to dividends each year and assets on liquidation? The answer is simple: while holders of preferred stock are given precedence with regard to assets and dividends, they do not have the right to vote on company policy. Preferred shareholders have no voice in company management. They are, in fact, more like long-term bondholders (creditors) than owners: Both receive a fixed payment each year as dividend or interest, both have preference over common stockholders as to assets on liquidation, but neither has a vote in company management. Long-term bondholders will eventually be repaid their investment—the debt principal—while preferred stockholders will not.

To explain fully preferred stock, we must address three other points: dividend calculation, obligation for missed dividend payments, and conversion privileges.

1. *Dividend calculation:* The dividend rate for preferred stock is a set amount each year and is usually stated as a dollar amount per share (i.e, a $5 preferred stock pays $5 dividends)

or as a percentage of par value (i.e., an 8 percent, $100 par value preferred share pays $8 dividends).

2. *Obligation for missed dividend payments:* If the dividend agreement on preferred stock is cumulative, a company must catch up any missed dividend payments to preferred shareholders before dividends can be paid to common shareholders. This is important because a company has no legal obligation to pay dividends until they are declared by the board of directors; thus, even though holders of preferred stock are entitled to dividends at a set rate, there is no guarantee that they will be paid until the dividends are declared by the board. For example, assume dividends to preferred shareholders would total $100,000 per year, but the company does not declare and does not pay dividends for years one and two. In year three, the board declares total dividends of $350,000. If the dividend agreement for preferred shareholders specifies that dividend payments are cumulative, the preferred shareholders must receive the dividend payments they missed before common shareholders can receive payments. A cumulative distribution schedule for the above example is shown below:

For Preferred Stock:

Current year dividend (Year 3)	$100,000
Prior year dividends (Years 1 and 2)	200,000
Total dividends for preferred stockholders	$300,000
Residual amount available for dividends to common stockholders	50,000
Total dividends paid	$350,000

In contrast, if a preferred stock does not have a cumulative dividend payment agreement, the company does not have to pay dividends missed before paying dividends to common shareholders. A noncumulative distribution of the same $350,000 under the conditions described is shown below:

For Preferred Stock:

Current-year dividend (year three)	$100,000
Prior-year dividend (years one and two)	-0-
Total dividends for preferred stock holders	$100,000
Residual amount available for dividends to common stockholders	250,000
Total dividends paid	$350,000

3. *Conversion privilege:* Some preferred stock agreements contain an option allowing the preferred stock to be exchanged for common shares. Since common shares do not have a fixed dividend rate, they carry more risk; however, they offer more opportunity for market price increases. To make preferred shares more attractive to investors, the stock may be convertible to common shares in some ratio (ten shares of common for one share of preferred, for example).

Preferred stock, like common stock, is shown in the balance sheet stockholders' equity section and is separated into "Par Value" and "Capital Paid in Excess of Par":

Preferred Stock (at Par)	$500,000
Paid in Capital in Excess of Par	100,000

Again, the number of shares issued and authorized is disclosed.

Treasury Stock

Stock issued by a company may later be reacquired by the company, which may then retire or cancel it. Reacquired stock that is not retired or canceled is referred to as "treasury stock."

Treasury stock is not an asset; a company cannot create an asset by holding stock in itself. Treasury stock represents a decrease in outstanding stock, just as if the shares had been retired, but the reduction in shares outstanding is not made and the treasury stock is shown as a reduction in stockholders' equity in one of two ways. (Under either method, total stockholders' equity is decreased by the purchase of treasury shares.)

1. The treasury stock may be shown at par value as reduction in common stock.

Stockholders' Equity

Contributed capital:		
Common stock at par	500,000	
Less treasury stock at par	100,000	
	400,000	
Paid in capital in excess of par	80,000	480,000
Retained earnings		200,000
Total stockholders' equity		680,000

2. The treasury stock may be shown at reacquisition cost as a reduction of total stockholders' equity.

Stockholders' Equity

Common stock at par	40,000	
Paid in capital in excess of par	50,000	90,000
Retained earnings		100,000
Total		190,000
Less treasury stock at cost		10,000
Total stockholders' equity		180,000

Just as treasury stock is not an asset, an income statement loss or gain cannot result from treasury stock transactions. Events transpire that you and I would call a "loss" (reacquiring treasury stock for $20 per share and later reissuing it for $12) or a "gain" (reacquiring treasury shares at $30 and reissuing the shares at $40). But it is illegal for a company to produce a gain or loss, in accounting terms, on transactions involving its own stock. When total stockholders' equity is decreased by treasury stock transactions, the decrease is usually taken directly from retained earnings, and no loss is recorded on the income statement. When total stockholders' equity is increased by treasury stock transactions, the increase is recorded as a separate source of capital called "paid-in capital from treasury stock transactions."

Subscribed Stock

Companies may issue stock outright—selling the stock and receiving cash, property or services in exchange—or on a subscription basis. A stock subscription is a legally binding contract between the issuing company and the subscriber or purchaser of the stock. Stock subscription agreements allow payment for the stock to be deferred and accomplish two goals:
1. They give the company a legal claim for the contract price of the stock.
2. They give the purchaser the legal status of a stockholder (unless specific rights are withheld by state law or contract).

The company's legal claim to the stock contract price is recorded in the balance sheet (usually as a current asset) as "Stock Subscriptions Receivable." Stock subscriptions are like other company receivables: The purchaser/stockholder pays against the outstanding balance according to the contract agreement. The stock certificates are ordinarily not issued until the contract price is paid in full.

When the subscription agreement is signed, the source of the new asset "Subscription Receivable" is shown in the owners' equity section of the balance sheet as an increase in two accounts:

1. The par value of the stock is recorded in an account called "Common Stock Subscribed."
2. Any excess over par value is recorded in the account "Premium on Common Stock" or "Paid-in Capital in Excess of Par."

When the subscribed stock is fully paid, there will no longer be a "Subscription Receivable" category carried in current assets, and "Common Stock Subscribed" will be transferred to "Common Stock."

Although a stock subscription agreement is a legal contract and the subscription receivable is a legitimate receivable, corporate policy and state law vary as to how a defaulted subscription is treated. When a subscriber defaults, the company may take any of the following actions:

1. It can refund the amount received.
2. It can refund the amount received less the cost of reselling the stock.
3. It can declare as forefeited the amount received from the subscriber.
4. It can issue shares equal to the amount already received.

Donated Capital

When property or services are donated to a company, the value of the asset is recorded and the source of the asset is shown as a corresponding increase in owners' equity, called "Paid-in Capital from Donations." If the donation is very large, the nature of the donation may be identified, as in "Paid-in Capital from Donated Plant Site."

RETAINED EARNINGS

Retained earnings is the dollar amount of assets furnished by company earnings that were not distributed as dividends. The primary key to understanding retained earnings is to realize that retained earnings do not represent cash—they represent only a source of assets and not any particular asset.

If a company earns $500,000 and does not declare dividends, retained earnings are increased by the $500,000 retained in the business. But what does a company do with $500,000 received as profits? They may use it to expand the business (to buy new equipment or increase inventories, for instance) or to repay an outstanding loan. They would certainly *not* keep the $500,000 as cash in the bank. The $500,000 increase in retained earnings documents a source of net assets (assets minus liabilities) but does not indicate which assets were provided by the income.

In addition to being a source of assets, retained earnings are also the maximum amount that can be distributed to stockholders as dividends. The company probably does not have cash available to pay dividends in the amount of retained earnings (nor would the company wish to, if earnings could be reinvested in the business). A company frequently distributes a portion of each year's earnings as dividends in some general pattern, perhaps some amount per share or some percentage of earnings; the remainder is retained and invested in the business.

Appropriations of Retained Earnings

When a company embarks on a special project, it may limit dividend payments until the project is completed, either because it is required to do so by a major creditor or because it wishes to preserve cash for expansion. When management limits dividend payments, there are two methods of notifying stockholders:

1. Through the notes to the financial statements
2. By appropriating a portion of retained earnings

That portion of retained earnings listed as appropriated in the owners' equity section of the balance sheet is not available for dividend payments. Since, as we have stressed, retained earnings constitute only the source of the assets, not an asset, no cash or any other resource need be set aside to fund the project undertaken.

When the project is completed, appropriated retained earnings are unappropriated and become available for dividend payments. Cash may have been spent on the project (building a plant, retiring bonds) and the composition of assets changed, but retained earnings are unaffected except for changing the designation of the appropriated component back to unappropriated.

Companies may use an appropriation of retained earnings simply to reduce the size of unappropriated retained earnings "available" for dividends. Uninformed investors may believe they should receive more of the earnings retained in the business, or labor unions may believe that wages should be higher—neither group realizing that the earnings retained are reinvested to buy new equipment, build new plants, and create more profit for owners and wages for workers.

CHAPTER PERSPECTIVE

This chapter has discussed the accounts and balance sheet captions you are most likely to encounter in the liability and owners' equity sections of the balance sheet. Liabilities are usually divided into current and noncurrent categories; owners' equity may divide capital into contributed and earned capital. Each category may include many different account titles. To understand the broad array of items that you may encounter in this part of the balance sheet, you must understand how accountants treat the different events affecting these items and you must read the balance sheet and other financial statements, including the notes to the financial statements, carefully.

The Income Statement: Operating Income

INTRODUCTION AND MAIN POINTS

Accountants and financial-statement readers usually consider information in the income statement to be more important than information in the balance sheet. If, for example, a company has a high level of debt, an investor may still believe the company will be successful—*if* the company has a strong earnings record. But if a company has a more moderate level of debt, an investor may doubt the company's ability to survive—*if* the company's earnings record is poor. This chapter is the first of two chapters covering the components of the income statement.

This chapter describes each component in a classified income statement and discusses in detail the components of operating income. Different inventory flow methods are introduced and the difference between inventories held by manufacturers and inventories held by retailers is discussed. Chapter 7 covers the remainder of the classified income statement, nonoperating revenues, and expenses.

After studying the material in this chapter:

 You will know the components of a classified income statement.

 You will understand the difference that different inventory accounting flow methods can produce.

 You will know the difference between the kinds of inventories that may be held by a manufacturer and by a retailer.

 You will know how accountants determine operating income and the significance of this portion of the income statement.

INCOME STATEMENT COMPONENTS

The income statement reports the results of business activities for a period of time, typically a fiscal year. These results are classified as revenues and expenses. Revenues measure the inflow of new assets to the business from the earnings process; expenses measure the outflow of assets or the using up of assets in that same process. Net income represents an increase in assets and owners' equity, while a net loss represents a decrease in assets and owners' equity.

Annual business income or loss is computed by subtracting the expenses that occurred during the year from the revenues earned during the year. If revenues exceed expenses, the business has earned income; if expenses exceed revenues, a loss has occurred. Revenues and expenses are recorded at the time they are earned or occur, regardless of when cash is received or paid, according to the accrual concept used by accountants to measure business activity and income.

THE INCOME STATEMENT

Each income statement contains information unique to the company preparing it. Depending on the activities of the company, an income statement may contain the following sections:

Sales or Operating Revenues:	Net sales revenues (sales less returns) or service revenues are reported in this section.
Cost of Goods Sold:	This is the amount the company paid for the inventory it sold. A service organization does not have this expense.
Gross Profit:	This is the difference between net sales revenues and the cost of goods sold. From this profit margin, the company must cover all other costs if it expects to have net income. A service organization does not report a gross profit; a company may or may not calculate gross profit.
Operating Expenses:	These include selling, general, and administrative expenses.
Other Revenues:	These increases in asset value occur from transactions that are not directly related to operations; for instance, interest earned on investments arises from a decision related to managing idle cash, not trying to earn a profit through sales or by providing services.
Other Expenses:	These decreases in asset value occur from transactions not directly related to operations. For

instance, interest expense arises from the decision to finance operations by increasing debt. That decision is not related to trying to earn a profit through sales or by providing services.

Pretax Income Continuing Operations:

This figure is the sum of all the revenues from and expenses related to the portion of the business that is continuing.

Income Tax Expense:

This figure is a function of pretax income from continuing operations and the appropriate tax rates.

Income from Continuing Operations:

This is the after-tax income of the portion of the business that is continuing.

Discontinued Operations:

This may either be an after-tax gain or loss on a segment of the business that management intends to sell.

Income Before Extraordinary Items:

This is a subtotal.

Extraordinary Items:

These are after-tax gains or losses on transactions that are unusual and that are not expected to reoccur.

Cumulative Effect of a Change in Accounting Principle:

A change in accounting principle occurs when management changes from one acceptable accounting principle to another. This is a catch-up adjustment. For example, suppose we change depreciation methods to a method that would have recorded more depreciation expense than was recorded under the old method. To make the records look as if we have always used the new method, we must take the additional depreciation—the cumulative effect of the change in accounting principle.

When a company reports a change in accounting principle, it also shows pro forma income figures in a schedule attached to the income statement. These pro forma income figures show what past net incomes would have been if the new principle had been used in those reporting years.

Net Income (Loss): This is the total of all reported revenues (gains) and expenses (losses).

Earnings Per Common Share: Publicly traded companies that are required to present several ratios summarize the assumed income earned by each holder of a share of common share. Earnings-per-share ratios are an income figure divided by an average number of common shares assumed to be outstanding.

Not all income statements include the sections presented above. For instance, in a year in which a company does not have discontinued operations or a change in accounting principle, those sections drop out of the income statement. Care should be taken when comparing income statements over time; for example, income from continuing operations is comparable only to a later year's net income taken from an income statement that does not have discontinued operations, extraordinary items, or a change in accounting principle. Figure 6-1a contains an example of a simple income statement taken from actual financial statements; Figure 6-1b contains a more complex example.

REVENUE FROM SALES AND SERVICES

Revenues (the price charged by the company for its merchandise or services) are generally recorded at the time of sale or completion of the service. However, two conditions must be met before revenue can be recorded: The earnings process must be substantially complete, and the company must be reasonably certain the revenue can be collected.

The earnings process is not substantially complete if:
- The seller and buyer have not agreed on the price of the merchandise or service.
- The buyer does not have to pay the seller until the merchandise is resold.
- The buyer does not have to pay the seller if the merchandise is stolen or physically destroyed.
- The buyer and seller are related parties (for example, parent company and subsidiary).

STATEMENTS OF INCOME
(Years ended December 31)

(Dollars in thousands except per share)

	1989	1988
Sales	$ 1,655,830	$ 1,599,751
Cost and expenses		
Cost of products sold............	1,306,758	1,263,978
Selling, general and administrative expenses.....................	161,546	148,417
Interest expense	29,440	25,175
Acquisition consolidation charges		
Income from operations before income taxes	158,086	162,181
Taxes on income (Note 16)	60,906	67,029
Income from operations before equity in earnings of affiliates	97,180	95,152
Equity in earnings of affiliates (Note 10).............................	6,381	1,125
Net income	$ 103,561	$ 96,277
Average shares outstanding	43,897,002	43,816,224
Net income	$2.36	$2.20
Dividends per share..............	$.81	$.64

FIG. 6-1a *A simple income statement.*

▬ The seller must still provide significant services to the buyer or aid in reselling the product.

If substantial performance has occurred and the collectibility of the revenue is reasonably certain, the sale of product or service can be recorded. If a company cannot estimate the collectibility of a sale, it records revenue as the customer makes payments. This has the effect of recording the sale on a cash basis rather than when it is earned.

Accountants use one of two methods to record revenue as the customer makes payments: the installment method or the cost-recovery method. The *installment method* records part of each payment as revenue. Suppose, for example, we sold merchandise that cost us $40 for $100. The gross profit on the sale is $60 ($100 − $40) or 60 percent of the sales price ($60/$100). As the customer makes payments, $.60 of each $1 collected is reported as revenue. (The remaining $.40 is cost of goods sold expense.)

Statement of Income

In the thousands except per share amounts For the years ended December 31	1988	1987	1986
Net sales	$3,021,352	$2,647,900	$2,799,481
Cost of goods sold	2,264,736	1,947,335	2,105,587
Administrative, selling and service engineering expenses	471,120	431,986	455,457
Restructure of operations	—	—	23,000
Operating income	285,496	268,579	215,437
Interest expense	32,672	38,641	60,900
Other income (expense), net	(24,603)	(26,233)	(16,592)
Dresser-Rand income (loss)	2,567	(42,569)	—
Nonrecurring gains	—	—	33,694
Nonrecurring charges	—	—	17,305
Earnings before income taxes, extraordinary item and cumulative effect of accounting change	230,788	161,136	154,334
Provision for income taxes	69,200	53,200	53,700
Earnings before extraordinary item and cumulative effect of accounting change	161,588	107,936	100,634
Extraordinary item—(net of income tax benefit of $5,673)	—	—	(6,660)
Cumulative effect of accounting change—(net of income tax provision of $9,004)	—	9,755	—
Net earnings	$ 161,588	$ 117,691	$ 93,974
Earnings per share of common stock:			
Net earnings before extraordinary item and cumulative effect of accounting change	$3.00	$1.98	$1.92
Extraordinary item	—	—	(.13)
Cumulative effect of accounting change	—	.19	—
Net earnings per share	$3.00	$2.17	$1.79

Pro forma amounts, assuming the new method of accounting had been applied retroactively for 1987 and 1986, are $107.9 million ($1.98 per share) and $100.1 million ($1.91 per share), respectively, for earnings before extraordinary item and $107.9 million ($1.98 per share) and $93.4 million ($1.78 per share), respectively, for net earnings.
See accompanying notes to consolidated financial statements.

FIG. 6-1b *A detailed income statement.*

The revenue that has not yet been collected is recorded as "Deferred Gross Profit" in the liability section of the balance sheet.

In contrast, the *cost-recovery method* does not record revenue until the customer has paid the seller an amount equal to the cost of the merchandise sold. Using the example given above, we have to recover the $40 cost from the customer before any revenue is recorded. After we recover the $40 cost of the merchandise, each dollar received is recorded as revenue.

Long-Term Contract

If a company provides services on a long-term contract, revenue may be recorded over the life of the contract. For example, the construction industry records revenue on major long-term contracts as the work is performed rather than at the point of sale. If dependable estimates of selling price, construction costs, and the stage of construction exist, the construction company records revenue as the work is performed. Accountants refer to this as the percentage-of-completion method.

For instance, suppose we are involved in a three-year construction project. At the end of the first year, we estimate the project is one-third completed; after the second year, it is two thirds complete. We finish the project in the third year. We record one third of the estimated gross profit (sales price less the total estimated construction cost) as revenue in the first year, and another third of the estimated gross profit in the second year ($\frac{2}{3} - \frac{1}{3}$ reported the first year). The final one-third is recorded as revenue in the third year.

While the percentage-of-completion method departs from the concept of recording revenue at the point of sale, it is consistent with the accrual concept of measuring activities in the period in which they occur. If a company does not have dependable estimates of the sales price, construction costs, and stage of construction, it does not recognize revenue until the project is complete (year three in our example).

COST OF GOODS SOLD AND INVENTORIES

Inventories were discussed in Chapter 3 as a component of the current assets section of the balance sheet. This discussion explains the relationship between cost-of-goods-sold category in the income statement and the balance-in-inventory-on-hand category in the balance sheet.

The total inventory available for sale each year is the total of the beginning inventory (that available at the beginning of the year) and the inventory purchased during the year. At year end, the total inventory available for sale each year is either still on hand or sold. The total available for sale is split between ending inventory in the balance sheet and cost of goods sold in the income statement.

At first glance, this may seem to be no problem—and if all units were purchased at the same price all year, there would in fact be no problem. A problem develops, however, because companies purchase units at many different prices, and, depending on the method used to flow costs through inventory, ending inventory and cost of goods sold can be any one of several different figures—all of which are acceptable for financial reporting.

For example, suppose that a company has no beginning inventory and purchases three identical units during the first quarter of the year: one in January, one in February, and one in March. The units were purchased for $4, $6, and $8, respectively. Now assume that one unit is sold for $10. What would the gross profit be?

If the company charges the $4 cost of the first unit purchased to cost of goods sold, gross profit is $6 and ending inventory is $14 ($6 + $8) for the two units still on hand. If the company charges the $6 cost of the second unit purchased to cost of goods sold, gross profit is $4 and ending inventory is $12 ($4 + $8). Finally, if the last unit purchased is expensed first, gross profit and ending inventory will be $2 and $10, respectively. These three possibilities are shown below.

	Possibility 1	Possibility 2	Possibility 3
In the income statement:			
Selling price	$10	$10	$10
Cost of goods sold	4	6	8
Gross Profit	6	$ 4	$ 2
In the balance sheet:			
Ending inventory	$14	$12	$10
	($6 + $8)	($4 + $8)	($4 + $6)

There are three inventory accounting methods in common use; depending upon which is used, any one of these results described above is possible. The three methods are First-In-First-Out (FIFO), Last-In-First-Out (LIFO), and Weighted Average.

FIFO Inventory

Accountants using FIFO inventory flow record costs the way merchants typically flow goods: The oldest units are sold first, and the most recently purchased units wind up in ending inventory. In the above example, using a FIFO inventory flow produces the first possibility.

The key to understanding inventory and cost of goods sold is to realize that when units are identical, accountants are free to flow costs through the accounting records in ways that do not mimic the way the actual goods are handled.

LIFO Inventory

The third possibility in the example given above results from the use of the LIFO (Last-In-First-Out) method of inventory flow, by which the cost of the most recent purchases are charged to cost of goods sold and the old costs remain in inventory, regardless of how the company flows the physical units.

To understand the accounting logic behind LIFO inventory, think about the result of the sale. How much better off is the company after selling one unit for $10? Is it $6 better off? Or $4? Or $2? To answer this question, you must consider replacement costs. If the company is to remain in business, management must replace any units sold. How much will the next unit purchased cost? The last unit purchased cost $8. Prices have been rising from $4 to $6 to $8 per unit. The next unit probably will cost $8 per unit or more. If the company, having sold one unit for $10, must replace the unit sold, it is only $2 better off ($10 − $8 = $2). The logic that supports LIFO increases the accuracy of the income statement, flowing costs in a LIFO pattern regardless of the flow pattern of physical units.

Figure 6-2 contains one company's note disclosure of inventory methods and the difference between values obtained using LIFO and FIFO.

Weighted-Average Inventory

Weighted-average inventory, the third method, is a compromise between flowing costs as merchants flow inventory and maximizing the accuracy of the income statement. This method charges both ending inventory and cost of goods sold with the weighted average cost of all units available for sale. The weighted-average cost per unit for our example is $4 + $6 + $8 or $18, divided by three units, or $6 per unit. This result is shown in possibility 2.

Inventories are stated at the lower of cost or market. The last-in, first-out (LIFO) method was used to determine costs of approximately 45% of the total inventories in 1989 and 49% in 1988. The remaining inventories are determined on the first-in, first-out (FIFO) method.

Inventories at December 31 are summarized as follows:

(Dollars in thousands)	1989	1988
Finished and in process........	$ 65,989	$ 60,367
Materials and supplies.........	85,660	103,339
	$151,649	$163,706

If the FIFO method of accounting had been used for all inventories, the totals would have been higher by $11,536,000 in 1989 and $8,057,000 in 1988.

FIG. 6-2. *Note disclosure of inventory methods and the difference between results based on LIFO and FIFO.*

MANUFACTURERS' INVENTORIES

A manufacturer may have several different kinds of inventory: raw materials, work in process, and finished goods held for sale (in contrast to a retail company which has only an inventory of units held for sale). In addition, manufacturing costs differ from nonmanufacturing costs in the timing of their charge against earnings. Nonmanufacturing costs, such as selling or administrative costs, are called *period costs* because they generally become expenses as a result of the passing of time. When a sales salary is paid, it is immediately charged to sales salaries expense, because the benefit of the salary (the salesperson's work) was consumed in the period during which the salesperson made sales calls. In contrast, when a year's insurance is paid on the corporate office building, the insurance cost is expensed month by month and the insurance (with its benefit as an asset) expires over a period of time.

Manufacturing costs, in contrast, are assets (the cost of inventory of manufactured units) until the units are sold. When an assembly-line worker or factory foreman is paid, the wages are charged, not to a wage expense account, but directly, or through overhead, to an inventory of unfinished work in process (an asset). When prepaid insurance on the factory expires month by month, it is charged, not to insurance expense, but through overhead to an inventory of unfinished work in process (an asset).

All manufacturing costs—labor, materials, and overhead—are charged to the asset work-in-process inventory. When financial statements are prepared, work-in-process inventory is shown in the current assets section of the balance sheet or disclosed in the notes to the financial statements.

When units are completed, the costs charged to work-in-process inventory are transferred to finished-goods inventory, another asset account. Only when the finished goods are finally sold are the manufacturing costs transferred to an expense account, cost of goods sold. Because manufacturing costs are not expensed until the product is sold, manufacturing costs are called *product costs*.

The flow of manufacturing costs is illustrated below:

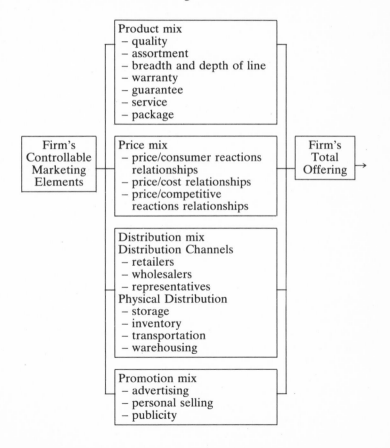

Inventory might appear in a note to the financial statements, supporting both the balance sheeet amount and the calculation of cost of goods sold as shown below.

Inventories
Raw materials	$1,050,000
Work in process	2,790,000
Finished goods	10,500,500
Total inventories	$14,340,500

Factory Overhead

Factory overhead is the total of all the indirect costs of production (all manufacturing costs except raw materials and labor used directly in the product). Factory overhead includes the costs of supervisory labor, maintenance, factory and equipment depreciation, manufacturing supplies used, energy, insurance, and any other manufacturing cost associated only indirectly with individual units produced.

Distorted Profit

The accounting method that charges all manufacturing costs to units produced is called *full* or *absorption costing*. Because absorption costing charges fixed capacity costs (such as supervision and factory depreciation) to individual units produced, net income is biased optimistically (high) when inventories are increasing and pessimistically (low) when inventories are decreasing. The full explanation of why this happens is very complex, but the net effect is that in times of growth, when inventories are increasing, profits may not be quite as great as reported, and in times of recession, when inventories are shrinking, profits may not be as dismal as financial statements indicate.

OTHER OPERATING EXPENSES

In a business that sells merchandise, the major operating expense is the cost of goods sold. Other operating expenses are reported on the income statement after gross profit on sales and are generally divided into selling and administrative expenses.

Selling Expenses

Selling expenses are the costs associated with producing sales. They include sales personnel salaries and commissions, sales manager and office staff salaries, payroll taxes expense (related to the sales staff), pension expense (related to the sales staff), travel and entertainment, advertising expense, delivery expense and shipping supplies expense, sales office supplies expense, telephone expense (related to sales staff), and sales equipment depreciation expense.

Administrative Expenses

Administrative expenses are the costs associated with managing the company. They include officers' salaries, office staff salaries, payroll taxes expense (related to the administrative staff), pension expense (related to the administrative staff), legal and professional services, research-and-development expense, utilities expense, telephone expense (related to the administrative staff), insurance expense, building depreciation expense, office equipment depreciation expense, office supplies expense, and miscellaneous office expenses.

The foregoing are only representative of the types of costs that are classified as selling or administrative expenses. Actual costs and breakdowns vary, depending on the nature of the company's business. For instance, a service-oriented business such as a dentist's office may not break out its expenses into the selling and administrative categories.

CHAPTER PERSPECTIVE

This chapter, the first of two on the components of the income statement, introduced the classified income statement. The components of operating income were discussed in detail: sales, cost of goods sold, selling expenses, and administrative expenses. The different inventory flow methods—LIFO, FIFO, and weighted average—were introduced and their logic explained. The difference between inventories held by a manufacturer and a retailer was discussed and the flow of costs in a manufacturing company was introduced.

The Income Statement: Nonoperating Items, Deferred Taxes, and Earnings Per Share

INTRODUCTION AND MAIN POINTS

Accountants make the income statement easier to understand by separating the income (or loss) generated by ongoing, normal operations from income that is derived from activities or events that are not expected to be ongoing or are neither normal nor ongoing. This chapter discusses the two most frequently occurring items in these categories: discontinued operations and extraordinary items.

Accountants also seek to make the income statement more informative by calculating and displaying earnings per common share, but this effort results in a much-used statistic that is poorly understood by accountants and financial-statement readers alike. The second half of the chapter discusses earnings per share and deferred income taxes, another controversial area that affects both the income statement and the balance sheet.

After studying this material:

━ You will understand the impact of a decision to discontinue a business operation and will see how accountants present that impact in the financial statements.

━ You will be able to distinguish gains and losses that are classified as extraordinary and will see how accountants present these items in the income statement.

━ You will understand why tax expense on the income statement is not always the same as the taxes paid during the year and will understand how accountants resolve this difference.

━ You will understand the basic calculation of earnings per share and the multitude of factors that complicate this otherwise simple statistic.

DISCONTINUED OPERATIONS

The decision by a company to discontinue one of its business operations creates a contingency. In Chapter 2, we defined a contingency as a situation in which the company stands to gain or lose as the result of a past transaction or event. Only the amount of gain or loss that is dependent on another transaction or event is "contingent." At the point management decides to sell a segment of the business (the event giving rise to future gain or loss) a contingency exists, because management may not know whether the sale will result in a gain or loss. Management may intend to sell and not yet have a buyer lined up, or, even if management has a buyer, the exact gain or loss may not be known until the disposal date.

While the precise amount of gain or loss may be unknown at the point management decides to sell, the contingency is classified as "likely to occur" because the decision to sell makes the incurrence of either a gain or loss certain. Therefore, disclosure of discontinued operations follows the guidelines for disclosure of "likely" contingencies as discussed in Chapter 2. If management expects a loss on disposal, the loss is reported on the income statement in the period in which management makes the decision to sell. If management expects a gain on the disposal, the gain is postponed until the fiscal year in which the actual disposal occurs. (Remember, conservatism, which governs the reporting of contingencies, favors recording losses that are likely to occur before they occur but recording gains when they actually occur.)

Separate Disclosure
Gains or losses on discontinued operations are reported on the income statement in a special section that follows income from continuing operations and precedes extraordinary items. Discontinued operations are reported net of their tax effects. (Gains on disposal of such an operation generally give rise to additional taxes, while losses generally result in tax savings.) It is necessary to report discontinued operations net of their tax consequences because of the structure of the income statement. Income tax expense has been computed on income from continuing operations. Gains or losses reported on the income statement below the continuing operations section either increase tax expense or save taxes.

In the year in which management decides to sell the segment, two categories of discontinued operations may appear on the income statement: a gain or loss from operating the discontinued segment, and a gain or loss on disposal of the segment. The gain or loss from operating the discontinued segment is the segment's net income or loss from the beginning of the fiscal year to the date when management adopts the plan of disposal. The second component, gain or loss on disposal of the segment, is the contingency—the anticipated gain or loss generated by segment from the adoption of the disposal plan to the actual date of disposal. This includes winding-down operations as well as actual disposal of the segment's assets.

Discontinued Operations—An Illustration

Most dispositions are reported on more than one annual income statement. Because disposal of a large business segment is a lengthy process, it is seldom accomplished within one fiscal period. Let's look at a simple example of a disposal.

Whatsit, Inc., decides to sell the Widget division to Sangsung, Ltd. The decision to sell is made at the October 1, 1990 board meeting. From January 1 to October 1, 1990 Widget experienced an after-tax operating loss of $1 million. Whatsit estimates that operations from October 1, 1990, through September 1, 1991 (the date Sangsung will take over operations), and the actual sale will generate a $5 million after-tax loss. Whatsit's income statement for the year ended December 31, 1990, will show discontinued operations of:

1990

Discontinued Operations:

Loss from Operating Widget Division	$1,000,000
Estimated Loss on Disposal of Widget	5,000,000
	$6,000,000

Remember that the estimated loss on disposal is a contingency. Because Whatsit is estimating a loss, it will record the loss in the fiscal year in which the disposal decision was made. If, instead of estimating a loss on disposal, Whatsit had estimated a gain, only the "Loss from Operating Widget Division" would have been reported on the 1990 income statement. The gain would be recorded in 1991 when operations are actually turned over to Sangsung.

Because Whatsit must use estimates to recognize the "Loss on Disposal of Widget Division," the difference between the estimated loss and the actual loss will be reported in 1991. Suppose Whatsit experiences an actual after-tax "Loss on Disposal" of $5,750,000. The discontinued operations section of Whatsit's 1991 income statement will appear as follows:

1991
Discontinued Operations:
   Loss on Disposal of Widget Division $750,000

Together, the 1990 and 1991 income statements report the full loss on disposal ($5,750,000).

Notice that Whatsit did not report any gain or loss from operating the Widget division during 1991. There cannot be additional "gain or loss from operating" the discontinued segment in 1991; gains or losses from operations experienced after the decision to sell has been made are part of the gain or loss on disposal of the segment.

Now suppose that instead of the estimated $5 million loss on disposal, Whatsit's actual loss is $4,800,000. The discontinued operations section of Whatsit's 1991 income statement would then appear as follows:

1991
Discontinued Operations
   Gain on Disposal of Widget Division $200,000

Together, the 1990 and 1991 income statements report the full loss on disposal of $4,800,000 ($5 million estimated loss in 1990 minus the $200,000 gain reported in 1991).

Disposals That Are Not Discontinued Operations

Segregating gains or losses on discontinued operations on the income statement is important. Segregation alerts the reader of the financial statements to the fact that a major portion of the business will no longer be contributing to the company's earnings. In this situation, income from continuing operations (rather than net income) becomes the important figure when trying to forecast the future earnings ability of the company. However, not all sales of business assets, segments, or divisions are reported as discontinued operations.

Only those operations that represent a completely separate line of product (service) or class of customer (client) are considered segments when reporting discontinued operations. Gains or losses on disposal of business assets, segments, or divisions that are not sales of a completely separate product line or class of customer are reported as part of income from continuing operations.

EXTRAORDINARY ITEMS

Before a company can classify a gain or loss as an extraordinary item, two criteria must be met:

1. the gain or loss must come from a transaction or event that is unusual. An unusual transaction or event is one that is unrelated to the typical activities of the business.
2. that transaction or event must be nonrecurring—that is, one that management does not expect to occur again.

The classification as extraordinary is company-specific. A natural disaster such as an earthquake, for example, meets the definition of unusual (unrelated to the typical activities of the business). But, if our business is located in Southern California on the San Andreas Fault, the quake would not be considered nonrecurring and therefore could not be considered extraordinary. On the other hand, an earthquake in New York City would give rise to an extraordinary loss. In general, the criteria of "unusual" and "nonrecurring" must be looked at from the perspective of the reporting company: Is the transaction or event unusual given the nature of that company's business and its geographical location?

Presentation of Extraordinary Items

Extraordinary gains or losses are reported in their own section on the income statement, between discontinued operations and the cumulative effect of a change in accounting principle. A net extraordinary gain (gain less additional income taxes) increases income, while a net extraordinary loss (loss reduced by income tax savings) decreases income. Accountants report extraordinary items net of their tax consequences because of the structure of the income statement: Income tax expense has been computed on income from continuing operations. Gains or losses reported on the income statement below the continuing operations section either increase tax expense or save taxes.

Segregating extraordinary gains or losses on the income statement is important. By classifying a gain or loss as extraordinary, management is saying, "This is an unusual gain or loss and we do not expect it to reoccur." Segregating extraordinary items also allows comparability between years. Because extraordinary items are not expected to reoccur, "Income Before Extraordinary Items" can be compared to "Net Income" in years when there are no extraordinary gains or losses. Companies required to report earnings per share must report "Per Share Income Before Extraordinary Items" so that figure may also be compared to "Per Share Net Income" for years in which there were no extraordinary gains or losses.

Exceptions to the Rules

There are exceptions to the criteria for evaluating gains and losses. Accounting principles require that certain types of gains and losses not be treated as extraordinary items, while other gains and losses must be given extraordinary item treatment.

Gains or losses that may not be treated as extraordinary items include:

1. losses from the write-down or write-off of receivables, inventories, equipment, or intangible assets (a write-down or write-off of an asset occurs when an asset's value has been impaired, and the asset is reduced or written down)
2. gains or losses related to exchanging foreign currencies
3. gains or losses from the sale of a business segment
4. gains or losses from the sale or abandonment of property, plant, or equipment that has been used in the business
5. losses resulting from strikes by employees

The company's type of business and geographical location are not important, because these gains or losses may not receive extraordinary-item treatment.

Gains or losses on settlement of debt before its due date (the difference between the recorded value of the debt and the amount paid to settle the debt) are reported as extraordinary items. Again, the company's type of business and geographical location are not important because these gains or losses must receive extraordinary-item treatment. Figure 7-1 presents the income statement and footnote disclosure for our extraordinary item from the 1989 annual report of Forest City Enterprises.

TAXES AND TAX DEFERRALS

Income tax regulations do not always require that a company use the same accounting method on the tax return that it has used on the income statement. Tax expense as shown on the income statement is derived from the revenues and expenses listed on the income statement. In other words, taxes are recorded on the income statement in the same year as the revenues and expenses giving rise to the taxes. This is done in adherence to the matching concept. However, the taxes actually due the government are derived from the figures on the tax return. The difference in these two tax amounts is called "deferred taxes."

Different Depreciation Methods

Suppose we decide to use a different method of depreciation on the income statement than we use on the tax return (which both the accounting profession and the government allow us to do). Depreciation expense on the income statement and tax return will be different at various times in the equipment's useful life. Consider this example:

Annual Depreciation

	Year 1	Year 2	Year 3	Year 4	Total
Income Statement	$10,000	$10,000	$10,000	$10,000	$40,000
Tax Return	$13,332	$17,780	$ 5,924	$ 2,964	$40,000
Difference *	($ 3,332)	($ 7,780)	$ 4,076	$ 7,036	$ -0-
× Tax Rate of 30 percent	$ 1,000	($ 2,334)	($ 1,223)	($ 2,111)	$ -0-

*A negative (or parenthetical) difference in this example means that more depreciation will be recorded on the tax return, decreasing the amount of taxes currently due.

In years 1 and 2, this company records more depreciation on the tax return than on the income statement ($3,332 and $7,780, respectively). This causes it to pay less in tax than it is showing as tax expense on its income statement ($1,000 and $2,334, respectively). By claiming more depreciation on the tax return, the company postpones taxes in years 1 and 2.

In years 3 and 4 the company shows more depreciation on the income statement than on the tax return ($5,924 and $2,964, respectively). This causes it to pay more taxes than are showing in tax expense for years 3 and 4 ($1,223 and $2,111, respectively). This is the payment of the postponed taxes from years 1 and 2.

FIG. 7-1 *Consolidated statements of earnings for Forest City Enterprises, Inc. and Subsidiaries*

	For the Years Ended January 31,		
	1990	1989	1988
	(in thousands, except per share data)		
Revenues			
Sales and operating revenues	$324,249	$293,150	$276,381
Interest and other income	17,046	17,566	14,948
Equity in earnings of affiliates	1,128	1,702	2,251
Total revenues	342,423	312,418	293,580
Operating costs excluding depreciation and amortization			
Interest incurred	120,086	96,983	78,609
Less interest capitalized for projects under development	30,600	17,077	11,641
	89,486	79,906	66,968
Operating costs of rental properties	134,051	117,957	109,266
Other operating expenses	82,239	84,795	90,603
	305,776	282,658	266,837
Operating earnings before depreciation and amortization and gain on disposition of properties and other provisions	35,647	29,760	26,743
Depreciation and amortization	31,341	25,450	20,844
Operating earnings before gain on disposition of properties and other provisions	5,306	4,310	5,899
Gain on disposition of properties and other provisions	5,760	10,753	597
Earnings from continuing operations before income taxes	11,066	15,063	6,496

Income taxes

Current	(287)	571	(950)
Deferred	5,562	6,659	3,749
	5,275	7,230	2,799
Net earnings from continuing operations	5,791	7,833	3,697
Net loss from discontinued operations	(1,565)	—	(511)
Net earnings before extraordinary gain and cumulative effect of an accounting change	4,226	7,833	3,186
Extraordinary gain, net of tax	1,690	—	—
Cumulative effect on prior years of a change in accounting principle relating to income taxes	—	—	9,187
Net earnings	$ 5,916	$ 7,833	$ 12,373

Earnings (loss) per share

Continuing operations	$ .70	$ .99	$ .47
Net discontinued operations	(.19)	—	(.06)
Extraordinary gain, net of tax	.21	—	—
Cumulative effect of a change in accounting principle	—	—	1.15
Net earnings	$ .72	$ .99	$ 1.56

Extraordinary Gain

The Company signed an agreement on November 15, 1989 with a savings and loan association, settling a dispute that arose over the Company's right to extend the maturity dates of various loans on certain of its land parcels. The Company had commenced a civil action against the lender but the civil action was settled by a compromise agreement whereby the Company agreed to retire the outstanding debt at a reduced cost, resulting in a gain before income taxes of $4,611,000.

In connection with the early extinguishment of certain letters of credit, the Company has expensed the unamortized procurement costs and early cancellation penalties and fees totaling $1,634,000. These letters of credit, which are required under the related debt agreements, guarantee repayment by the Company of principal and interest on certain tax-exempt Industrial Revenue Bonds issued by various community redevelopment agencies.

The net effect of these transactions resulted in an extraordinary gain of $1,690,000, net of tax.

Notice that there is no difference between the total depreciation taken on the income statement and tax return over the four-year period. Over the four-year period, tax expense also equals the amount of taxes due. The difference is simply in the timing of the reporting.

In this example, a liability for future taxes is created in years 1 and 2. This liability is paid in years 3 and 4. The balance sheet prepared at the end of year 1 shows the "deferred tax liability" as noncurrent (since it will not come due in the next year). The balance sheet prepared at the end of year 2 shows $1,223 of the "deferred tax liability" as current (the amount due in the next year) and $2,111 as a noncurrent liability (the amount not due until year 4).

Timing Differences

Recording revenues and expenses on the income statement and tax return in different periods can also produce a "deferred tax asset." Suppose that our fiscal year ends on December 31 and that in December 19X1 we collect January 19X2 rents. Income tax regulations require that we pay tax on the rents in 19X1, the year in which they are collected. Under the accrual accounting concept (see Chapter 1), the rents are not earned until January 19X2 and are not reported as revenue on the 19X1 income statement. They are unearned at year end 19X1 and are reported as a current liability on the December 31, 19X1 balance sheet (we must furnish the premises or return the rent money). The 19X1 tax payment (which includes tax on the rent received) is more than the expense showing on the income statement; we have paid taxes on revenue we have not yet earned. This prepayment is treated as an asset—"deferred tax asset"—which is essentially a "prepaid" tax.

Changing Tax Rates

If the company experiences a change in tax rates, it must revise the recorded amount of the "deferred tax liability" or "deferred tax asset." This adjustment is made through tax expense. Suppose the income statement shows $10,000 more in revenue than does the tax return. At a 30 percent rate, this creates a $3,000 "deferred tax liability." If the tax rate increases to 40 percent, the "deferred tax liability" must be increased by $1,000 [($10,000 x 40 percent) − $3,000]. This adjustment is made by increasing income tax expense by $1,000 when the tax rate changes, either by legislation or because the company moves into a higher (or lower) tax bracket through changes in earnings.

A company should use timing differences to its advantage. If income tax regulations allow, it can use methods on the tax return that minimize the amount of taxes currently due, creating a "deferred tax liability." This postpones the payment of tax to a later period. Postponing the payment of tax as long as legally possible allows the company to use those funds to earn additional profits.

EARNINGS PER SHARE

Earnings per share (EPS) is a simple, almost intuitive accounting measure carried (of necessity) to its most complicated, confusing extreme. Generally accepted accounting principles require a publicly held company to calculate its earnings per share and display that figure on its income statement. The official pronouncement on EPS is 35 pages long and is so complicated and confusing in its original form that an official explanation—125 pages long—was written to explain the original opinion. Still, earnings per share is often cited as the single most used financial ratio; it can be understood if you ignore the complications and concentrate on the purpose of this ratio.

Basic EPS

Earnings per share is simply the earnings of the company divided by the number of shares of stock outstanding. When a financial-statement reader examines a company's earnings per share over a period of several years, a pattern of growth or contraction may become apparent. Reducing the company's total earnings to a measure of earnings per ownership share helps an investor determine how successful the company is in creating earnings for individual shareholders. If a company sells additional shares of stock, for instance, you would expect total earnings to increase as a result of the additional investment received from owners; the additional shareholder investment might be used to build a new plant or to expand operations in some other way.

An increase in total earnings achieved in this way can be misleading. Suppose a company with 100,000 shares of stock outstanding issues an additional 20,000 shares of stock and expands production facilities with the cash received. Assume that, as a result, the company's earnings increase from $200,000 to $220,000 per year. If an investor looks only at total earnings, an increase of 10 percent may appear good. But if we look at the earnings per share for the two years, we see that the earnings per share of ownership actually fell:

Before investment: EPS = $200,000/$100,000 shares = $2.00/share After investment: EPS = $220,000/120,000 shares = $1.83/share

As companies increase and decrease the number of shares outstanding, by issuing or retiring shares of stock, by combining with other companies, or by fulfilling obligations to convert bonds or meet employee stock options, the earnings per share figure relates the company's reported earnings to the number of shares of stock outstanding. The basic equation for earnings per share is:

Basic EPS = Earnings / number of shares outstanding

EPS Complications

But now for the complications. Suppose there are preferred stockholders as well as common stockholders. In that case, some of the company's earnings must be paid as dividends to preferred stockholders just as interest must be paid on debt. Dividend payments to preferred stockholders, like interest, are a cost of capital and must be subtracted from earnings to determine the earnings available to common stockholders. (Interest is already deducted as an operating expense in calculating earnings.) So, if we are interested in the earnings per share for common stockholders, we must modify the EPS equation to read:

$$\text{EPS} = \text{Earnings available to common stockholders} / \text{number of shares outstanding}$$

Suppose further that the company issues or retires common stock during the year. A correct calculation now requires that a weighted-average number of shares be used as the denominator.

$$\text{EPS} = \text{Earnings available to common stockholders} / \text{weighted-average number of shares outstanding}$$

When a company has issued bonds or preferred stock that is convertible to shares of common stock or has stock warrants or options outstanding, the calculation of EPS becomes even more complex.

Stock warrants entitle the holder to acquire shares of stock at a fixed price within a specified period. The holder may sell the warrants or exercise them by paying the fixed price and converting the warrants into shares of common stock. Stock warants are purchased in the open market from individual investors or from an issuing corporation. The warrants are issued either separately or as part of other securities, such as bonds or preferred stock. When issued with other securities, the warrants are used as a *sweetener* to make the securities more attractive to potential investors. An investor can detach the warrants and sell them or, if he chooses, exercise them.

Corporate employees and officers are issued stock rights under *stock option* plans, which are similar to warrants. These selected individuals are given the option of purchasing common stock at a specified price over a stipulated period of time. Corporations adopt stock option plans for a variety of reasons: 1) to attract and retain high-quality personnel, 2) to raise capital for expansion, and 3) to spread ownership of common stock among employees. Figure 7–2 presents the footnote disclosure relating to Zenith Electronics Corporation's stock option plan from its 1989 annual report.

Preferred stock warrants and options can be thought of as essentially shares of common stock (if it is obvious that they will be exercised and increase the number of shares outstanding). Conversely, it may be obvious that other items will never be exercised and will not result in an increase in common stock outstanding. On some items, even experts may disagree.

To calculate a useful measure of EPS, the number of shares is increased to reflect the increase resulting from those items that are essentially shares of common stock (called common stock equivalents). The number of shares should not be increased to include those items that will never be exercised. Those that may be exercised (but that are not common stock equivalents) might cause some confusion; to prevent this, accountants calculate two measures of EPS and publish both of them with the income statement in the annual report. The two measures of EPS are called *primary* earnings per share (containing only a weighted average of common shares and common stock equivalents in the denominator) and *fully diluted* earnings per share (representing a worst-case scenario with all items that could reasonably be converted to common stock counted as common shares in the denominator).

When accountants treat an item as if it were converted into common stock—increasing the number of shares outstanding—an adjustment must frequently be made to the numerator as well. For example, if an issue of convertible bonds is treated as if it were converted into common stock in an EPS calculation, the accountant must also correct earnings by adding back the interest expense that would not have been subtracted if the bonds had actually been converted. Corrections must also be made for dividends that would not accrue to preferred shareholders if convertible preferred shares are treated as converted to common stock.

A portion of the consolidated statements of income for the Valero Energy Corporation is presented in Figure 7-3. Notice that net income is reduced in arriving at the net income applicable to common stock (the numerator in the EPS calculation). Primary and fully diluted EPS for 1989 are $.98 and $.95, respectively.

	Year Ended December 31,		
	1989	1988	1987
NET INCOME.	$ 41,501	$ 30,575	$ 12,909
Less: Preferred and preference stock dividend requirements	13,347	16,537	11,371
NET INCOME APPLICABLE TO COMMON STOCK	$ 28,154	$ 14,038	$ 1,538
EARNINGS (LOSS) PER SHARE OF COMMON STOCK ASSUMING NO DILUTION:			
Continuing operations	$ .98	$ .54	$ .80
Discontinued operations	.	.	(.56)
Extraordinary item	.	.	(.45)
Cumulative effect of accounting change	.	.	.27
Total	$ .98	$ .54	$ .06
EARNINGS (LOSS) PER SHARE OF COMMON STOCK ASSUMING FULL DILUTION:			
Continuing operations	$ .95	$ .54	$ .80
Discontinued operations	.	.	(.56)
Extraordinary item	.	.	(.45)
Cumulative effect of accounting change	.	.	.27
Total	$ .95	$ .54	$ .06
CASH DIVIDENDS DECLARED PER SHARE OF COMMON STOCK	$ .15	$.	$.

FIG. 7-3 *Valero Energy Corporation and Subsidiaries consolidated statements of income.*

Note 11—Stock options and awards

The 1987 Stock Incentive Plan authorizes the granting of incentive and non-qualified stock options, restricted stock awards and stock appreciation rights to key management personnel. Stock options have been granted and are currently outstanding under this and prior plans. The purchase price of shares under option is the market price of the shares on the date of grant. Options expire 10 years from the date granted.

Transactions in 1989 are summarized below:

	Shares	Price per Share
Options outstanding at Jan. 1, 1989	1,572,351	$10\frac{3}{8}-26\frac{5}{8}$
Granted	107,750	$16\frac{1}{2}-20$
Exercised	(44,705)	$10\frac{3}{8}-15\frac{3}{8}$
Cancelled or expired	(162,430)	$12\frac{3}{8}-26\frac{5}{8}$
Options outstanding at Dec. 31, 1989	1,472,966	$10\frac{3}{8}-26\frac{5}{8}$
Options exercisable at Dec. 31, 1989	1,407,616	
Shares available for grant at Dec. 31, 1989	679,773	

The company had 92,400 and 121,900 restricted stock awards issued and outstanding as of December 31, 1989 and 1988, respectively. The market value of the restricted shares is deferred in the additional paid-in capital account and amortized over the years the restrictions lapse. Total compensation expense in 1989 and 1988, related to these awards, was not material.

FIG. 7-2 *Footnote disclosure relating to stock option plan of Zenith Electronics Corporation.*

CHAPTER PERSPECTIVE

Accountants make the income statement easier to understand by separating the income (or loss) generated by ongoing, normal operations from income that is derived from discontinued operations and extraordinary items. We have defined the terms associated with these nonoperating items and given examples of how each is presented in an income statement. The chapter also discussed deferred income taxes, explaining why tax expense on the income statement is not always the same as the taxes paid during the year, illustrating how accountants present the difference in the financial statements, and explaining the calculation of deferred income taxes. The chapter explained the basic calculation of earnings per share and discussed the factors that complicate this otherwise simple statistic.

The Statement of Cash Flows and Consolidated Statements

INTRODUCTION AND MAIN POINTS

In this chapter we introduce the Statement of Cash Flows (SCF), the third statement (in addition to the balance sheet and the income statement) required in published financial statements such as annual reports. The primary purpose of the SCF is to furnish information regarding a company's cash receipts and cash payments for a period of time. A secondary purpose is to explain the change in cash over that same period. The SCF is a flow statement like the income statement and shows the results of activities over a period of time—a quarter or a year, for example. All cash flows are presented in the SCF as either operating, investing, or financing cash flows. Financial-statement readers can use the SCF to examine a company's liquidity and cash management.

The final portion of this chapter discusses consolidated financial statements issued by companies that own controlling interest in other companies, called subsidiaries. Almost all large companies publish consolidated financial statements; of the 600 industrial and merchandising companies cited in the 1989 edition of *Accounting Trends and Techniques*, published by the American Institute of Certified Public Accountants, only ten companies did not publish consolidated financial statements for 1988.

After studying the material in this chapter:

■ You will understand the purpose and general structure of the SCF.

■ You will know the general sources and uses of cash.

■ You will be able to distinguish among operating, investing, and financing cash flows.

■ You will understand why companies publish consolidated financial statements.

■ You will see how the statements of affiliated companies are combined to show the relationship and economic activity of the consolidated group.

CASH VERSUS ACCRUAL ACCOUNTING

Before you can understand the usefulness of the Statement of Cash Flows, you must clearly understand the difference between accrual accounting—as used to create the income statement—and cash-basis accounting. Accrual accounting attempts to translate into dollars of profit or loss the actual activities of the fiscal period. Remember from Chapter 1 that the accrual principle is a combination of two ideas: revenue recognition and matching.

Revenue Recognition

The revenue recognition principle provides that revenue (sales price) be recorded when the necessary activities to sell a good or provide a service have been completed. Revenue is recorded at the point of sale regardless of whether cash is collected or a receivable from the customer is created at that time.

Matching

The matching principle tells the accountant when to record a production cost as expense. Costs directly associated with producing a certain revenue are expensed in the same period that the revenue is recorded. The accountant expenses the cost of long-lived assets over their expected lives. Other costs that benefit only the current period are expensed as they arise.

Under the matching principle, an expense can be recorded before, after, or at the time a cost is actually paid. From the accountant's point of view, it is the earnings activity that gives rise to the conversion of cost to expense. It does not matter whether that cost has been paid or a liability created.

Cash-basis reporting, on the other hand, is concerned only with the business's checkbook. Cash inflows are treated as revenues of the period; cash outflows are treated as the period's expenses. Cash flows do not capture the earnings activities of the period. For instance, a company sells merchandise to a customer at the end of the year and the customer makes payment next period. On the cash basis, the sale is not recorded until the collection is made, even though the effort to generate the sale was made this period. Similarly, if the salesperson will not be paid for that day's work until next period, their salary is not an expense on the cash basis.

Accrual accounting provides a measure of the period's earnings activities. Comparing accrual income measures over time can give us a feel for what the company can do in the future, but it does not provide us with a measure of the company's liquidity—its ability to pay its debts as they come due.

Cash-flow accounting does not isolate the earnings activities of the period. However, it does provide us with a liquidity measure. Combining accrual income measures with cash flow measures creates a base from which to estimate future operations, measure liquidity, and determine the timing between producing sales and collecting on sales. This combination takes place when we use all the financial statements together—the balance sheet, the income statement, and the statement of cash flows.

THE STATEMENT OF CASH FLOWS

The statement of cash flows is like a bridge. The balance sheet tells us what a business's assets, liabilities, and owners' equity are at a point in time. But what about the changes that have occurred in the business between two balance-sheet dates (from the end of one fiscal year to the end of another)? The statement of cash flows provides this bridge. It describes all of the changes that have occurred in the balance sheet during the fiscal year in terms of their effect on cash. What changes in the assets, liabilities, and owners' equity provided cash? What changes in assets, liabilities, and owners' equity used cash? These are the questions a statement of cash flows answers.

A company can obtain cash from operations, of course. It can also issue stock, borrow, and sell assets other than inventory. These are the four general sources of cash.

The general uses of cash are corollaries of the sources of cash, with one addition. Operations can consume cash (instead of providing cash), the company may reacquire its stock, repay debt, and buy assets other than inventory; it may also pay dividends. The general sources and uses of cash are shown in Figure 8-1.

Sources	Uses
Operations	Operations
Issue Stock	Reacquire Stock
Borrow	Repay Debt
Sell Assets	Buy Assets
	Pay Dividends

FIG. 8-1 *General sources and uses of cash.*

A company is required to present its sources and uses of cash according to three classes of activities: operating activities, investing activities, and financing activities. Figure 8-2 shows the general format of a statement of cash flows incorporating the three classes of activities. In this example, operating activities provided $70,000 in cash, financing activities (issuing stock and borrowing, perhaps) provided $30,000, and investing activities (lending money or buying stock in other companies, perhaps) used $50,000. Cash was $40,000 at the beginning of the year and $90,000 at year end.

Cash provided by (or used in):	
Operating Activities	$70,000
Investing Activities	(50,000)
Financing Activities	30,000
Increase (or decrease) in cash or cash equivalents	$50,000
Cash and cash equivalents, beginning of year	40,000
Cash and cash equivalents, end of year	$90,000

FIG. 8-2 *Statement of cash flows for the year ended December 31, 1991.*

Operating Activities
Cash from operating activities is cash-basis net income. It includes all collections during the year from sales of merchandise or providing services. It also includes dividends and interest received from investments. It is reduced by the payment of operating costs, including interest and taxes. A schedule reconciling accrual-based net income for the year to the cash collected from operating activities must accompany the SCF if it is not included in the body of the statement. Figure 8-3 presents this information from an actual Statement of Cash Flows.

Investing Activities
Cash from or for investing activities refers to changes in the company's long-term assets. Decreases in investments, property, plant and equipment, intangibles, and other assets indicate that sales or disposals that provide the company with cash have taken place. Increases in these same assets indicate that the company has purchased additional assets—a major use of cash.

Financing Activities
Often shown as "Net cash provided (used) by financing activities," financing activities are changes in a company's long-term

Consolidated Statements of Cash Flows

Fiscal Year Ended (dollars in thousands)	May 2, 1990	May 3, 1989	April 27, 1988
Operating Activities:			
Net income	$504,451	$440,230	$386,014
Adjustments to reconcile net income to cash provided by operating activities:			
Depreciation and amortization	168,523	148,104	133,348
Deferred tax provision	37,921	65,271	27,560
Other items, net	(31,572)	(45,454)	(10,595)
Changes in current assets and liabilities, excluding effects of acquisitions and divestitures:			
Receivables	(104,818)	(69,818)	(72)
Inventories	(86,549)	(134,582)	(12,251)
Prepaid expenses and other current assets	17,634	(13,650)	19,908
Accounts payable	46,751	25,290	38,145
Accrued liabilities	(35,837)	19,855	18,940
Income taxes	11,333	(18,929)	(33,837)
Cash provided by operating activities	527,837	416,317	567,160
Investing Activities			
Capital expenditures	(355,317)	(323,325)	(238,265)
Acquisitions, net of cash acquired	(56,328)	(167,470)	(287,597)
Proceeds from divestitures	6,398	72,712	18,880
Purchases of short-term investments	(342,228)	(382,550)	(513,408)
Sales and maturities of short-term investments	368,767	412,365	666,272
Other items, net	10,434	12,627	5,005
Cash (used for) investing activities	(368,274)	(375,641)	(349,113)
Financing Activities:			
Proceeds from long-term debt	231,584	227,291	45,108
Payments on long-term debt	(28,095)	(34,683)	(165,832)
Proceeds (payments) on short-term debt	87,596	49,110	(41,305)
Dividends	(207,500)	(178,474)	(154,573)
Purchase of treasury stock	(279,899)	(97,508)	(123,519)
Exercise of stock options	56,752	30,393	23,463
Cash loaned to ESOP, net	(47,000)	—	—
Sale of treasury stock to ESOP	50,000	—	—
Other items, net	—	(1,590)	1,589
Cash (used for) financing activities	(136,562)	(5,461)	(415,069)
Effect of exchange rate changes on cash and cash equivalents	211	(8,098)	280
Net increase (decrease) in cash and cash equivalents	23,212	27,117	(196,742)
Cash and cash equivalents at beginning of year	102,605	75,488	272,230
Cash and cash equivalents at end of year	$125,817	$102,605	$ 75,488

FIG. 8-3 *Portion of cash flows statement showing operating, investing, and financing activities.*

liabilities and/or owners' equity. Increasing long-term debt or selling stock (ownership) provides the company with cash, while decreasing liabilities (indicating payment of debt) and distributing dividends to shareholders are major uses of cash.

Other Activities

Some transactions do not have a direct effect on cash. That is, these transactions affect assets or liabilities, but not cash. For example, a purchase of land on a long-term mortgage with no cash down payment does not affect the company's cash balance. However, for the statement of cash flows to be a complete bridge between two balance sheets (describing all the changes that have occurred in assets, liabilities, and owners' equity), this transaction must be reported. Major investing and financing activities that do not directly affect cash are summarized in a schedule that accompanies the statement of cash flows or in narrative form.

Figure 8-4 contains an expanded presentation of the statement of cash flows assuming that land costing $1,000,000 was acquired by agreeing to pay a 20-year mortgage payable for $1,000,000.

Cash Flows From Operating Activities:	
Received from customers	$2,418,500
Paid suppliers and employees	(1,255,000)
Dividends and interest received	150,000
Interest paid	(260,500)
Taxes paid	(320,000)
Net cash provided by operating activities	$ 733,000
Cash Flows From Investing Activities:	
Received—sale of plant	3,000,000
Received—sale of equipment	550,000
Paid—new equipment purchases	(1,015,000)
Paid—new plant	(4,950,000)
Net cash used in investing activities	(2,415,000)
Cash Flows From Financing Activities:	
Received—sale of bonds	2,000,000
Paid—dividends to shareholders	(100,000)
Net cash provided by financing activities	1,900,000
Net Increase in Cash	218,000
Cash at the Beginning of the Year	50,000
Cash at the End of the Year	$ 268,000

Low cash investing and financing activities:
  Acquisition of land by incurrence of mortgage
    payable $1,000,000

FIG. 8-4 *Delmar-Higgins, Ltd. statement of cash flows for the year ended December 31, 1991.*

CONSOLIDATED STATEMENTS

To understand consolidated financial statements, you must realize that they are more or less the sum of the parts—that is, they are the combined financial statements of a parent company and its subsidiaries. A parent/subsidiary relationship is created when a company acquires more than 50 percent of the common stock of another company. Because common stock is the voting stock of a corporation, acquiring more than 50 percent entitles the acquiring company (parent) to majority representation on the board of directors of the acquired company (subsidiary). This allows the acquiring company to control the affairs of the acquired company.

The Concept of Consolidating Statements

When management of a parent company owns stock in any company that it intends to hold for more than one year, the stock is shown both in the accounts and on the balance sheet of the parent as a noncurrent asset, "Investments." When the parent company owns a majority of the stock in a company, creating a subsidiary, the two companies are, for all practical purposes, combined; the financial statements of the two companies are consolidated and shown as if the two companies were one economic entity and the parent and its subsidiary (or subsidiaries) are referred to as affiliated companies. Accounting principles require that the assets, liabilities, revenues, and expenses of majority-owned subsidiaries be included in the financial statements of their parents.

An economic entity is an activity for which separate accounting records can be created. The parent and its subsidiary are each economic entities for which separate accounting records are kept and for which separate financial statements are issued. But because of the common control by stockholders who control the parent and, through it, the subsidiary, the combined companies can also be treated as a single economic entity. Stockholders, creditors, and others must see the financial statements of the combined entity if they are to understand the relationship between the companies and its economic implications. The requirement that affiliated companies publish consolidated financial statements reflects the concept of substance over form: The affiliated companies are, in substance, one economic entity, regardless of their separate legal form. As we stated at the outset of the chapter, virtually all large companies issue consolidated statements. The requirement to consolidate does not preclude the affiliated companies from also issuing separate individual financial statements.

The Mechanics of Consolidating Statements

Suppose Acme, Inc., buys 100 percent of the stock of Baker Company for the book value of its owners' equity (common stock plus retained earnings). The balance-sheet equation for Baker is shown below:

$$\text{Assets} = \text{Liabilities} + \text{Owners' Equity}$$
$$\$400,000 = \$300,000 + \$100,000$$

The Acme purchase of Baker stock is recorded on the Acme books by creating "Investment in Baker, $100,000," and reducing cash by $100,000. But what has Acme purchased? Since the value of the Baker owners' equity is $100,000, Acme has purchased $100,000 of property rights. If Acme shows the stock in its balance sheet simply as an investment of $100,000, the true nature of its relationship with Baker is not disclosed. Now Acme owes every debt that Baker owes and owns every asset that Baker owns. If Acme is to properly disclose its ownership of Baker, its balance sheet must show every debt owed and asset owned by Baker.

The balance-sheet equation for Acme before and after the purchase of the Baker stock is shown in Figure 8-5. Total assets for Acme are the same before and after the investment in Baker (the $100,000 asset "cash" has been traded for an equal asset, "Investment in Baker.")

	Assets	=	Liabilities	+	Owners' Equity
Before	$1,000,000	=	$700,000	+	$300,000
minus cash	(100,000)				
plus stock					
investment	100,000				
After	$1,000,000	=	$700,000	+	$300,000

FIG. 8-5 *Effect of Baker Purchase on Acme balance sheet.*

When Acme wishes to prepare financial statements, Acme must remove the $100,000 "Investment in Baker" and replace it with the individual assets and liabilities of Baker, as shown in Figure 8-6. The process of combining the companies is called *consolidation*, and the financial statements of a parent company combined with its subsidiary are called *consolidated financial statements*. Note that the total owners' equity of Acme is not changed by the consolidation.

	Assets	=	Liabilities	+	Owners' Equity
Acme before					
consolidation	$1,000,000	=	$700,000	+	$300,000
less the investment	(100,000)				
plus the assets and					
liabilities of Baker	400,000		300,000		
Acme's consolidated	$1,300,000	=	$1,000,000	+	$300,000
balance sheet					

FIG. 8-6 *Acme and Baker Consolidated.*

Eliminating Intercompany Transactions

In preparing the consolidated financial statements, accountants eliminate any transactions between the parent and its subsidiaries. If these transactions were not eliminated, assets, liabilities, revenue, and expense of the combined company would be overstated.

Consider another example. If a parent company "Y" has lent $5 million to its subsidiary "X," it will have a $5 million "Receivable from Subsidiary X" (an asset) recorded and Subsidiary X will have a $5 million "Payable to Parent Y" (a liability) recorded. Because parent and subsidiary are treated as one company in the consolidated financial statements, it does not make sense to include the $5,000,000 "Receivable from Subsidiary X" and the $5,000,000 "Payable to Parent Y" in assets and liabilities. As one company we cannot borrow from or owe to itself. When the consolidated balance sheet is prepared, the parent's $5 million "Receivable from Subsidiary X" cancels the subsidiary's $5 million "Payable to the Parent Y"; if this were not done, consolidated assets and liabilities would be reported as $5 million more than they actually are.

Because transactions between the parent and its subsidiaries are eliminated, consolidated financial statements reflect only the transactions that have taken place between the combined companies and outsiders. However, when consolidating the financial statements of a parent and those subsidiaries that are not wholly owned (that is, in which the parent does not own 100 percent of the voting stock), "minority interest"—the owners' equity of the other shareholders of the subsidiary—is created. If we own 60 percent of a subsidiary, there is a 40 percent minority interest. Because accounting principles allow all of the assets and liabilities of a subsidiary to be reported in the consolidated financial statements, the portion of those assets and liabilities that belong to the minority shareholders must be labeled "minority interest" and may be shown on the consolidated balance sheet as either a liability (the amount the parent "owes" the minority shareholders) or as a part of consolidated owners' equity.

Goodwill

Another account that frequently appears on the consolidated balance sheet is "Excess of Cost Over Net Assets Acquired," or purchased goodwill. Purchased goodwill is an intangible asset that is amortized (expensed) over a period of time that does not exceed forty years.

Additional information on the activities of the subsidiaries is included in the notes to the financial statements dealing with "segments." A business segment is a major product line, an industry, a class of customer, domestic operations, or foreign operations.

When Affiliated Companies Need Not Consolidate

We have stated that affiliated companies always issue consolidated statements; however, there are exceptions to this statement. Each company in an affiliated group (parent or subsidiary) may issue separate financial statements for regulatory agencies or for special purposes such as obtaining financing or credit from suppliers. Additionally, consolidated statements are not required if control is only temporary or if control does not rest with the majority owners.

CHAPTER PERSPECTIVE

This chapter has described the Statement of Cash Flows, the third statement required in published financial statements. We discussed the general sources and uses of cash common to all companies and the way companies are required to present cash flows in the Statement of Cash Flows—separated into flows from operating, investing, and financing activities. Finally, we explained the organization of consolidated financial statements, the type of financial statement published by most companies, and showed how to combine statements to show the relationship and economic activity of an affiliated group.

Quarterly Statements, Reports on Specified Elements, Reviews, and Compilations

CHAPTER

9

INTRODUCTION AND MAIN POINTS

Financial statements included in an annual report have been audited by an independent Certified Public Accountant (CPA); because the statements are audited, financial-statement readers can rely on the fairness of the financial-statement presentation. But there are other statements, such as interim, or quarterly, reports issued by publicly held companies and financial statements by nonpublic companies, that may have been reviewed by a CPA at a lower level of thoroughness than that required for a full audit. Accountants may also be called upon to issue reports on specified elements, accounts, or items in a financial statement.

This chapter discusses these other types of evaluations that are often requested of CPAs. After studying the material in this chapter:

━━ You will understand the levels of assurance and the conclusions expressed by the accountant, in engagements other than audits.

━━ You will understand the form of the financial statements issued by the CPA when he or she reviews unaudited interim financial statements or information (the quarterly report) of a public company.

━━ You will understand the form of the financial statements issued by the CPA who reviews the financial statements of a nonpublic company.

━━ You will understand the types of financial information presented by the CPA who reports on specified elements, accounts, or items in a financial statement.

━━ You will understand the types of financial information presented by the CPA who performs agreed-upon procedures.

━━ You will understand the type of report issued by the CPA who compiles the financial statements of a nonpublic company.

■ You will understand the reporting responsibilities assumed by the CPA for each type of engagement.

TYPES OF ENGAGEMENTS

A CPA may be called upon to prepare a variety of reports relating to financial statements. In an *audit*, the accountant performs the *attest* function; that is, the accountant gathers a sufficient amount of competent evidence to provide a high level of assurance that the information contained in the financial statements is presented fairly in accordance with generally accepted accounting principles (GAAP) or some other comprehensive basis of accounting. This high level of assurance by the CPA regarding the credibility of the financial statements is sometimes referred to as positive assurance.

CPAs provide other types of *attestation* services in which they issue written communications expressing a conclusion as to the reliability of the financial statements or other financial information being reported on.

A review is another example of an attestation service offered by a CPA. The procedures performed by the accountant during a review are not as extensive as those performed in the course of an audit and normally consist of client inquiries and analytical review. As you might expect, a review provides only a moderate level of assurance—normally referred to as negative assurance—compared to a full audit. When giving negative assurance, the auditor, in effect, says only "I know of nothing wrong." In contrast, positive assurance says, in effect, "Having tested, I believe the statements to be presented fairly." There is a big difference.

Reports on specified elements, accounts, or items in a financial statement normally fall into one of two categories:

1. Reports expressing an *audit opinion* on one or more specified elements or accounts. In these, the CPA expresses positive assurance in the audit report only for the item or items audited.

2. Reports issued by the CPA after performing *agreed-upon procedures*, procedures agreed to by the accountant, the party requesting the engagement, and the intended users of the accountant's report. The accountant's report in such a case expresses negative assurance.

A *compilation*, a check of financial statements for form, appropriateness, arithmetic accuracy, is not an attestation service because the accountant does not express a conclusion regarding the financial statements and specifically disclaims any level of assurance regarding those statements. However, because some limited procedures have been performed by the accountant, he or she is associated with the financial statements and a report accompanies the statements.

A sample report for each type of engagement is provided in this chapter. Figure 9-1 summarizes the evidence examined and the types of conclusions reached by CPAs in different situations.

Type of Engagement	Amount of Evidence Collected	Level of Assurance	Conclusion Reached
Audit	Substantial	High	Positive
Review	Significant	Moderate	Negative
Audit of Specified Elements, Accounts, or Items	Substantial	High	Positive
Agreed Upon Procedures	Varying	As Agreed Upon	Negative Disclaimer
Complication	None	Minimal	(none)

FIG. 9-1 *Summary of types of engagements.*

QUARTERLY STATEMENTS OF A PUBLIC COMPANY

Both the New York Stock Exchange and the Securities and Exchange Commission (SEC) require that listed or registered companies provide their shareholders with quarterly financial statements. (The content of the quarterly report (the 10-Q) filed with the SEC is discussed in Chapter 10.) Quarterly financial statements are prepared for the first three quarters of a company's fiscal year; fourth-quarter statements are unnecessary because annual financial statements are issued at that time. However, many companies do issue fourth-quarter statements to their shareholders and other interested parties.

Quarterly financial statements look much the same as annual financial statements; however, there are some major differences. For one thing, because accounting principles require that the same methods of recording revenues, expenses, assets, and liabilities be used in the quarterly statements and the annual statements, it is necessary to estimate some key figures. For instance, because taking a physical inventory count is time-consuming and costly, it is done only once a year. In order to prepare the quarterly financial statements, ending inventory for the quarter is therefore estimated. The annual tax rate must also be estimated so that quarterly taxes can be recorded at the rate the company actually expects to pay.

Accounting principles also require that seasonality in the quarterly statements be pointed out. For instance, if second-quarter sales are normally greater than sales in the other quarters, this fact should be indicated in the second quarter's financial statements. This has the effect of reminding the reader that sales are not level throughout the year.

A third difference is that footnote disclosure is minimal in quarterly statements. However, certain items must be disclosed if they are applicable. These items are significant changes in estimates or provisions for income taxes; contingent items; changes in accounting principles or estimates; significant changes in financial position; and disposal of a segment of a business and extraordinary, unusual, or infrequently occurring items. The reader may find the details of one or more of these items in a section of the quarterly report normally authored by the company president or chairman of the board.

A final difference is that quarterly financial statements are unaudited. Although public companies whose securities are listed on a stock exchange are required to have their annual financial statements audited and to release interim financial information quarterly, a review of the interim reports by an independent CPA is not required.*

Figure 9-2 shows the quarterly report for the Chevron Corporation for the first quarter of 1990. Notice that in addition to the quarterly financial statements, it includes a discussion of earnings and of the annual stockholders' meeting by the chairman of the board, as well as news briefs related to Chevron Corporation, and that there is no review report by an independent CPA. Normally, the basic financial data presented in the quarterly report closely parallel those found in the annual

---

*In fact, many companies do have a review performed by their independent CPA, but the review report is not published with the interim financial statements because of management's concern that the review report might be misinterpreted as an audit report. Currently, the SEC is considering a proposal to require firms that must file form 10-Q to have a review and publish that review report in its filings with the Commission.

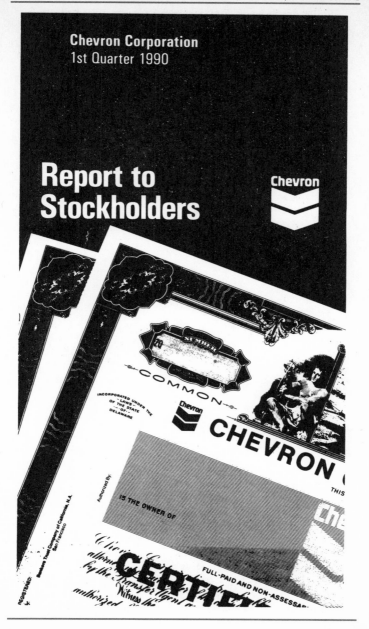

Results at a glance

	First Quarter		
	1990	1989	Change
Revenues	$9.3 bil.	$7.7 bil.	+21%
Earnings	$473 mil.	$313 mil.	+51%
Earnings per share	$1.33	$0.91	+46%

Dividend declared

On April 25, Chevron Corporation declared a quarterly dividend of 70 cents a share, payable June 11 to stockholders of record May 7. The dividend rate is unchanged from the preceding quarter.

Chevron Corporation

225 Bush St., Room 1109
San Francisco, CA 94104

Chairman's Letter

Earnings surge of 51 percent brightens first quarter results

Chevron reported first quarter earnings of $473 million, an increase of 51 percent from the $313 million earned in the first quarter 1989. Earnings per share increased 46 percent, from 91 cents to $1.33. Total revenues were $9.3 billion for the quarter, compared with $7.7 billion last year.

Higher prices for crude oil and natural gas, as well as increased worldwide production, contributed significantly to the earnings increase. Our production of natural gas set company records in January and February, reflecting, in part, the development of Gulf of Mexico properties purchased from Tenneco in 1988. These results convincingly demonstrated the benefit of our being the largest U.S. producer of this increasingly important fuel.

Refining and marketing earnings were aided not only by higher product prices, but also by higher refinery runs and sales volumes. Prices were particularly strong for jet fuel, and we are the leading U.S. supplier of that product.

Chemical operations recorded one-time benefits from product licensing agreements related to the restructuring of our agricultural chemicals business. However, industrial chemical earnings were hurt by lower commodity prices industrywide.

Worldwide capital and exploratory expenditures, including the company's share of affiliates' expenditures, were $807 million in the quarter, down slightly from the $833 million in the first quarter of 1989.

Because of continued volatility in crude oil prices, our operating outlook for the second quarter remains uncertain. However, sales of marginal producing properties and other assets should result in net gains over the balance of the year. Furthermore, key initiatives, such as the restructuring of our U.S. exploration and production operations and the ongoing modernization of our refineries and service stations, will help us remain competitive despite recurring fluctuations in crude oil prices.

K. T. Derr (signature)

K. T. DERR
Chairman of the Board

May 1990

Review of operations

U.S. petroleum operations earned $214 million in the first quarter, compared with $77 million last year. Exploration and production contributed $155 million, compared with $70 million in the 1989 quarter. Average crude oil prices were up about $3.50 per barrel to more than $18.50. Liquids production declined about 3 percent, but natural gas production increased 13 percent. Average natural gas prices were up 15 percent to just over $1.90 per thousand cubic feet. This year's quarter included charges for organizational restructuring and a prior year's tax adjustment.

Refining and marketing earned $59 million, up from $7 million in 1989. Average product sales prices advanced about 17 percent from 1989, and sales volumes were up almost 6 percent.

Non-U.S. petroleum operations earned $200 million in the first quarter, compared with $159 million last year. Liquids production was up 3 percent. Increases in Indonesia and Australia more than offset declines in Canada and the United Kingdom. Natural gas production increased 33 percent, reflecting higher production in Canada and the mid-1989 start-up of the North West Shelf Project in Australia.

The increase in refining and marketing earnings was due mainly to higher sales margins and favorable foreign exchange effects.

Chemical operations earned $123 million, compared with $131 million last year.

Total foreign exchange effects resulted in a loss of $15 million for the quarter, compared with a gain of $22 million for the 1989 period.

CONSOLIDATED STATEMENT OF INCOME
—Millions of Dollars (Unaudited)

	First Quarter	
Revenues	**1990**	**1989**
Sales and other operating revenues	**$9,184**	$7,537
Equity in net income of affiliated		
companies and other income	**138**	193
	9,322	7,730
Costs and Other Deductions		
Purchased crude oil and products		
and other operating expenses	**6,474**	5,278
Exploration expenses	**129**	144
Depreciation, depletion and amortization	**709**	655
Taxes other than on income	**874**	805
Interest and debt expense	**164**	156
	8,350	7,038
Income Before Income Tax Expense	**972**	692
Income Tax Expense	**499**	379
Net Income	**$ 473**	$ 313
Net Income Per Share of Common Stock	**$ 1.33**	$ .91
Dividends Per Share of Common Stock	**$ .70**	$ .70
Average Number of Shares (000's)	**354,943**	340,928

EARNINGS BY MAJOR OPERATING AREA
—Millions of Dollars (Unaudited)

	First Quarter	
U.S. Petroleum Operations	**1990**	**1989**
Exploration and Production	**$155**	$ 70
Refining, Marketing and Transportation	**59**	7
Total U.S. Petroleum	**214**	77
Non-U.S. Petroleum Operations		
Exploration and Production	**129**	116
Refining, Marketing and Transportation	**71**	43
Total Non-U.S. Petroleum	**200**	159
Total Petroleum Operations	**414**	236
Chemicals	**123**	131
Minerals	**19**	6
Corporate and Other[1]	**(83)**	(60)
Total Earnings	**$473**	$313

[1] Includes interest expense, interest income on cash and marketable securities, other corporate items, and real estate and insurance activities.

[2] Condensed from the Dec. 31, 1989, audited balance sheet.

[3] Includes interests in affiliates.

CONSOLIDATED BALANCE SHEET
—Millions of Dollars

	March 31, 1990	Dec. 31, 1989[2]
Assets	(Unaudited)	
Cash and cash equivalents	$ 1,091	$ 1,152
Other current assets	7,688	7,468
Total current assets	8,779	8,620
Investments and advances	1,823	1,806
Properties, plant and equipment—net	22,967	23,040
Other	382	418
Total Assets	$33,951	$33,884
Liabilities		
Short-term debt	$ 140	$ 126
Other current liabilities	7,444	7,457
Total current liabilities	7,584	7,583
Long-term debt and capital lease obligations	7,360	7,390
Deferred income taxes	3,431	3,436
Deferred credits and other liabilities	1,444	1,495
Total Liabilities	19,819	19,904
Stockholders' Equity	14,132	13,980
Total Liabilities and Stockholders' Equity	$33,951	$33,884

CONSOLIDATED STATEMENT OF CASH FLOWS
—Millions of Dollars (Unaudited)

	First Quarter	
	1990	1989
Operating Activities		
Net Income	$ 473	$ 313
Adjustments		
Depreciation, depletion and amortization	709	655
Net (increase) decrease in operating working capital	(284)	196
Other	(92)	(210)
Net cash provided by operating activities	806	954
Investing Activities		
Capital expenditures	(618)	(648)
Other	53	89
Net cash used in investing activities	(565)	(559)
Financing Activities		
Net repayments of debt	(22)	(115)
Cash dividends paid	(248)	(238)
Purchase of treasury shares	(39)	—
Net cash used in financing activities	(309)	(353)
Effect of Exchange Rate Changes on Cash and Cash Equivalents	7	(10)
Net Change in Cash and Cash Equivalents	(61)	32
Cash and Cash Equivalents at Beginning of Year	1,152	1,297
Cash and Cash Equivalents at End of Period	$1,091	$1,329

CAPITAL AND EXPLORATORY EXPENDITURES[3]
—Millions of Dollars (Unaudited)

	First Quarter	
	1990	1989
United States		
Exploration and Production	$230	$245
Refining, Marketing and Transportation	147	79
Chemicals	39	40
Other	39	98
Total United States	455	462
Non-U.S.		
Exploration and Production	249	215
Refining, Marketing and Transportation	97	135
Chemicals	2	14
Other	4	7
Total Non-U.S.	352	371
Worldwide	$807	$833

OPERATING STATISTICS[3]

	First Quarter	
	1990	1989
Net Liquids Production (MB/D)		
United States	484	497
Non-U.S.	479	464
Worldwide	963	961
Net Natural Gas Production ($\overline{M}CF/D$)		
United States	2,901	2,565
Non-U.S.	434	327
Worldwide	3,335	2,892
Natural Gas Sales ($\overline{M}CF/D$)		
United States	3,057	2,799
Non-U.S.	445	311
Worldwide	3,502	3,110
Natural Gas Liquids Sales (MB/D)		
United States	159	215
Non-U.S.	40	41
Worldwide	199	256
Refined Products Sales (MB/D)		
United States	1,518	1,435
Non-U.S.	771	752
Worldwide	2,289	2,187
Refinery Input (MB/D)		
United States	1,394	1,348
Non-U.S.	507	493
Worldwide	1,901	1,841

Stockholder questions target politics and the environment

Stockholder questions at the Annual Meeting focused mainly on Chevron's political neutrality in non-U.S. operations and on environmental, health and safety issues.

A stockholder urged that Chevron's payments to the government of Angola, resulting from company operations in Cabinda, be placed in an escrow account because of the civil war in that country. Chairman Ken Derr responded, "This is not a viable option. We have to pay taxes to the duly constituted governments where we operate."

Various stockholders expressed interest in Chevron's ongoing negotiations in the Soviet Union to form a joint venture for oil and gas exploration and production. Derr commented that the political situation in the Soviet Union "was a moving target. Dramatic changes have occurred since we began the negotiations." He assured the audience that Chevron would proceed only "when we have worked out the proper economics."

One stockholder asked about the merits of double-hulled tankers. Derr said it's generally recognized that two hulls would not have lessened the spill from the *Exxon Valdez* last year, but the company was awaiting the findings of a study on tanker architecture being conducted by the National Academy of Sciences.

Representatives from two groups commended Chevron on its commitment to a public dialogue on issues of health and safety. The West County Toxics Coalition of Richmond, Calif., and the Congregation of Divine Providence of San Antonio, Texas, both urged the company to continue monitoring the effects of its operations on surrounding communities and to continue its policy of open communication.

One stockholder questioned Chevron's concern about rising oil imports. Derr said, "As OPEC production increases, we stand a greater risk of price shocks or supply disruptions."

report. The discussion of earnings, announcements by management, and selected news briefs are included to keep investors and analysts informed of interim changes in the company's operations and financial position.

A review of interim financial information provided by a public company is viewed in the framework of an annual audit of its annual financial statements; that is, the scope of the review and the sufficiency of evidence collected by the CPA are influenced by findings from the previous annual audit. The accountant's standard report on the review of interim financial information of a public company appears in Figure 9-3

We have made a review (describe the information or statements reviewed) of XYZ Company and consolidated subsidiaries of September 30, 19X1, and for the 3-month and 9-month periods then ended, in accordance with standards established by the American Institute of Certified Public Accountants.

A review of interim information consists principally of obtaining an understanding of the system for the preparation of interim financial information, applying analytical procedures to financial data, and making inquiries of persons responsible for financial and accounting matters. It is substantially less in scope than an audit in accordance with generally accepted auditing standards, the objective of which is the expression of an opinion regarding the financial statements taken as a whole. Accordingly, we do not express such an opinion.

Based on our review, we are not aware of any material modifications that should be made to the accompanying financial (information or statements) for them to be in conformity with generally accepted accounting principles.

FIG. 9-3 *Standard review report for interim information.*

The review report states that the review was made in accordance with AICPA standards and identifies the interim information reviewed. The report also contains a brief description of the procedures for a review of interim information. The CPA essentially says nothing more than "I do not know of any material changes that must be made to make the statements conform to GAAP" (see Chapter 1 for a discussion of GAAP). But the accountant has not made tests of the underlying accounting records to see if they support the figures in the financial statements—to do so would be to conduct an audit. And the reader is put on notice that a review is substantially narrower in scope than an audit.

Reviews are normally performed at the request of the board of directors so that the accountant can report to management, the board, and the stockholders on significant matters found through inquiry and analytical procedures. Reviews thereby protect the company from potential legal liability by alerting management to unusual or irregular matters found during their review.

FINANCIAL STATEMENT REVIEWS OF NONPUBLIC COMPANIES

Many CPAs work with nonpublic client companies that do not need audits, perhaps because the business is closely held, has little debt, or is not subject to government regulations that require an audit. Examples of such companies include small (sometimes family-owned) businesses and professional firms or partnerships such as those formed by doctors and lawyers. Many times these companies need tax services or assistance preparing unaudited financial statements in order to obtain credit; you may occasionally run across a set of financial statements for a nonpublic company that has been reviewed by an independent CPA. These reviews do not carry the same weight as a formal audit, which concludes with an opinion by the CPA on the fairness of financial-statement presentation.

Figure 9-4 is an example of a review report for a nonpublic company.

We have reviewed the accompanying balance sheet of ABC Company as of December 31, 19X0, and the related statements of income, retained earnings, and changes in financial position for the year ended, in accordance with standards established by the American Institute of Certified Public Accountants. All information included in these financial statements is the representation of the management of ABC Company.

A review consists principally of inquiries of company personnel and analytical procedures applied to financial data. It is substantially less in scope than an examination in accordance with generally accepted auditing standards, the objective of which is the expression of an opinion regarding the financial statements taken as a whole. Accordingly, we do not express such an opinion.

Based on our review, we are not aware of any material modifications that should be made to the accompanying financial statements in order for them to be in conformity with generally accepted accounting principles.

FIG. 9-4 *Review report for a nonpublic company.*

The report for a nonpublic company is substantially the same as that prepared for a public company. The essential difference is that in the review report relating to the interim financial statements for a public company, the CPA makes reference to "obtaining an understanding of the system for the preparation of interim financial information."

Like those in a review for a public company, the procedures performed for a review for a nonpublic company are limited to inquiry of company personnel and analytical review. Notice that the CPA states in the review report that he or she is not aware of any material changes needed to make the financial statements conform to GAAP. The report also states that the financial statements were not audited, and no opinion is expressed as to their fairness of presentation.

PROCEDURES PERFORMED IN AUDITS AND REVIEWS

Whether a public or a nonpublic company, a review consists of questioning management about the preparation of the financial statements and analyzing past and present financial statements to determine if unusual relationships exist. For instance, assume that for the last several years accounts receivable have averaged $2 million, but this year they are reported at $4 million. What is the cause of the unexpected relationship? Have the sales been recorded twice? It is up to the CPA to determine if the statements are wrong. The CPA does not investigate relationships that appear normal.

There are procedural differences between conducting an audit and a review. When performing an audit, the CPA is present at the counting of year-end inventories; in a review, the CPA merely asks questions about the procedures used to count inventories. Auditing standards require the CPA to obtain written confirmations from customers of the amounts they owe the company (accounts receivable) and from suppliers confirming the amounts owed by the business (accounts payable); the CPA would not perform such procedures in a review and would merely ask management whether all sales and payments from customers and all purchases and payments to suppliers have been recorded.

REPORTS ON COMPONENTS OF A FINANCIAL STATEMENT

A CPA may be requested to report on some specific aspect of a financial statement, a financial statement item, a forecast or projection, or a schedule; typical components are trade accounts receivable, projected income statement, and the schedule of royalties under a licensing agreement. As we stated, these types of engagements generally fall into one of two categories: reports on components that express an audit opinion and reports based on applying agreed-upon procedures.

Reports Expressing an Audit Opinion on Components

Suppose a shopping mall charges its tenants rent in accordance with a lease agreement that specifies that the rent is based on a percentage of the tenant's gross sales. The mall management might require an audit report on the fair presentation of those gross sales figures in accordance with GAAP. The tenant then engages an auditor to perform an examination of the sales account. The auditor's unqualified opinion on a schedule of gross

---

Independent Auditor's Report

We have audited the accompanying schedule of gross sales (as defined in the lease agreement dated March 24, 1991, between Smith Company, as lessor, and Jones Stores Corporation, as lessee) of Jones Stores Corporation at its Yellowstone Street store, Pocatello, Idaho, for the year ended December 31, 1991. This schedule is the responsibility of Jones Store Corporation's management. Our responsibility is to express an opinion on this schedule based on our audit.

We conducted our audit in accordance with generally accepted auditing standards. Those standards require that we plan and perform the audit to obtain reasonable assurance about whether the schedule of gross sales is free of material misstatement. An audit includes examining, on a test basis, evidence supporting the amounts and disclosures in the schedule of gross sales. An audit also includes assessing the accounting principles used and significant estimates made by management, as well as evaluating the overall schedule presentation. We believe that our audit provides a reasonable basis for our opinion.

In our opinion, the schedule of gross sales referred to above presents fairly, in all material respects, the gross sales of Jones Stores Corporation at its Yellowstone Street store, Pocatello, Idaho, for the year ended December 31, 1991, as defined in the lease agreement referred to in the first paragraph.

This report is intended solely for the information and use of the boards of directors and managements of Jones Stores Corporation and Smith Company and should not be used for any other purpose.

FIG. 9-5 *Report relating to amount of sales for the purpose of computing rental.*

sales is shown in Figure 9-5. Similar reports might be requested to determine royalty agreements or participation in profit-sharing plans.

There are several similarities and differences between an audit report on specified elements and the auditor's standard audit report (discussed in Chapter 2).

Similarities

1. The report title includes the word "independent."
2. The report states that the specified elements, accounts, or items identified in the report have been audited.
3. The report states that the specified elements, accounts, or items are the responsibility of the company's management and that the auditor is responsible for expressing an opinion on the specified elements, accounts or items based on the audit.
4. The second paragraph regarding generally accepted auditing standards and the definition of an audit is the same as that found in the standard audit report except that the reference is to the specified element rather than to the financial statements as a whole.
5. The opinion paragraph is the same as the standard report except that reference is made to the identified element rather than to the financial statements as a whole.

Differences

1. While not included in the sample report shown in Figure 9-6, an additional paragraph might be needed above the opinion paragraph to describe the accounting basis on which the specified elements, accounts, or items are presented if different from GAAP. If necessary, the auditor should also comment in this paragraph on the sources of significant client interpretations relating to the provisions of a relevant agreement (such as the lease agreement).
2. Our example contains a paragraph after the opinion paragraph restricting the distribution of the report to Smith Company and Jones Stores Corporation. This restriction is necessary because the basis of presentation is determined by reference to a document (the lease agreement) that is not generally available to other third parties. A similar restriction is necessary if the presentation of the element, account, or item was not in conformity with GAAP. On the other hand, if a CPA were engaged to simply audit a schedule of accounts receivable for a company, such a restriction would be unnecessary.

Reports Based on Applying Agreed-Upon Procedures

When the scope of an examination of specified elements, accounts, or items is limited, the engagement becomes one based on *agreed-upon procedures*. This means that the accountant is applying selected auditing procedures, rather than the full set of procedures that would normally be performed in an audit.

When this type of engagement is performed, the parties involved arrive at an understanding of the specific audit procedures to be performed by the CPA through discussions; this understanding is stated in a draft copy of the report or in the engagement letter distributed to the concerned parties, who are asked to respond with any comments before a report is issued.

The accountant's report contains the following information:

1. The specified elements, accounts, or items to which the agreed-upon procedures were applied.
2. The intended distribution of the report.
3. The procedures applied, along with the accountant's findings.
4. A disclaimer of opinion (negative assurance) with respect to the specified elements, accounts, or items.
5. A statement that the report relates only to the specified elements, accounts, or items and not to the client's financial statements taken as a whole.

Figure 9-6 provides an example of an agreed-upon procedures engagement in which the accountant has performed limited procedures on a statement of investment performance statistics for a company fund. The reference in the report to "Note 1" refers to footnote 1. In footnote 1, the CPA enumerates the measurement and disclosure criteria used to evaluate the fund. That is, the CPA identifies the established, stated, or agreed-upon criteria in this footnote.

To ABC Company and XYZ Fund

We have applied the procedures enumerated below to the accompanying Statement of Investment Performance Statistics of XYZ Fund for the year ended December 31, 19X1. These procedures, which were agreed to by ABC Company and XYZ Fund, were performed solely to assist you in evaluating the investment performance of XYZ Fund. This report is intended solely for your information and should not be used by those who did not participate in determining the procedures.

Our procedures and findings are as follows: (This paragraph enumerates the procedures and findings).

These agreed-upon procedures are substantially less in scope than an examination, the objective of which is the expression of an opinion on the Statement of Investment Performance Statistics. Accordingly, we do not express an opinion.

Based on the application of the procedures referred to above, nothing came to our attention that caused us to believe that the accompanying Statement of Investment Performance Statistics is not presented in conformity with the measurement and disclosure criteria set forth in Note 1. Had we performed additional procedures or had we made an examination of the Statement of Investment Performance Statistics, other matters might have come to our attention that would have been reported to you.

FIG. 9-6 *Report on agreed-upon procedures for the statement of investment performance statistics of XYZ Fund.*

COMPILATION REPORTS FOR NONPUBLIC COMPANIES

When doing a compilation, the CPA reads the financial statements, decides whether they are in proper form and appear to contain appropriate disclosures, and checks the mathematics of the statements (for instance, for the balance sheet, do assets equal liabilities plus owners' equity?). The CPA is not required to analyze relationships or to ask management questions about the preparation of the statements. However, the accountant should be familiar enough with the company's business transactions and the proper accounting to be used to know if the information supplied by the company has obvious flaws.

The accountant's report should state that a compilation has been performed and that a compilation is limited to presenting information that is the representation of management or the owners. The report must state that the accountant has not audited or reviewed the financial statements and is not expressing an opinion as to their fairness of presentation. Compilations can be performed on the financial statements taken as a whole or on only one financial statement. Figure 9-7 shows a sample compilation report on the financial statements of PLT Company

We have compiled the accompanying balance sheet of PLT Company as of December 31, 19X1, and the related statements of income, retained earnings, and cash flows for the year then ended, in accordance with standards established by the American Institute of Certified Public Accountants.

A compilation is limited to presenting in the form of financial statements information that is the representation of management. We have not audited or reviewed the accompanying financial statements and, accordingly, do not express an opinion or any other form of assurance on them.

FIG. 9-7 *Accountant's Compilation Report*

An accountant who is not independent of a company can still compile the financial statements of the company and issue a report. In this instance, an additional paragraph is added noting that the accountant is not independent of the company.

CHAPTER PERSPECTIVE

In this chapter we described services other than full audits that can be provided by CPAs. These services include reviews of both public and nonpublic companies; audits of specified elements, accounts, or financial statement items; agreed-upon procedures engagements; and engagements to compile the financial statements of nonpublic companies.

Each of these engagements carries a different assurance. These levels of assurance are communicated through the report issued by the CPA and may be positive (as in an unqualified audit opinion), negative (as in a review of a nonpublic company), or unstated (as in a disclaimer of opinion in a compilation engagement of a nonpublic company).

We described the reports and responsibilities of the CPA when performing reviews of public and nonpublic companies, audits of specified elements, agreed-upon procedures engagements, and compilations of the financial statements of nonpublic companies. We also included in each section an illustration of a CPA's report for that particular engagement.

Reports to the SEC

INTRODUCTION AND MAIN POINTS

While annual reports containing audited financial statements are used by a number of groups, including some government agencies, the Securities and Exchange Commission (SEC) requires that companies under its jurisdiction file separate reports according to specified formats. The SEC filings discussed in this chapter include the registration, the required annual filing (Form 10-K), the required quarterly filing (Form 10-Q), and the required filing of significant changes (Form 8-K). After studying the material in this chapter:

▬ You will understand the general goal of the SEC in ensuring equal access to information.

▬ You will understand the accountant/auditor's involvement in the SEC registration process and the information contained in a registration statement.

▬ You will know what an auditor's comfort letter is and why underwriters request them.

▬ You will know the difference between Forms 10-K, 10-Q, and 8-K and the information they require.

▬ You will know which forms contain audited data and which do not.

Prior to the establishment of the SEC, many states enacted legislation to curb abuses relating to the issuance of securities. The state laws dealing with the regulation of securities became known as "blue sky laws," a phrase that originated more than fifty years ago in a judicial comment denouncing speculative schemes that were an intangible as "so many feet of blue sky." "Blue sky law" is often used interchangeably with "state law" to refer to state laws that govern issuance and trading of securities.

State laws never really proved to be totally effective in regulating the securities markets, largely because companies that were engaged in interstate commerce could simply choose to issue securities in a state where there were no regulations governing their issuance. Also, in states where regulations existed, exemptions were commonplace, along with selective prosecution of those companies found to have violated the law.

Because the state laws proved to be ineffectual, a large number of state and local officials looked to the federal government for action regarding the regulation of the securities markets. The results were the Securities Acts of 1933 and the Securities Exchange Act of 1934.

THE REASON FOR SEC REPORTING REQUIREMENTS

If the markets for both debt and stock are to be orderly and if investors are to make informed investment decisions, all parties must have equal access to reliable information about the companies that borrow money or issue stock. Part of the job of the SEC is to ensure that current and potential investors and creditors have equal access to information about companies whose securities are publicly traded. In attempting to ensure that investors are provided with the information necessary to make informed investment decisions, the SEC has expanded its regulations to encompass four areas:

1. Offerings of securities, both as original issuances and as secondary distributions
2. The information a prospective investor is entitled to receive
3. The information an investor is entitled to receive periodically
4. Disclosure of significant events

The SEC accomplishes its mission by requiring publicly held companies to provide financial information at regular intervals. This information is then made available to potential investors or others with an interest in it.

By overseeing the filing of information—determining what information should be filed and how it should be presented—the SEC acts as a kind of clearinghouse. (However, requests for annual reports should be addressed to the company and requests for SEC filings should be addressed to the company or the SEC.) This chapter discusses the registration process and SEC Forms 10-K, 10-Q, and 8-K. These reports are compared in Figure 10-1.

Form	Filing Frequency	Contains Audited Data?
Registration (including S-1)	At issue	yes
10-K	Annually	yes
10-Q	Quarterly	no
8-K	as needed (following significant changes)	no

FIG. 10-1 *Forms required by the SEC*

REGISTRATION

Registration is the process of filing information about stock and the issuing company with the proper regulatory agency. At the federal level, registration statements are filed with the SEC. The SEC does not approve the company or its stock issue, but looks only at the adequacy of the information disclosed. State laws may also require registration.

The registration process normally begins with the selection of an investment banker or underwriter. The underwriter agrees to assist the company in the registration process by marketing and distributing the securities. The underwriter usually requests a *comfort letter* from the independent CPA auditor to indicate that the company has fulfilled all of the necessary accounting requirements in the registration process. The comfort letter says, in essence, that the CPA knows of nothing wrong with the financial information provided by the company issuing the securities.

Underwriters request comfort letters to acquire information and to show their reliance on the CPA auditor. Comfort letters are not required by the SEC or by any of the securities acts. They are simply one way accountants are involved with stock issues.

The registration statement is a document presented in narrative form, similar to a brochure. The SEC requires companies to file a registration statement before a public offering of stock is made in interstate commerce or through the mails, unless the offering qualifies for an exemption. Exemptions are divided into two categories: exempt securities and exempt transactions. Securities offered by banks, nonprofit organizations, common carriers, state governments, as well as intrastate offerings, are examples from the first category. Exempt transactions are private offerings to a limited number of persons or institutions who already have access to the type of information that registration would disclose and who do not intend to redistribute the securities. The SEC also has the authority to exempt other offerings when the amount of capital to be raised is small and the offering is limited to a modest group of investors. This "small issue exemption" has a $5 million limit on the amount that can be solicited. Exemption from registration does not relieve the company from legal liability. The registration statement, which is available to the public, serves only to provide investors with a source of information and does not imply approval of the investment by the SEC.

A company selects one form from over twenty different forms. The most common are *Form S-1, Form S-2,* and *Form S-3.*

A Form S-1 consists of two principal parts: a prospectus, or selling document, that must be furnished to all purchasers of the stock, and a supplemental part containing more detailed information, such as a listing of expenses related to issuing the securities, information about officers and directors, and additional exhibits and financial statement schedules.

Form S-1 is the basic, most commonly used form for full registration of an initial stock offering. Instructions for the financial statement portions of the registration forms are found in Regulation S-X and, for the nonfinancial aspects of registration, in Regulation S-K. The company must provide whatever information is necessary to make the registration statement complete and not misleading.

As stated, a prospectus is included in Form S-1. A prospectus is any offer made in writing to sell stock; as used by the SEC, the term refers to the document the SEC requires companies to provide to prospective investors in stock registered with the SEC. It is unlawful to sell registered stock in interstate commerce without providing the investor with a prospectus.

The registration statement does not become effective immediately when it is filed, and no sales of stock can be made until it becomes effective. Nonetheless, expressions of interest can be solicited from investors by showing them a preliminary prospectus called a "red herring." This document includes on its face a legend in red ink stating that the registration statement has not become effective and that a formal offer to sell can be made only after the effective date of the registration. Ordinarily, information about offering price, commissions to dealers, and proceeds accruing to the issuer is excluded from the red herring.

Though the SEC does not pass judgment on the value of the offering as an investment, it frequently requires amendments to the registration to improve disclosure. The accountant may assist in the preparation of tables and other data contained in the registration statement in addition to the audited statements, but must make it clear he or she does not assume responsibility for any matters not within his or her expertise as an accountant.

In some states, an effective federal registration fulfills all state blue sky requirements. State securities administrators can provide this information.

THE ANNUAL FILING (FORM 10-K)

Form 10-K must be filed annually with the SEC by publicly traded companies within ninety days after the close of the company's fiscal year. Form 10-K requires much the same information that companies include in their annual reports but also asks for additional information. Some companies issue a combined annual report and 10-K, a procedure allowed under the SEC's integrated disclosure rules.

The 10-K is divided into four parts, each of which is subdivided into individual items. If information has been provided elsewhere, the company may reference those sources rather than repeating the information. The financial statements contained in the 10-K are audited; the 10-K contains a copy of the auditor's report (Item 8, below) as do the financial statements in the annual report.

The contents of the 10-K are:

Part 1

Item 1   A description of the company's business, including information on different segments of the company (for example, product lines, industries, domestic and foreign operations, and major classes of customers).

Item 2   A description of the company's property.

Item 3   A description of any legal proceedings in which the company is involved.

Item 4   A discussion of matters that have been voted on by the shareholders.

Part 2

Item 5   A description of the market for the company's common stock, including disclosures of the principal American markets on which the company's common stock is traded, quarterly high and low stock prices for the last two years, the approximate number of shareholders, the number of times and the amount of cash dividends paid in the last two years, and any restrictions on the company's ability to pay dividends.

Item 6   A five-year summary of selected financial data, including net sales (operating revenues), income or loss from continuing operations, income or loss from continuing operations per common share, total assets, long-term debt and redeemable preferred stock, and cash dividends per common share.

Item 7   Management's discussion of the company's financial condition, changes that have occurred in financial condition, and the results of operations. This discussion includes management's analysis of the company's liquidity, resources, and operations, the impact of inflation, the cause of major changes in the financial statements that have occurred during the year, and any material contingencies.

Item 8   The financial statements, supplementary data, and auditor's report.

Item 9   Changes in accounting principles and disagreements with the company's auditors.

Part 3

Item 10   The company's directors and executive officers.

Item 11   Compensation of the executive officers.

Item 12   Company securities owned by management and major stockholders.

Item 13   Information on related-party transactions, including transactions between the company and management, its subsidiaries, and major stockholders.

Part 4

Item 14   Exhibits, financial-statement schedules, and reports on Form 8-K.

Figure 10-2 provides excerpts from the 1989 10-K report of American Capital Management & Research, Inc.

FORM 10-K

SECURITIES AND EXCHANGE COMMISSION
Washington, D.C. 20549

[X] ANNUAL REPORT PURSUANT TO SECTION 13 OR 15(d) OF THE
SECURITIES EXCHANGE ACT OF 1934

For the fiscal year ended December 31, 1989

[ ] TRANSITION REPORT PURSUANT TO SECTION 13 OR 15(d) OF THE
SECURITIES EXCHANGE ACT OF 1934

For the transition period from .... to ....

Commission file number 1-9084

(Exact name of registrant as specified in its charter)

Delaware	**74-1623159**
(State or other jurisdiction of incorporation or organization)	(I.R.S. Employer Identification No.)
2800 Post Oak Blvd.	
Houston, Texas	**77056-6198**
(Address of principal executive offices)	(Zip Code)

Registrant's telephone number, including area code: (713) 993-0500

Securities registered pursuant to Section 12(b) of the Act:

Title of each class	Name of each exchange on which registered
Common Stock, par value $.10 per share	New York Stock Exchange

Indicate by check mark whether the registrant (1) has filed all reports required to be filed by Section 13 or 15(d) of the Securities Exchange Act of 1934 during the preceding 12 months (or for such shorter period that the registrant was required to file such reports), and (2) has been subject to such filing requirements for the past 90 days.

Yes ..✓..   No. .....

The aggregate market value of the voting stock held by non-affiliates of the registrant as of February 28, 1990 was approximately $35,867,442.

As of February 28, 1990, the registrant had 24,387,400 shares of common stock outstanding.

DOCUMENTS INCORPORATED BY REFERENCE

Document	Form 10-K Part
Proxy Statement for 1990 Annual Meeting of Shareholders	Part III

AMERICAN CAPITAL MANAGEMENT & RESEARCH, INC. AND SUBSIDIARIES
FORM 10-K ANNUAL REPORT
FOR YEAR ENDED DECEMBER 31, 1989

TABLE OF CONTENTS

PART I

ITEM 1: BUSINESS

(a) General Development of Business

    American Capital Management & Research, Inc. and its subsidiaries (the "Company" or the "Registrant"), currently provide investment management and advisory services, distribution services and transfer agency services for the American Capital complex of investment companies ("American Capital Funds") and investment advisory services to the Common Sense^{TM} Trust, a diversified, open-end management investment company operated through joint ventures with The A. L. Williams Corporation ("ALW"), a wholly-owned subsidiary of Primerica Corporation ("Primerica"). At December 31, 1989, the Company provided investment advisory services to 28 portfolios of open-end management investment companies ("American Capital Mutual Funds"), five portfolios of the Common Sense^{TM} Trust, and four portfolios of closed-end management investment companies ("Closed-end Funds") (together, the "Funds") with various investment objectives. The Company, a Delaware corporation founded in 1968, and its predecessors have been in the investment advisory business since 1926. At December 31, 1989, Fund assets under management, including American Capital Funds and the Common Sense^{TM} Trust were $13.4 billion. The Company also provided investment management services for insurance company subsidiaries of Primerica. At December 31, 1989, such assets were $1.6 billion. However, the Company has been informed by Primerica, that Primerica intends to manage the investments of its insurance subsidiaries' assets internally and therefore, effective January 1, 1990, these assets are no longer managed by the Company.

    The Company operates through subsidiaries, principal among which are: American Capital Asset Management, Inc. ("Capital Management"), which acts as the investment adviser to each of the American Capital Funds and sub-adviser to the Common Sense^{TM} Funds; American Capital Marketing, Inc. ("Capital Marketing"), a broker/dealer registered under the Securities Exchange Act of 1934, as amended (the "Exchange Act"), which acts as the national distributor for all shares of the publicly offered American Capital Mutual Funds; Advantage Capital Corporation ("Advantage Capital"), a retail broker/dealer registered under the Exchange Act, which sells shares of the publicly offered American Capital Mutual Funds as well as other securities products directly to the public through a licensed sales force located throughout the United States; American Capital Companies Shareholder Services, Inc. ("ACCESS"), which serves as transfer agent and shareholder service agent for most of the American Capital Mutual Funds; American Capital Trust Company ("Trust Company"), which serves as a custodian and retirement plans administrator; and American Capital Services, Inc. ("Capital Services"), which oversees shareholder service operations and provides corporate administrative services. Other subsidiaries of the Company market products relating to the American Capital Funds and provide necessary services to the American Capital organization.

    The Company is a majority-owned (approximately 83%-owned) subsidiary of Primerica, a Delaware Corporation, which, through its subsidiaries, is principally engaged in (i) consumer services, (ii) insurance services, and (iii) investment services. The filings of Primerica and its other subsidiaries who file reports under the Exchange Act, Commercial Credit Company and Primerica Holdings, Inc., ("Primerica Holdings"), provide

ITEM 1: BUSINESS (Continued)

additional business and financial information about those companies. Primerica Corporation, a New Jersey corporation ("old Primerica"), acquired the Company in 1983 from American General Corporation. The Company operated as an indirect wholly-owned subsidiary of old Primerica until the public offering in 1986 of approximately 17% of the Company's common stock. Effective December 15, 1988, old Primerica was merged into Primerica Holdings, a newly formed wholly-owned subsidiary of Commercial Credit Group, Inc. Thereupon, Commercial Credit Group, Inc. changed its corporate name to Primerica Corporation.

(b) Financial Information About Industry Segments

The Company is engaged in one business segment, investment services, primarily investment management, distribution and transfer agency services. Its clients include the Funds as well as institutional and other clients.

(c) Narrative Description of Business

The Company's principal products and services are investment management advice to the Funds, distribution and marketing of the American Capital Mutual Funds' shares, and shareholder and transfer agency services for the American Capital Mutual Funds.

The goal of Capital Management is consistent above-average performance. Two teams of analysts, traders and portfolio managers are used to accomplish this goal. One team manages bond or "fixed income" investments; the other engages in stock or "equity" market activities.

The Fixed-Income Department utilizes a computer-based system for tracking the bond markets and the thousands of individual securities that trade within them. The Department is organized into groups that manage corporate, municipal, government and money market securities.

The Equity Department uses a combination of quantitative analysis techniques and traditional stock selection methods to build equity portfolios. Initially, thousands of stocks are screened by computer to identify those that may be undervalued based on factors such as price, book value and earnings per share. Fundamental analysis techniques are used by the research staff to independently assess the growth prospects for these companies, utilizing Wall Street sources, interviews with management and reviews of the competitive environment before making their recommendations to portfolio managers who determine which stocks to buy, sell or hold. Benchmark portfolios for each Fund help portfolio managers maintain desired portfolio characteristics.

ITEM 6: SELECTED FINANCIAL DATA

AMERICAN CAPITAL MANAGEMENT & RESEARCH, INC. AND SUBSIDIARIES
SELECTED CONSOLIDATED FINANCIAL DATA
(In thousands, except per share amounts)

	Years Ended December 31,				
	1989	1988	1987	1986	1985
Revenues					
Investment management and advisory fees	$ 58,795	$ 60,259	$ 67,839	$ 59,553	$ 39,372
Commissions, net of commissions paid	5,363	7,747	25,684	53,353	43,810
Transfer agent fees	22,177	18,317	–	–	–
Equity in earnings of joint ventures	7,124	4,789	2,170		
Other income, principally custodial fees	8,350	8,093	11,033	8,975	8,266
	$101,809	$ 99,205	$106,726	$121,881	$ 91,448
Net Income	$ 19,796	$ 23,325	$ 29,835	$ 36,772	$ 26,558
Earnings per share of common stock	$ .81	$ .96	$ 1.23	$ 1.52	$ 1.10
Cash Dividends declared per share following public offering(1)(2)	$ .70	$ 1.00	$ 1.40	$ .45	$ –
SELECTED BALANCE SHEET DATA AT DECEMBER 31					
Total assets	$ 73,260	$ 72,129	$ 76,128	$ 90,423	$ 76,678
Bank term loan and revolving credit agreement	$ –	$ 8,650	$ 7,750	$ 14,350	–
Stockholders' equity(2)	$ 49,187	$ 45,494	$ 45,080	$ 49,852	$ 48,956

(1) The Company was a wholly-owned subsidiary of Primerica Corporation from September 10, 1983 until a public offering of its stock on March 14, 1986, at which time it became an approximately 83%-owned subsidiary.

(2) On April 18, 1989, the Board of Directors reduced the quarterly cash dividend from $.25 to $.15 per share. The Company paid cash dividends of $.25 per share for the first quarter and $.15 per share for the remaining three quarters. The Board of Directors declared and paid cash dividends of $.25 per share for each quarter of 1988. On January 20, 1987, the Board of Directors increased the quarterly cash dividend from $.15 to $.25 per share and declared an extraordinary dividend of $.40 per share. The Board of Directors declared and paid cash dividends of $.25 per share for each quarter of 1987. On February 6, 1986, the Company paid a cash dividend of $25 million and cash dividends of $.15 per share for each of the first three quarters of 1986. The Board of Directors declared and paid cash dividends of $22.5 million in 19^5.

ITEM 7: MANAGEMENT'S DISCUSSION AND ANALYSIS OF FINANCIAL CONDITION AND RESULTS OF OPERATIONS

General

Revenues are derived principally from investment management and advisory fees received from the Funds managed by the Company, transfer agency fees received from the Funds, commissions received from the sales of Fund shares and other securities, and from equity in joint ventures. The joint ventures are engaged in the same aspects of the mutual fund business managing a diversified open-end management investment company marketed under the registered name of the Common Sense[TM] Trust (the "Trust"). Investment management and advisory fees are based on the value of assets of Funds under management calculated at various rates which tend to decrease with increases in Fund asset size. Transfer agent fees are based on the estimated cost of providing these services. Net commissions from Fund sales tend to fluctuate directly with sales volume and also are affected by the mix of equity and fixed-income Fund shares sold.

Total assets under management were $15.0 billion, $14.3 billion and $14.9 billion at December 31, 1989, 1988 and 1987, respectively. Included in total assets under management at December 31, 1989, 1988, and 1987 are $1.6 billion, $1.0 billion and $.9 billion, respectively, of assets of certain insurance subsidiaries of Primerica, and $1.3 billion, $.8 billion and $.4 billion, respectively, of assets of the Trust. Redemptions have exceeded sales of American Capital Funds since mid 1987. The industry had net sales in 1989, while American Capital Funds have remained in a net redemption position. During 1989, the favorable market performance of mutual fund assets and dividend reinvestments by shareholders offset partially this negative trend. There is no way to predict future shareholder activity or whether favorable market and investment performance will continue. During this three-year period and continuing into the first quarter of 1990, there have been sharp market movements, both positive and negative, which also influence shareholder purchases and redemptions.

Total sales at net asset value were $1.28 billion, $1.31 billion, and $3.00 billion for 1989, 1988, and 1987, respectively. The 1989 sales include $48.8 million of investments in the American Capital Reserve Fund, Inc. made by the Company for its own cash management purposes. Such investments in prior years were not significant. Total sales for 1988 exclude $136 million for sales of a closed-end fund. Included in total sales for 1989, 1988, and 1987 were $556.4 million, $485.6 million, and $452.1 million of sales of the Trust which began in April 1987.

The Company has been informed by Primerica that Primerica intends to manage the investments of its insurance subsidiaries' assets internally and, therefore, beginning in the first quarter of 1990, these assets are no longer managed by the Company. Revenues related to these services for 1989, 1988, and 1987 amounted to approximately $2.5 million, $1.9 million, and $2.0 million, respectively.

ITEM 7: MANAGEMENT'S DISCUSSION AND ANALYSIS OF FINANCIAL CONDITION AND RESULTS OF OPERATIONS (CONTINUED)

Results of Operations

Net income was $19.8 million, or $.81 per share, for the year ended December 31, 1989, $23.3 million, or $.96 per share, for the year ended December 31, 1988, and $29.8 million, or $1.23 per share, for the year ended December 31, 1987. Investment management and advisory fees have decreased to $58.8 million for 1989 from $60.3 million in 1988 and $67.8 million in 1987, due primarily to the decline in average assets under management of the American Capital Funds, the basis upon which fees are determined. On March 2, 1990, the Board of Directors for the American Capital Mutual Funds approved a new investment management and advisory fee schedule for three equity funds comprising 35% of the American Capital Mutual Fund assets under management as of December 31, 1989. The new fee schedule is subject to Fund shareholder approval and the increase, if approved, is expected to be effective July 1, 1990. Based on asset levels at February 28, 1990, the annualized effective fee increase would be approximately $3.6 million.

Commission revenue has continued a downward trend to $5.4 million for 1989 from $7.7 million for 1988 and $25.7 million in 1987. American Capital Fund sales, excluding money market and closed-end funds, which generate the majority of commission income, decreased 28% to $507.5 million for 1989 from $673.5 million for 1988, which had decreased 78% from $2,998.2 million for 1987. In an effort to stimulate sales, a change in the commission structure was effected in 1989 whereby the front-end sales charge on most American Capital Funds was reduced, thereby reducing the retained commission. This reduction, along with 100% dealer concession incentive programs, further compounded the decrease in commission revenues brought about by lower sales volumes.

Effective February 29, 1988, American Capital Companies Shareholder Services, Inc. ("ACCESS") acquired for $2.6 million substantially all of the assets of Shareholders Investor Service Corporation, the shareholder service and dividend disbursing agent for most of the managed Funds. Pursuant to an agreement with the Funds' boards of directors, ACCESS agreed to enhance transfer agent services and provide such services at their approximate costs. Transfer agent fees were $22.2 million for 1989, representing 12 months of activity versus $18.3 million for 10 months of activity in 1988. Rates charged per account for transfer agent services, which are competitive with rates charged throughout the industry, are approved annually by the boards of directors of the managed Funds.

The Company recorded equity in the earnings of its joint ventures with The A.L. Williams Corporation (a subsidiary of Primerica) of $7.1 million, $4.8 million, and $2.2 million for 1989, 1988, and 1987, respectively. The joint ventures distribute, manage and administer the portfolios of the Common Sense™ Trust. Assets under management of the Trust have grown steadily since inception of the Trust.

ITEM 7: MANAGEMENT'S DISCUSSION AND ANALYSIS OF FINANCIAL CONDITION AND RESULTS OF OPERATIONS (CONTINUED)

Total expenses increased $7.7 million to $71.3 million in 1989 from $63.6 million in 1988. Expenses for 1988 were $7.2 million higher than 1987 expenses of $56.4 million. After netting out the transfer agent costs of approximately $22 million and $18 million for 1989 and 1988, respectively, expense increases were primarily a result of the installation of a performance-based compensation program for portfolio management and other areas of the Company, promotional expenses and other costs of investments made to enhance the Company's service and marketing areas. From 1987 to 1988, excluding transfer agency costs, overall expenses decreased, reflecting lower sales activity and the effect of cost reduction programs.

Liquidity and Capital Resources

At December 31, 1989, 1988, and 1987, the Company had $22.1 million, $16.0 million, and $15.3 million, respectively, of cash and cash equivalents. Management believes the Company's cash resources, plus funds generated from operations and credit arrangements discussed below, are sufficient to meet the Company's foreseeable capital and liquidity requirements.

During 1989, the Company paid off the remaining balance of its bank term loan. At December 31, 1988 and 1987, the outstanding balance relating to the bank term loan was $5.2 million and $7.8 million, respectively. The weighted average interest rate was 11.5% during 1989. In addition, the Company has a $10 million revolving credit agreement with a bank that expires April 1, 1991. At December 31, 1989, no amounts were outstanding related to the revolving credit agreement. At December 31, 1988, $3.5 million was outstanding under the revolving credit agreement and paid during 1989, in addition to $2.0 million borrowed and paid during the year. Primerica has provided the Company with a line of credit of $95 million for general corporate purposes. The amount available under this line of credit is reduced by borrowings or the amounts available for borrowing under the bank term loan and revolving credit agreement, respectively. At December 31, 1989, $85 million was available under Primerica's line of credit.

The Company's broker/dealer subsidiaries are subject to rules and regulations of the Securities and Exchange Commission ("SEC") which require the maintenance of minimum net capital and reserve accounts. At December 31, 1989, the amount of net capital required for all three subsidiaries pursuant to such rules and regulations aggregated $.5 million. The net capital of each of the broker/dealer subsidiaries, which separately met all requirements, aggregated $5.6 million. Additionally, at December 31, 1989, the Company was required to segregate $2.7 million of cash or cash equivalents to comply with an SEC reserve requirement.

On April 18, 1989, the Board of Directors reduced the quarterly cash dividend from $.25 to $.15 per share. The Company paid cash dividends of $.25 per share for the first quarter and $.15 per share for the remaining three quarters. On January 16, 1990, the Company's Board of Directors declared a cash dividend of $.15 per share payable February 27, 1990 to shareholders of record on January 31, 1990.

ITEM 7: MANAGEMENT'S DISCUSSION AND ANALYSIS OF FINANCIAL CONDITION AND RESULTS OF OPERATIONS (CONTINUED)

Impact of Inflation

The Company's business is not capital intensive and management believes that financial results as reported would not have been affected significantly had such results been adjusted to reflect the effects of inflation and price changes. However, inflation affects the cost of operations, in particular salaries and related benefits. Although the impact of inflation upon revenues is difficult to predict, management believes revenues would change in relation to changes in the cost of operations.

INDEPENDENT AUDITORS' REPORT

To the Board of Directors and Stockholders of
American Capital Management & Research, Inc.:

We have audited the accompanying consolidated statement of financial position
of American Capital Management & Research, Inc. and Subsidiaries as of
December 31, 1989, and the related consolidated statements of income, changes
in stockholders' equity and cash flows and the financial statement schedules
I, II, IX and X for the year then ended. These consolidated financial
statements and financial statement schedules are the responsibility of the
Company's management. Our responsibility is to express an opinion on these
financial statements and financial statement schedules based on our audit.

We conducted our audit in accordance with generally accepted auditing
standards. Those standards require that we plan and perform the audit to
obtain reasonable assurance about whether the financial statements are free of
material misstatement. An audit includes examining, on a test basis, evidence
supporting the amounts and disclosures in the financial statements. An audit
also includes assessing the accounting principles used and significant
estimates made by management, as well as evaluating the overall financial
statement presentation. We believe that our audit provides a reasonable basis
for our opinion.

In our opinion, the financial statements referred to above present fairly, in
all material respects, the financial position of American Capital Management &
Research, Inc. and Subsidiaries as of December 31, 1989, and the results of
their operations and their cash flows for the year then ended in conformity
with generally accepted accounting principles. Also in our opinion, the
related financial statement schedules, when considered in relation to the
basic consolidated financial statements taken as a whole, present fairly, in
all material respects, the information set forth therein.

                              KPMG PEAT MARWICK

Houston, Texas
January 26, 1990

AMERICAN CAPITAL MANAGEMENT & RESEARCH, INC. AND SUBSIDIARIES
CONSOLIDATED STATEMENT OF INCOME
(In thousands, except per share amounts)

	Years Ended December 31,		
	1989	1988	1987
Revenues			
Investment management and advisory fees	$ 58,795	$60,259	$ 67,839
Commissions, net of commissions paid	5,363	7,747	25,684
Transfer agent fees	22,177	18,317	–
Equity in earnings of joint ventures	7,124	4,789	2,170
Other income, principally custodial fees	8,350	8,093	11,033
	101,809	99,205	106,726
Expenses			
Employee compensation and benefits	33,776	30,966	26,593
Other operating, general and administrative	37,495	32,636	29,791
	71,271	63,602	56,384
Income before income taxes	30,538	35,603	50,342
Provision for income taxes	10,742	12,278	20,507
Net income	$ 19,796	$ 23,325	$ 29,835
Earnings per share of common stock	$ .81	$ .96	$ 1.23
Weighted average number of shares outstanding	24,377	24,367	24,324

See Notes to Consolidated Financial Statements.

AMERICAN CAPITAL MANAGEMENT & RESEARCH, INC. AND SUBSIDIARIES
CONSOLIDATED STATEMENT OF FINANCIAL POSITION
(In thousands, except shares)

	December 31	
	1989	1988
Assets		
Cash and cash equivalents ($2.7 million and $.3 million, respectively, segregated for customers)	$22,097	$15,987
Management fees and other receivables from Funds	11,042	7,831
Receivables from related parties	308	3,439
Other accounts receivable	5,783	6,768
Marketable equity securities	7,153	9,719
Unamortized cost of contracts purchased, net	9,797	11,818
Equipment, leasehold improvements and furniture, net	9,225	10,215
Investments in joint ventures	6,003	4,488
Other assets	1,852	1,864
	$73,260	$72,129
Liabilities		
Accounts payable	$ 8,070	$ 6,542
Accrued compensation	5,732	4,835
Payables from security transactions	2,971	995
Bank term loan and revolving credit agreement	–	8,650
Payables to related parties	3,104	947
Deferred compensation	4,196	4,666
	24,073	26,635
Stockholders' Equity		
Common stock ($.10 par value; 50,000,000 shares authorized, shares issued and outstanding- 24,381,200 in 1989, 24,367,800 in 1988)	2,438	2,437
Capital in excess of par value	23,951	23,677
Retained earnings	23,403	20,669
Deferred compensation-restricted stock	(508)	(768)
Net unrealized depreciation of marketable equity securities	(97)	(521)
	49,187	45,494
	$73,260	$72,129

See Notes to Consolidated Financial Statements.

AMERICAN CAPITAL MANAGEMENT & RESEARCH, INC. AND SUBSIDIARIES
CONSOLIDATED STATEMENT OF CASH FLOWS
(In thousands)

	Years Ended December 31,		
	1989	1988	1987
Operating Activities			
Net income	$ 19,796	$ 23,325	$ 29,835
Adjustments to reconcile net income to net			
cash provided by operating activities:			
Depreciation and amortization	4,724	4,285	3,827
Undistributed earnings of joint ventures	(1,515)	(1,503)	(985)
Deferred taxes	427	697	275
Realized loss (gain) on sale of			
marketable equity securities	(1)	719	(254)
Change in assets and liabilities:			
Decrease (increase) in receivables	(2,226)	(385)	7,540
Decrease (increase) in receivables			
from related parties	2,783	(2,751)	(243)
Increase (decrease) in payables to			
related parties	2,157	135	(44)
Increase (decrease) in accounts			
payable and other liabilities	4,039	(2,103)	(4,322)
Decrease (increase) in other assets	(82)	10	(482)
Net cash provided by operating			
activities	30,102	22,429	35,147
Investing Activities			
Additions to equipment, leasehold			
improvements and furniture	(1,619)	(4,115)	(1,299)
Investments in joint ventures	-	-	(1,000)
Repayment of loans to officers and			
employees	348	284	247
Purchase of marketable equity securities	(1,523)	(1,541)	(12,488)
Proceeds from sale of marketable equity			
securities	4,514	9,565	6,881
Net cash provided by (used in)			
investing activities	1,720	4,193	(7,659)
Financing Activities			
Borrowings under line-of-credit			
agreements	2,000	8,200	10,000
Repayments under line-of-credit			
agreements	(5,500)	(7,200)	(7,500)
Repayments on bank term loan	(5,150)	(2,600)	(6,600)
Dividends paid	(17,062)	(24,368)	(33,978)
Net cash used in financing activities	(25,712)	(25,968)	(38,078)
Net increase (decrease) in cash and			
cash equivalents	6,110	654	(10,590)
Cash and cash equivalents at beginning			
of year (1)	15,987	15,333	25,923
Cash and cash equivalents at end of			
year (1)	$ 22,097	$ 15,987	$ 15,333

(1) Cash and cash equivalents included $2.7 million, $.3 million, $4.0 million,
and $5.4 million as of December 31, 1989, 1988, 1987, and 1986,
respectively, segregated for customers and restricted as to withdrawal.

See Notes to Consolidated Financial Statements.

AMERICAN CAPITAL MANAGEMENT & RESEARCH, INC. AND SUBSIDIARIES
CONSOLIDATED STATEMENT OF CHANGES IN STOCKHOLDERS' EQUITY
Three Years Ending December 31, 1989
(In thousands)

| | Common Stock | | Capital In | | Deferred Compen- sation - Restricted | Net Unrealized Depreciation of Market- able Equity |
	Shares Issued	Par Value	Excess of Par Value	Retained Earnings	Stock	Securities
December 31, 1986	24,260	$2,426	$21,735	$25,855	$ (164)	$ -0-
Issuance of restricted stock	83	8	1,444		(860)	
Net income				29,835		
Dividends to:						
Parent				(28,175)		
Other stockholders				(5,803)		
Net unrealized depreciation of marketable equity securities						(1,221)
December 31, 1987	24,343	2,434	23,179	21,712	(1,024)	(1,221)
Issuance of restricted stock	25	3	498		256	
Net income				23,325		
Dividends to:						
Parent				(20,125)		
Other stockholders				(4,243)		
Change in net unrealized depreciation of marketable equity securities						700
December 31, 1988	24,368	2,437	23,677	20,669	(768)	(521)
Issuance of restricted stock	13	1	274		260	
Net income				19,796		
Dividends to:						
Parent				(14,087)		
Other stockholders				(2,975)		
Change in net unrealized depreciation of marketable equity securities						424
December 31, 1989	24,381	$2,438	$23,951	$23,403	$ (508)	$ (97)

See Notes to Consolidated Financial Statements.

AMERICAN CAPITAL MANAGEMENT & RESEARCH, INC. AND SUBSIDIARIES
NOTES TO CONSOLIDATED FINANCIAL STATEMENTS

1. ORGANIZATION AND BUSINESS

American Capital Management & Research, Inc. is an approximate 83%-owned subsidiary of Associated Madison Companies, Inc. ("Associated Madison" or "Parent Company") which is a wholly-owned subsidiary of Primerica Holdings, Inc., which is a wholly-owned subsidiary of Primerica Corporation ("Primerica"). Effective December 15, 1988, Primerica Holdings, Inc. ("old Primerica") merged into a wholly-owned subsidiary of Commercial Credit Group, Inc. ("CCG") at which time the name of CCG was changed to Primerica Corporation.

American Capital Management & Research, Inc. and Subsidiaries (the "Company") are engaged in one business segment, investment services. The principal activities of the Company consist of providing investment management, distribution, transfer agency, and investment account custodial services for the American Capital complex of Funds ("Funds"). The Company also provides investment services through a sub-advisory agreement to the Common Sense™ Trust through a joint venture relationship. (See Note 7.)

2. SUMMARY OF SIGNIFICANT ACCOUNTING POLICIES

Principles of Consolidation:

The consolidated financial statements include the accounts of American Capital Management & Research, Inc. and its subsidiaries, all of which are wholly owned, and investments in unconsolidated 50%-owned joint ventures which are accounted for by the equity method. All material intercompany accounts and transactions have been eliminated in consolidation.

Revenue Recognition:

Investment management and advisory fees are recorded as income for the period in which the services are performed. Commissions related to security transactions are accrued on the trade date.

Income Taxes:

Federal income taxes payable currently are provided principally on a separate consolidated return basis under an income tax allocation arrangement with Primerica. Deferred income taxes represent the tax effect of temporary differences in the recognition of income and expense for tax purposes and financial reporting purposes and are provided based on the tax rate at which the items of income and expense are expected to be settled in Primerica's consolidated tax return.

Cash Equivalents and Marketable Equity Securities:

In 1989, the Company changed its investment strategy and began to invest excess cash in American Capital Reserve Fund, Inc. ("Reserve Fund"), a money market fund managed by a subsidiary of the Company, rather than reverse repurchase agreements with a bank. At December 31, 1989, the Company had $11 million invested in the Reserve Fund, classified as cash equivalents. Such investments in prior years were not significant.

AMERICAN CAPITAL MANAGEMENT & RESEARCH, INC. AND SUBSIDIARIES
NOTES TO CONSOLIDATED FINANCIAL STATEMENTS--(CONTINUED)

2. **Summary of Significant Accounting Policies** (Continued)

Other cash equivalents, principally U.S. government obligations, reverse repurchase agreements, and certificates of deposit with maturities at date of purchase of three months or less, are carried at cost plus accrued interest, which approximates market value.

Marketable equity securities are carried at the lower of aggregate cost or market value. Unrealized depreciation of equity securities is reflected directly in stockholders' equity and, accordingly, has no effect on net income. Gross unrealized gains and losses were $323,000 and $420,000, respectively, at December 31, 1989, and $128,000 and $649,000, respectively, at December 31, 1988.

Unamortized Cost of Contracts Purchased:

The cost of purchasing certain Fund advisory and management contracts is amortized over 10 years using the straight-line basis. Accumulated amortization at December 31, 1989 and 1988 was $16.1 million and $14.1 million, respectively.

Equipment, Leasehold Improvements, and Furniture:

Equipment, leasehold improvements, and furniture are stated at cost. Equipment and furniture are depreciated on a straight-line basis over their estimated useful lives ranging from 5 to 10 years. Leasehold improvements are amortized on a straight-line basis over the remaining lease term including renewal options. When assets are sold or retired, the cost and related accumulated depreciation are removed from the accounts and the resulting gain or loss is included in income.

Earnings Per Share:

Earnings per share of common stock is computed based on the weighted average number of common shares outstanding during each year.

Reclassifications:

Certain reclassifications have been made to the Company's prior years' consolidated financial statements to conform with the current year classifications.

3. **EQUIPMENT, LEASEHOLD IMPROVEMENTS, AND FURNITURE**

Equipment, leasehold improvements, and furniture at December 31, 1989 and 1988 were comprised of the following (in thousands):

	1989	1988
Equipment, furniture, and fixtures..............	$13,736	$12,295
Leasehold improvements.........................	3,630	3,461
	17,366	15,756
Less accumulated depreciation and amortization..	(8,141)	(5,541)
	$ 9,225	$10,215

AMERICAN CAPITAL MANAGEMENT & RESEARCH, INC. AND SUBSIDIARIES
NOTES TO CONSOLIDATED FINANCIAL STATEMENTS--(CONTINUED)

4. BANK BORROWING ARRANGEMENTS

In 1986, the Company entered into a term loan and revolving credit agreement with a bank that expires in April 1991 which provides for maximum borrowings in the amounts of $25 million and $10 million (reduced from $20 million during 1989), respectively. At December 31, 1989, no amounts were outstanding related to either the term loan or the revolving credit agreement. At December 31, 1988, $5.2 million was outstanding related to the term loan and $3.5 million was outstanding under the revolving credit agreement, both of which were paid during 1989. An additional $2.0 million was borrowed and paid back on the revolving credit agreement during 1989.

The bank term loan and revolving credit agreement provides for interest on borrowings based on a variety of possible rates defined in the agreement. The weighted average interest rates on borrowings under the term loan and revolving credit agreement were 11.5% and 11.3%, respectively, in 1989. The Company pays a commitment fee of 1/4 of 1% per year computed on the average daily unused portion of the revolving commitment.

Bank borrowing arrangements permit the distribution of cash dividends to the extent that net cash flow (as defined) exceeds the Company's debt service under the borrowings determined quarterly, provided specified minimum levels of tangible net worth are maintained.

Interest expense on bank borrowings for 1989, 1988 and 1987 was $432,000, $569,000, and $1,044,000, respectively. Interest paid on borrowings was $452,000, $528,000 and $1,137,000 for 1989, 1988, and 1987, respectively.

5. INCOME TAXES

The provision for income taxes consists of (in thousands):

	1989	1988	1987
Current	$10,315	$11,581	$20,232
Deferred	427	697	275
	$10,742	$12,278	$20,507

The Company's effective income tax rate approximates the Federal statutory rate of 34% for 1989 and 1988 and 40% for 1987. Deferred income taxes result primarily from accrued expenses which are not deductible for tax purposes until paid, temporary differences between book and tax depreciation, and amortization of the cost of management contracts. Actual income taxes paid to the Parent Company in each of the years ended December 31, 1989, 1988, and 1987 were $9.3 million, $13.9 million, and $19.7 million, respectively. The Company's liability of $1,875,000 and $683,000 as of December 31, 1989 and 1988, respectively, for its portion of income taxes payable currently is included in payables to related parties.

6. BENEFIT PLANS

The Company has a Thrift and Incentive Plan which is based on contributions made through payroll deductions and matched partially by the

AMERICAN CAPITAL MANAGEMENT & RESEARCH, INC. AND SUBSIDIARIES
NOTES TO CONSOLIDATED FINANCIAL STATEMENTS--(CONTINUED)

6. BENEFIT PLANS (Continued)

Company. The total employer cost of the 401(k) matching features of this plan was $459,000, $533,000, and $506,000 for 1989, 1988, and 1987, respectively.

In 1989, the Company terminated its defined benefit pension plan as of December 31, 1988 and adopted a defined contribution plan ("Profit Plus") effective January 1, 1989. Profit Plus was implemented by modifying the existing Thrift and Incentive Plan. The termination of the pension plan resulted in a $1.6 million curtailment gain, a $1.3 million loss on settlement of the pension obligations, and a $0.6 million gain from the pension plan asset reversion. As a result, a net pretax gain of $0.9 million has been recorded related to the pension plan termination.

Profit Plus involves fixed and discretionary Company contributions, subject to the approval of the Company's Board of Directors, in addition to the 401(k) features of the existing Thrift and Incentive Plan. The fixed portion of the contribution aggregated approximately $740,000 and the discretionary portion was estimated to be approximately $477,000. Pension expense for the years ended December 31, 1988 and 1987 was $530,000 and $472,000, respectively.

7. RELATED PARTY TRANSACTIONS

The Company has an agreement with Primerica under which Primerica provides the Company with certain services including but not limited to the following: investor relations, insurance and risk management, and shareholder records. The cost of these services was $258,000, $233,000, and $309,000 in 1989, 1988, and 1987, respectively, and approximates Primerica's actual cost of providing them. As of December 31, 1988, in connection with the December 15, 1988 merger between Primerica and CCG, the Company incurred $2.7 million of costs related to the solicitation of its managed mutual fund shareholders. Such costs were reimbursed by Primerica in May 1989.

The Company has from time to time borrowed funds from Primerica to meet short-term financing requirements. The Company paid interest based upon the rates that Primerica paid for its short-term borrowings. The Company has recorded interest expense and interest paid relating to advances from Primerica as follows (in thousands):

	1989	1988	1987
Interest Expense	$ —	$ 394	$ 157
Interest Paid	$ —	$ 465	$ 86

Primerica provides the Company with a $95 million line of credit which expires March 31, 1991. The credit available is $50 million available for general corporate purposes plus an amount up to $45 million that serves as a backup facility to the bank term loan and revolving credit agreement. The Company borrowed on the line of credit $4.7 million and $10.0 million during 1988 and 1987, respectively. Repayments of these borrowings were $7.2 million during 1988 and $7.5 million during 1987. There are no balances outstanding

AMERICAN CAPITAL MANAGEMENT & RESEARCH, INC. AND SUBSIDIARIES
NOTES TO CONSOLIDATED FINANCIAL STATEMENTS—(CONTINUED)

7. Related Party Transactions (Continued)

on the Primerica line of credit at December 31, 1989 or any borrowings during 1989; however, $10 million of the total line was committed to the backup facility at the bank. Interest expense on this line of credit was $394,000 and $157,000 and the weighted average interest rates, at Primerica's approximate cost of funds, were 8.0% and 8.8%, for the years ended December 31, 1988 and 1987, respectively.

The Company has provided investment advice concerning insurance portfolios to Associated Madison and has received a management fee for such services of $2,455,000, $1,896,000, and $2,007,000, in 1989, 1988, and 1987, respectively. The Company has been informed by Primerica that Primerica intends to manage the investments of its insurance subsidiaries' assets internally and therefore, effective January 1, 1990, these assets are no longer managed by the Company.

Sales generated by an affiliate, the parent of which is wholly-owned by Primerica, amounted to 12% of total American Capital Fund sales for 1989 and 15% for both 1988 and 1987.

The Company has entered into joint ventures with a subsidiary of Primerica. Under the joint venture arrangements, the partners are to invest capital and share in profits equally. These joint ventures distribute, manage and administer the portfolios of the Common Sense™ Trust (a diversified, open-end management investment company) which were introduced and offered to the public in April 1987. Combined unaudited summary information relating to these operations is as follows:

	December 31,	
	1989	1988
	(in thousands)	
Cash	$ 9,965	$ 7,472
Receivables	6,200	4,287
Equipment, leasehold improvements, and furniture, net	1,061	1,240
Other assets	823	761
Total assets	$18,049	$13,760
Accrued and other liabilities	$ 5,927	$ 4,784
Partners' capital	12,122	8,976
Total liabilities and partners' capital	$18,049	$13,760

AMERICAN CAPITAL MANAGEMENT & RESEARCH, INC. AND SUBSIDIARIES
NOTES TO CONSOLIDATED FINANCIAL STATEMENTS--(CONTINUED)

7. Related Party Transactions (Continued)

	Year ended December 31,		Period ended
	1989	1988	December 31, 1987
		(in thousands)	
Management, transfer agent, and custodial fees	$18,258	$11,958	$ 3,962
Underwriter concessions	6,135	5,941	5,729
Other income	520	294	124
Total revenues	24,913	18,193	9,815
Total expenses (1)	10,620	8,655	4,859
Net income	$14,293	$ 9,538	$ 4,956

(1) Includes fees charged by the Company to provide investment advice to one of the joint ventures of $1,848,000, $1,277,000, and $686,000 for the years ended December 31, 1989, 1988, and 1987, respectively. Such amounts appear in the accompanying consolidated statement of income in investment management and advisory fees.

8. REGULATORY REQUIREMENTS

The Company's broker/dealer subsidiaries are subject to rules and regulations of the Securities and Exchange Commission ("SEC") which require maintenance of minimum net capital and reserve accounts. At December 31, 1989, the amount of net capital required for all three subsidiaries pursuant to such rules and regulations aggregated $.5 million. The net capital of each of the broker/dealer subsidiaries which separately met all requirements, aggregated $5.6 million. Additionally, at December 31, 1989, the Company was required to segregate $2.7 million of cash equivalents to comply with an SEC reserve requirement.

9. MAJOR CUSTOMER INFORMATION

All fees attributable to the Government Securities Fund accounted for approximately 29%, 33%, and 39% of the Company's total revenues for the years ended December 31, 1989, 1988, and 1987, respectively. All fees attributable to the Pace Fund accounted for 17% of the Company's total revenues in each of the years 1989, 1988, and 1987.

10. STOCK INCENTIVES

During 1986, the Company established a plan under which up to 750,000 shares of the Company's common stock may be granted to the Company's key executives pursuant to stock options or awards of restricted or deferred stock. During 1988, the number of authorized shares was increased to 1,000,000. Stock options are granted at amounts not less than the fair market value at the date of grant for a period not to exceed 10 years. Deferred compensation expense associated with the restricted and deferred stock grants represents the market value of the Company's common stock at the date of grant and is recognized ratably over the vesting period. The shares associated with the restricted stock grant are considered issued and outstanding.

AMERICAN CAPITAL MANAGEMENT & RESEARCH, INC. AND SUBSIDIARIES
NOTES TO CONSOLIDATED FINANCIAL STATEMENTS—(Continued)

Combined information with respect to stock options, restricted and deferred stock grants is as follows:

(In shares)	1989	1988
Balance, beginning of year	536,400	664,050
Granted	–	46,000
Vesting of restricted and deferred stock grants ($17.125 to $20.50 per share)	(28,400)	(41,800)
Exercised	–	–
Expired or cancelled, including 14,400 and 12,600 shares of deferred stock in 1989 and 1988, respectively.....	(166,550)	(131,850)
Balance, end of year ($11.13 to $20.50 per share in 1989; $10.31 to $22.25 per share in 1988)................	341,450	536,400

The number of shares covered by stock options which were currently exercisable at December 31, 1989 and 1988 were 187,650 and 186,800, respectively. The number of shares vesting on January 1, 1990 and 1989 under the restricted and deferred stock grants were 21,200 and 28,400, respectively. The Company had 572,350 and 405,800 shares available for grant at December 31, 1989 and 1988, respectively.

11. COMMITMENTS AND CONTINGENCIES

In 1984, the Company entered into a 10-year noncancelable operating lease for office facilities in Houston, Texas, with options to renew for three additional five-year periods. In 1988, the Company entered into a 7-year lease for office facilities in Kansas City, Missouri, including a noncancelable period of three years. In addition, the Company has several noncancelable equipment leases expiring over the next three years.

At December 31, 1989, future minimum annual rentals under noncancelable operating leases are (in thousands):

1990	4,021
1991	3,271
1992	3,121
1993	3,121
1994	1,955
Later years	–
	$15,489

AMERICAN CAPITAL MANAGEMENT & RESEARCH, INC. AND SUBSIDIARIES
NOTES TO CONSOLIDATED FINANCIAL STATEMENTS--(CONTINUED)

11. COMMITMENTS AND CONTINGENCIES (Continued)

Rental expense, including data processing lease rentals and other equipment rentals, was $6,192,000, $6,381,000, and $5,392,000 for 1989, 1988, and 1987, respectively.

The Company is involved in lawsuits involving claims arising in the ordinary course of its business. In management's opinion, the ultimate resolution of such matters will not be material to the Company's consolidated financial position.

12. QUARTERLY FINANCIAL DATA (Unaudited)

| | 1989 | | | | |
	First	Second	Third	Fourth	Total
		(In thousands, except per share amounts)			
Revenues	$25,516	$25,734	$25,257	$25,302	$101,809
Income before income taxes	$ 7,949	$ 7,708	$ 6,929	$ 7,952	$ 30,538
Net income	$ 5,156	$ 4,993	$ 4,484	$ 5,163	$ 19,796
Earnings per share	$ .21	$ .21	$ .18	$ .21	$ .81

| | 1988 | | | | |
	First	Second	Third	Fourth	Total
		(In thousands, except per share amounts)			
Revenues	$22,774	$27,123	$25,304	$24,004	$ 99,205
Income before income taxes	$ 9,017	$ 9,634	$ 9,091	$ 7,861	$ 35,603
Net income	$ 5,837	$ 6,253	$ 5,997	$ 5,238	$ 23,325
Earnings per share	$ .24	$ .25	$ .25	$ .22	$ .96

EXHIBIT 22

American Capital Management & Research, Inc.
List of Subsidiaries

Name	State of Incorporation
Advantage Capital Corporation	New York
Advantage Capital Insurance Agency, Inc.	Missouri
Advantage Capital Insurance Agency of Hawaii, Inc.	Hawaii
Advantage Capital Insurance Agency of Ohio, Inc.	Ohio
American Capital Advisors, Inc.	Delaware
American Capital Asset Management, Inc.	Delaware
American Capital Companies Shareholder Services, Inc.	Delaware
American Capital Contractual Services, Inc.	New York
American Capital Custodial Services, Inc.	Delaware
American Capital Exchange Corporation (Subsidiary of American Capital Asset Management, Inc.)	California
American Capital Marketing, Inc.	Texas
American Capital Newco, Inc.	Delaware
American Capital Partner, Inc. (Subsidiary of American Capital Asset Management, Inc.)	Delaware
American Capital Sales, Inc.	Delaware
American Capital Services, Inc.	Delaware
American Capital Shareholders Corporation	Texas
American Capital T. A., Inc.	Delaware
American Capital Trust Company	Texas

THE QUARTERLY FILING (FORM 10-Q)

Form 10-Q must be filed with the SEC by a publicly traded company at the end of each of the first three quarters of its fiscal year. The filing deadline is forty-five days after the end of the quarter.

Form 10-Q contains only quarterly information. Just as with a company's published quarterly reports to stockholders, the quarterly financial statements contained in the 10-Q need not have been audited; they must only have been reviewed by the company's CPAs (the difference between an audit and a review is discussed in Chapter 9).

The contents of Form 10-Q are:

Part I: Financial Information

Item 1   Quarterly financial statements.

Item 2   Management's discussion of the company's financial condition, changes that have occurred in financial condition, and the results of operations.

Part II: Other Information

Item 1   A description of any legal proceedings in which the company is involved.

Item 2   Changes in securities.

Item 3   Defaults on senior securities.

Item 4   A discussion of matters that have been voted on by the shareholders.

Item 5   Other information.

Item 6   Exhibits and reports on Form 8-K.

Figure 10-3 is the November 1989 10-Q report for the H.J. Heinz Company.

THE FILING OF SIGNIFICANT CHANGES (FORM 8-K)

Form 8-K is the form most commonly used to report any significant changes in the information the company has filed with the SEC. Filing of the 8-K must take place within fifteen days of a significant change. Because the filing reports change so quickly, Form 8-K does not contain audited data. Much of the value of the Form 8-K information is its timeliness.

Examples of changes reported on Form 8-K are changes in the company's controlling ownership interest, major purchases or sales of assets, filing for bankruptcy or receivership, a change in the company's auditors, and resignations of directors.

A company required to file financial statements with the SEC must report a change in independent accountants on Form 8-K

SECURITIES AND EXCHANGE COMMISSION
WASHINGTON, D. C. 20549

FORM 10-Q

☒ QUARTERLY REPORT PURSUANT TO SECTION 13 OR 15(d) OF THE SECURI-
TIES EXCHANGE ACT OF 1934

For the quarterly period ended November 1, 1989

OR

☐ TRANSITION REPORT PURSUANT TO SECTION 13 OR 15(d) OF THE SECURI-
TIES EXCHANGE ACT OF 1934

For the transition period from _____ to _____

For the Six Months Ended November 1, 1989   Commission File Number 1-3385

H. J. HEINZ COMPANY

(Exact name of registrant as specified in its charter)

PENNSYLVANIA
(State or other jurisdiction of
incorporation or organization)

25-0542520
(I.R.S. Employer
Identification No.)

600 Grant Street, Pittsburgh, Pennsylvania
(Address of Principal Executive Offices)

15219
(Zip Code)

Registrant's telephone number, including area code: 412-456-5700

Indicate by check mark whether the registrant (1) has filed all reports required to be filed by section 13 or 15 (d) of the Securities Exchange Act of 1934 during the preceding 12 months (or for such shorter period that the registrant was required to file such reports), and (2) has been subject to such requirements for the past 90 days. Yes X No __

The number of shares of the Registrant's Common Stock, par value $.25 per share, outstanding as of November 29, 1989, was 256,339,018 shares.

PART I—FINANCIAL INFORMATION

Item 1. Financial Statements.

H. J. HEINZ COMPANY AND SUBSIDIARIES
CONSOLIDATED STATEMENTS OF INCOME

	Six Months Ended November 1, 1989	Six Months Ended October 26, 1988
	FY 1990	FY 1989
	(Unaudited) *(In Thousands, Except per Share Amounts)*	
Sales	$2,983,027	$2,804,134
Cost of products sold	1,825,090	1,693,041
Gross profit	1,157,937	1,111,093
Operating expenses	693,913	709,457
Operating income	464,024	401,636
Interest income	11,897	12,227
Interest expense	50,036	31,212
Other expense, net	13,546	15,381
Income before income taxes	412,339	367,270
Provision for income taxes	160,398	147,275
Net income	$ 251,941	$ 219,995
Net income per share	$ .95	$ .84
Cash dividends per share	$ .39	$ .33½

See Notes to Consolidated Financial Statements.

H. J. HEINZ COMPANY AND SUBSIDIARIES
CONSOLIDATED STATEMENTS OF INCOME

	Three Months Ended November 1, 1989	Three Months Ended October 26, 1988
	FY 1990	FY 1989
	(Unaudited) (In Thousands, Except per Share Amounts)	
Sales	$1,531,078	$1,424,639
Cost of products sold	942,238	868,782
Gross profit	588,840	555,857
Operating expenses	355,198	351,983
Operating income	233,642	203,874
Interest income	5,976	7,007
Interest expense	28,077	17,399
Other expense, net	6,655	6,650
Income before income taxes	204,886	186,832
Provision for income taxes	79,491	76,905
Net income	$ 125,395	$ 109,927
Net income per share	$ .47	$ .42
Cash dividends per share	$ .21	$ .18

See Notes to Consolidated Financial Statements.

H. J. HEINZ COMPANY AND SUBSIDIARIES
CONDENSED CONSOLIDATED BALANCE SHEETS

	November 1, 1989 FY 1990 (Unaudited)	May 3, 1989* FY 1989
	(Thousands of Dollars)	
ASSETS		
Current Assets:		
Cash and cash equivalents	$ 72,611	$ 102,605
Short-term investments, at cost which approximates market	176,707	135,124
Receivables, net..	602,360	507,475
Inventories	1,063,412	902,701
Prepaid expenses and other current assets	180,449	127,281
Total current assets	2,095,539	1,775,186
Property, plant and equipment...........................	2,301,132	2,184,106
Less accumulated depreciation	869,874	818,083
Net property, plant and equipment	1,431,258	1,366,023
Investments, advances and other assets	250,013	255,221
Goodwill	406,919	390,016
Other intangibles.......................................	222,883	215,361
Other noncurrent assets...............................	879,815	860,598
	$4,406,612	$4,001,807

*Summarized from audited fiscal year 1989 balance sheet.

See Notes to Consolidated Financial Statements.

H. J. HEINZ COMPANY AND SUBSIDIARIES
CONDENSED CONSOLIDATED BALANCE SHEETS

	November 1, 1989 FY 1990 (Unaudited)	May 3, 1989* FY 1989
	(Thousands of Dollars)	
LIABILITIES AND SHAREHOLDERS' EQUITY		
Current Liabilities:		
Short-term debt..	$ 368,988	$ 245,941
Portion of long-term debt due within one year	45,796	22,900
Accounts payable.......................................	412,049	407,050
Salaries and wages	80,694	75,470
Accrued marketing	111,102	85,954
Other accrued liabilities	201,142	224,306
Income taxes...	59,954	54,281
Total current liabilities	1,279,725	1,115,902
Long-term debt...	884,495	693,480
Deferred income taxes...................................	295,313	281,489
Other liabilities	130,013	133,698
	1,309,821	1,108,667
Shareholders' Equity:		
Capital stock	72,526	36,682
Additional capital	145,798	145,590
Retained earnings	2,415,489	2,263,829
Cumulative translation adjustments	(105,431)	(89,205)
	2,528,382	2,356,896
Less:		
Treasury stock at cost (30,809,775 shares at November 1, 1989 and 30,437,230 shares at May 3, 1989)	661,316	579,658
Deferred compensation	50,000	—
	1,817,066	1,777,238
	$4,406,612	$4,001,807

*Summarized from audited fiscal year 1989 balance sheet.

See Notes to Consolidated Financial Statements.

H. J. HEINZ COMPANY AND SUBSIDIARIES
CONDENSED CONSOLIDATED STATEMENTS OF CASH FLOWS

	Six Months Ended November 1, 1989 FY 1990	Six Months Ended October 26, 1988 FY 1989
	(Unaudited) (Thousands of Dollars)	
Net Cash Provided by Operating Activities	$ 61,663	$192,348
Cash Flows from Investing Activities:		
Capital expenditures	(157,614)	(144,208)
Acquisitions, net of cash acquired	(32,596)	(95,538)
Proceeds from divestitures........................	5,713	58,458
Purchases of short-term investments	(44,072)	(157,629)
Sales and maturities of short-term investments	4,029	127,664
Other items, net.................................	873	(2,852)
Net cash (used for) investing activities	(223,667)	(214,125)
Cash Flows from Financing Activities:		
Proceeds from long-term debt	234,978	274,085
Payments on long-term debt	(23,389)	(7,601)
Proceeds (payments) on short-term debt	123,983	(41,772)
Dividends	(100,281)	(85,893)
Purchases of treasury stock	(138,737)	(12,211)
Exercise of stock options	38,193	15,065
Cash loaned to ESOP	(50,000)	—
Sale of treasury stock to ESOP.....................	50,000	—
Net cash provided by financing activities	134,747	141,673
Effect of exchange rate changes on cash and cash equivalents .	(2,737)	(3,242)
Net (decrease) increase in cash and cash equivalents	(29,994)	116,654
Cash and cash equivalents at beginning of year............	102,605	75,488
Cash and cash equivalents at end of period	$ 72,611	$192,142

See Notes to Consolidated Financial Statements.

H. J. HEINZ COMPANY AND SUBSIDIARIES
NOTES TO CONSOLIDATED FINANCIAL STATEMENTS
(Unaudited)

(1) The Management's Discussion and Analysis of Financial Condition and Results of Operations which follows these notes contains additional information on the results of operations and the financial position of the company. Those comments should be read in conjunction with these notes. The company's annual report on Form 10-K for the fiscal year ended May 3, 1989 includes additional information about the company, its operations, and its financial position, and should be read in conjunction with this quarterly report on Form 10-Q.

(2) The results for the interim periods are not necessarily indicative of the results to be expected for the full fiscal year due to the seasonal nature of the company's business.

(3) In the opinion of management, all adjustments necessary for a fair statement of the results of operations of these interim periods have been included. Fiscal 1989 amounts reflect the two-for-one stock split in the form of a distribution of the company's common stock, effective September 27, 1989. Certain reclassifications were made to prior years' amounts to conform to Fiscal 1990 presentation.

(4) The composition of inventories at the balance sheet dates was as follows:

	November 1, 1989	May 3, 1989
		(Audited)
	(Thousands of Dollars)	
Finished goods and work-in-process....................	$ 756,375	$616,703
Packaging material and ingredients	307,037	285,998
	$1,063,412	$902,701

(5) In Fiscal 1989, the company adopted FASB Statement No. 95, "Statement of Cash Flows." The Consolidated Statement of Changes in Financial Position for the six months ended October 26, 1988 has been restated to conform with the new presentation.

(6) The provision for income taxes consists of provisions for federal, state, U.S. possessions and foreign income taxes. The company operates in an international environment with significant operations in various locations outside the United States. Accordingly, the consolidated income tax rate is a composite rate reflecting the earnings in the various locations and the applicable tax rates.

(7) In September 1989, the company established an Employee Stock Ownership Plan (ESOP) to replace in full or in part the company's cash matching contributions to the H. J. Heinz Company Employees Savings Plan (a 401(k) plan for salaried employees). The ESOP borrowed directly from the company $50 million and purchased 1,577,908 shares of treasury stock at $31.6875 per share. The ESOP debt is in the form of an intercompany interest-bearing note. The ESOP intends to refinance the note with third-party debt, guaranteed by the company, in the early months of calendar year 1990.

Item 2. Management's Discussion and Analysis of Financial Condition and Results of Operations.

RESULTS OF OPERATIONS
SIX MONTHS ENDED NOVEMBER 1, 1989 AND OCTOBER 26, 1988

Sales for the current six-month period were $2,983.0 million, up $178.9 million or 6.4% from the same period last year. Volume growth of 5.2% ($146.0 million) was primarily due to tuna, foodservice ketchup, and frozen potatoes. Price increases also contributed to the sales growth and more than offset the adverse impact on sales as a result of the U.S. dollar strengthening against most currencies. Price increases for the United Kingdom and Venezuela subsidiaries, as well as foodservice ketchup and corn syrup, more than offset lower tuna selling prices. The effect of acquisitions, net of divestitures, was immaterial.

The strong sales volume and price increases led to a $46.8 million increase in gross profit despite higher raw material costs (primarily tomatoes and potatoes) and a change in the company's product mix. The operating income margin increased 1.3% ($62.4 million) to 15.6% ($464.0 million) in the current year as a result of the company's ongoing efforts to lower operating costs.

Net interest expense increased $19.2 million in the six-month period, due to an increase in "net debt" as well as higher average interest rates for short-term borrowings. "Net debt" increased primarily due to the company's stock repurchase program and recent acquisitions.

The provision for income taxes is $160.4 million, which results in an effective rate of 38.9% versus 40.1% for the same period in Fiscal 1989. The effective tax rate for Fiscal 1989 included audit adjustments for prior years' taxes.

RESULTS OF OPERATIONS
THREE MONTHS ENDED NOVEMBER 1, 1989 AND OCTOBER 26, 1988

Sales for the second quarter increased $106.4 million or 7.5% from the second quarter of last year. The sales increase came primarily from volume (4.7%) and price (2.8%). Domestic tuna, frozen potatoes, Weight Watchers brand meals and Italian baby food were the primary contributors to the volume increase. Price increases were primarily in the company's foreign products as well as domestic foodservice ketchup and corn syrup. Foreign exchange rates had an adverse effect on sales as the result of the U.S. dollar strengthening against most currencies. In addition, acquisitions in the latter part of Fiscal 1989 contributed to the sales increase.

Operating income increased $29.8 million or 14.6%. The operating income margin increased to 15.3% from 14.3% for the same period last year. In addition to higher sales, the improved operating income can be attributed to benefits from the company's ongoing efforts to lower operating costs.

Net interest expense increased $11.7 million over the second quarter last year due to higher long-term borrowings and higher average short-term borrowing rates. The increase in long-term borrowings is the result of increased acquisition activity in the latter part of Fiscal 1989 and the company's stock repurchase program.

The second quarter provision for taxes was $79.5 million which results in an effective tax rate of 38.8%. The effective tax rate for the same period last year was 41.2%. The effective tax rate for the second quarter of Fiscal 1989 included audit adjustments for prior years' taxes.

Earnings per share increased 11.9% and net income increased 14.1% from the same period last year. The earnings per share increase is less than the net income growth as a result of the dilutive effect of the conversion of the company's convertible subordinated debentures in January 1989 and the effect of share price appreciation on common stock equivalents.

LIQUIDITY AND FINANCIAL POSITION

For the six months ended November 1, 1989, cash provided by operations was $61.7 million, down from $192.3 million for the same period last year. The decline is principally due to higher receivables and also due to higher costs of seasonally held inventory (tomatoes and potatoes) which are expected to be recovered through future sales. Investing activities required $223.7 million in Fiscal 1990, consisting primarily of capital expenditures related to productivity improvements at existing affiliates including Heinz USA, United Kingdom, Heinz Pet Products, Ore-Ida, Canada and Hubinger.

Net cash provided by financing activities was $134.7 million. This is primarily the result of increased borrowings offset by purchases of treasury stock and dividend payments. During the second quarter of this fiscal year, long-term line of credit agreements supporting commercial paper and bank debt totalling $347.0 million were replaced with similar agreements totalling $490.0 million. The increase of $235.0 million in long-term debt reflects the effects of these new agreements. The increased borrowings were principally used for purchases of treasury stock, dividend payments and capital expenditures. The dividend payments increased in Fiscal 1990 as a result of a quarterly dividend rate increase of 16.7% from 18 cents per share to 21 cents per share to shareholders of record as of September 21, 1989.

Financing activities included the repurchase of 4.8 million shares for the six-month period. To date, 8.9 million shares have been purchased as part of the ten-million-share repurchase plan, which began in September 1988. In November 1989, the board of directors authorized the repurchase of up to an additional ten million shares of common stock over an extended period of time. The board of directors also authorized a two-for-one stock split of the company's common stock (par value $.25 per share) in the form of a distribution, effective September 27, 1989.

In September 1989, the company established an employee stock ownership plan (ESOP). The purpose of the ESOP will be to fund company matching contributions to the H. J. Heinz Company Employees Savings Plan with company stock. The stock contributions will be used in full or in part to replace the company's cash matching contributions. (See Note 7 to the Consolidated Financial Statements.)

PART II—OTHER INFORMATION

ITEM 1. LEGAL PROCEEDINGS

Nothing to report under this item.

ITEM 2. CHANGES IN SECURITIES

Nothing to report under this item.

ITEM 3. DEFAULTS UPON SENIOR SECURITIES

Nothing to report under this item.

ITEM 4. SUBMISSION OF MATTERS TO A VOTE OF SECURITY HOLDERS

Reference is made to the Registrant's report of the September 6, 1989 Annual Meeting of Shareholders, which was mailed on November 10, 1989, to the Registrant's shareholders and which is enclosed as an exhibit to the report on this form.

ITEM 5. OTHER INFORMATION

In September 1989, the Registrant established an employee stock ownership plan (ESOP) for the purpose of replacing, in full or in part, the Registrant's cash matching contributions to the Registrant's Employees Savings Plan. (See Note 7 to the Registrants Consolidated Financial Statements.)

In November 1989, the board of directors authorized the repurchase of up to an additional 10,000,000 shares of its common stock. The purchases may take place over an extended period.

ITEM 6. EXHIBITS AND REPORTS ON FORM 8-K

(a) Exhibits required to be furnished by Item 601 of Regulation S-K are listed below and are filed as a part hereof. Documents not designated as being incorporated herein by reference are filed herewith. The paragraph numbers correspond to the exhibit numbers designated in Item 601 of Regulation S-K.

3. The Statement of Reduction of Authorized Shares dated July 12, 1989, amending the company's Articles of Incorporation.

11. Computation of net income per share.

23. Registrant's report of the September 6, 1989 Annual Meeting of Shareholders.

(b) Reports on Form 8-K

No reports on Form 8-K were filed during the quarter ended November 1, 1989.

Pursuant to the requirements of the Securities Exchange Act of 1934, the Registrant has duly caused this report to be signed on its behalf by the undersigned thereunto duly authorized.

H. J. HEINZ COMPANY
(Registrant)

Date: December 14, 1989

By /s/ R. DEREK FINLAY ....
R. Derek Finlay
Senior Vice President—Corporate Development
and Chief Financial Officer
(Principal Financial Officer)

Date: December 14, 1989

By /s/ DAVID R. WILLIAMS ....
David R. Williams
Vice President and Controller
(Principal Accounting Officer)

EXHIBIT 11

H. J. Heinz Company and Subsidiaries
COMPUTATION OF NET INCOME PER SHARE
(Unaudited)

	Six Months Ended	
	November 1, 1989 FY 1990	October 26, 1988 FY 1989
Primary income per share:		
Net income..	$251,941	$219,995
Preferred dividends	59	69
Net income applicable to common stock........................	$251,882	$219,926
Average common shares outstanding and common stock equivalents ...	266,172	263,110
Net income per share—primary	$ .95	$ .84
Fully diluted income per share:		
Net income..	$251,941	$219,995
Add-interest expense (after tax) for subordinated debentures due February, 2015 (1)	—	997
Net income applicable to outstanding and contingently issuable common stock....................................	$251,941	$220,992
Average common shares outstanding and common stock equivalents ...	266,172	263,110
Additional common shares assuming:		
Conversion of $1.70 third cumulative preferred stock.............	628	735
Additional common shares assuming options were exercised at the period-end market price...........................	1,305	759
Conversion of subordinated debentures due February, 2015 (1)	—	2,309
	268,105	266,913
Net income per share—fully diluted	$ .94	$ .83

(1) In January 1989, the Company called all of its 7¼% convertible subordinated debentures due 2015. The holders of the outstanding debentures elected to convert their debentures into approximately 1.2 million shares of the Company's common stock. The fully diluted income per share for Fiscal 1989 assumes this conversion as of the beginning of the year. The impact on primary income per share, assuming conversion at the beginning of the year, was not material.

All amounts in thousands except per share amounts.

within five business days. In addition, the company must provide a copy of the 8-K to the former accountants no later than the date of filing with the SEC.

CHAPTER PERSPECTIVE

The SEC seeks to give all investors equal access to information on publicly traded companies. To accomplish this, it requires companies to file a registration when stock is issued and to file Form 10-K annually, Form 10-Q quarterly, and Form 8-K whenever significant changes occur in the information that companies have filed with the SEC. The registration and Forms 10-K and 10-Q contain financial statements prepared by the companies' accountants; Form 8-K contains information about the changes that have occurred. The accounting data in the registration and Form 10-K are audited, but accounting data in Forms 10-Q and 8-K are not.

Ratio Analysis

INTRODUCTION AND MAIN POINTS

Published financial statements and their accompanying notes contain a wealth of information, presented in a uniform manner, consistent from period to period, and comparable (with limitations) from company to company. This chapter introduces you to the ratios used in financial statement analysis and shows you how to use them to evaluate a company's income performance, financial position, and stock. Specific ratios are used to examine a company's liquidity, profitability, activity, and debt to equity proportion.

After studying the material in this chapter:

■■■ You will know what a ratio is and what kind of information it can give.

■■■ You will begin to understand how to use ratios to evaluate a company using the company's past performance in comparison to others in its industry.

■■■ You will know which ratios to use to examine a company's profitability.

■■■ You will know which ratios to use to examine a company's activity.

■■■ You will know which ratios to use to examine a company's liquidity.

■■■ You will know which ratios to use to examine a company's debt and equity levels.

RATIO ANALYSIS

To understand ratio analysis—the basic analytical technique used in financial statement analysis—you must understand what it is and how financial analysts and other financial-statement readers use it to gain insight into the content of an annual report. It is also necessary to understand that financial statement analysis—using ratios and other tools—is hard work.

There is a common misunderstanding that learning the tools

of financial statement analysis immediately gives you secret knowledge or special insight into annual reports. This is not true. Ratio analysis is a valuable tool for use in understanding financial statements. But it is a tool in the way that a shovel is a tool—once you acquire the tool, hard work and diligence are required to obtain results.

WHAT ARE RATIOS?

First, what is a ratio? A *ratio* is a measure of relative size and is calculated by dividing one number into another.

A ratio can be expressed in a number of ways. All the following describe a ratio of four to three:

4 divided by 3
4/3
4:3
4 to 3
1.33

These expressions all show the ratio of four to three, but they are also the ratio of any other pair of numbers where the first is 1.33 times the second. Thus, they also are the ratio of 400 to 300, or 4 million to 3 million, or 1200 to 900, or 200 to 150, and so on. A ratio describes the relative size of two numbers or quantities but does not tell you the absolute size of the quantities being described. Each of the pairs listed (e.g., 200 to 150), expressed as a fraction, reduces to 4/3 or, divided, equals 1.33. Still, a ratio gives information about the two quantities used to generate the ratio.

Assume the ratio of weight (in pounds) to height (in feet) for Bill Jones is 45:1. Can you make judgments about Bill based only on this ratio? Would Bill be a good pick for a basketball team? Well, let's see. If Bill weighs 225 pounds, he is 5 feet tall (225/5 reduces to 45/1, or the ratio we expressed as 45:1). At 6 feet tall, Bill would have to weigh 270 pounds (6 × 45 = 270) to have a weight-to-height ratio of 45:1. So Bill is probably not a good pick for a basketball team. However, he may be a great pick for a football lineman. You cannot tell for sure, because you do not know the absolute values for his weight or height, but you can begin to form judgments from the relative measure of weight to height. Bill is a better pick for a football lineman, for instance, than is Ted Jones, a boy whose weight-to-height ratio is 35:2. At 6 feet tall, Ted would weigh only 105 pounds (35 × 6/2 = 105).

Ratios can be used to make assessments regarding financial statements. Assume a company has assets of $10 million and liabilities of $6 million. The ratio of assets to liabilities is therefore 5:3 (10:6 reduces to 5:3). What judgments can you make from this ratio? Is the company solvent? Yes, the company is solvent, for assets are greater than liabilities (the ratio of assets to liabilities is greater than one). But does the company have an ideal level of debt? Should the company have more debt? Less debt? Without a standard of comparison, you cannot tell. In the example above, the terms "basketball team" and "football lineman" provided a standard of reference for judging Bill and Ted. The same is true of ratio analysis for companies. If you know the ratio for assets to liabilities for the company's industry (a standard of reference) or for its major competitor (a comparison), you can make a judgment as to the desirability of an asset-to-liability ratio of 5:3.

A ratio for a company can be compared to each of the following:

1. the company's industry average or standard
2. another company in the same industry
3. the same ratio for the company in prior years.

Composite ratios for different industries are published by Dun and Bradstreet, Standard and Poor's Corporation, Robert Morris Associates, and the Federal Trade Commission. These references can be found in most public or college libraries. An example of industry ratios published by Robert Morris is shown in Figure 11-1.

A comparison with ratios of prior years gives a different perspective than does a comparison with ratios for the company's industry or competitors. A comparison with prior years may disclose a pattern in the company's functioning. Assume, for instance, that the ratio of assets to liabilities for a company has gone from 5:2 to 2:1 to 5:3 during the last three years. Debt is increasing—from 40 percent to 50 percent to 60 percent of total assets. Depending on other factors, this may be a cause of great concern.

Interpreting Ratios

It is important to note several points about ratios. First, financial ratios are only a starting point in analyzing a company's performance. Ratios do not give answers, but they do provide clues to what might be expected from the company's future performance. Second, ratios often give conflicting signals. For in-

Income Data

Net Sales	100.0
Gross Profit	26.0
Operating Expenses	22.3
Operating Profit	3.6
All Other Expenses (net)	1.6
Profit Before Taxes	2.0

Ratios

Current	2.2
	1.7
	1.4
Quick	1.5
	.8
	.6
Sales/Receivables	13.1
	8.4
	6.7
Cost of Sales/Inventory	7.8
	5.5
	3.7
Cost of Sales/Payables	14.7
	9.2
	8.2

FIG. 11-1 *Recent industry ratios and income statement data for the metal household furniture industry (published by Robert Morris and Associates).*

stance, on one hand, the more cash a company has, the better it is able to pay its debts. But having too much cash is bad because cash in the bank earns a limited, or no, return; the company could probably generate additional profits by investing its cash.

Finally, you should note that more than one ratio is needed to assess the financial statements in a company's annual report. Ratios are available that help in analyzing profitability, solvency, activity, and liquidity. A company's solvency ratios may be ideal, but if ratios that help analyze profitability and activity are bad (i.e., profits are down and sales are stagnant), a financial analyst would be concerned. You learn to use ratios in financial statement analysis only by diving in and doing a bit of hard work.

Additionally, financial-statement analysts use ratios for different purposes, because analysts' relationships to the company differ. For example, vendors generally have loans to the company of relatively short duration (under six months, perhaps a year); hence, they are concerned about the company's current debt-paying ability. Vendors want to know the likelihood that a company will be able to pay its obligations in the near future. On the other hand, banks, insurance companies, and pension funds, which make relatively long-term commitments ranging from one to thirty years, are concerned with the company's long-term solvency, rather than its short-term outlook. (They are concerned with the short term only because the company cannot get to the long term without surviving the short term.) Long-term creditors are interested in financial stability, overall financial strength, and earnings prospects. Their analysis is more difficult to do than that of a short-term investor.

Stockholders have the most difficult analytical task. A company can pay both its short-term debt and its long-term debt and still not earn enough to justify an investor's purchasing its common stock. Stockholders are concerned with profitability, earnings, dividends, and increases in the market price of a company's shares, in addition to liquidity and solvency.

There are four basic types of financial ratios, each of which measures a different aspect of company performance. In the remainder of this chapter, we discuss these ratios:

1. profitability ratios
2. activity ratios
3. liquidity ratios
4. overall (debt and equity) ratios

PROFITABILITY RATIOS

Profitability ratios are concerned primarily with income statement and stock performance and provide clues as to how well the company's managers are able to turn each dollar in sales into profit and support the price of the company's stock.

Profitability ratios are primarily "return on" ratios, in which some measure of profit (net income or gross margin, for example) is divided by some significant financial statement item. Profitability ratios measure some aspect of management's operating efficiency or stock performance. When measuring management's operating efficiency, the numerator of a profitability ratio is usually some measure of net income or profit, and the denominator is some aspect of management's responsibility.

Management Performance

Profitability ratios relate profit to some particular aspect of management performance, such as employing assets profitably, creating a return on owners' investment, or generating a profit on sales. Profitability ratios that measure management's performance on these three areas follow.

To measure employing assets profitability:

$$\text{return on assets} = \frac{\text{net income}}{\text{total assets}}$$

To measure the creation of a return on owners' investment:

$$\text{return on equity} = \frac{\text{net income}}{\text{owners' equity}}$$

To evaluate the profit generated on sales:

$$\text{gross profit ratio} = \frac{\text{gross profit (sales minus cost of goods sold)}}{\text{sales}}$$

$$\text{operating ratio} = \frac{\text{operating profit (sales minus operating expenses)}}{\text{sales}}$$

$$\text{return on sales} = \frac{\text{net income (sales minus all expenses)}}{\text{sales}}$$

Analysts draw conclusions based on these clues. For example, if the gross profit ratio is high while the operating ratio is low, an analyst might conclude that the company is using a high-priced promotion strategy. A high gross profit ratio indicates either high selling prices or low cost of goods sold; a low operating ratio (coupled with a high gross profit ratio) indicates high operating expenses, such as expensive advertising or promotion. However, other explanations are possible for high gross margin and low operating ratios, such as high administrative expenses, and the analyst must do a great deal more work before reaching the conclusion we did.

Stock Ratios

Another class of profitability ratios relates the earnings reported by the company to the dividend pattern established by management or to the price of the company's stock.

Dividend Ratios. Investors receive their return on investment from dividends and increases in the market value of their shares, rather than from earnings per share. The *dividend yield ratio* is the percentage of a share's market value paid annually in dividends; the *dividend payout ratio* is the percentage of common share earnings paid out in dividends.

$$\text{dividend yield} = \frac{\text{dividend per share}}{\text{market price per share}}$$

$$\text{dividend payout ratio} = \frac{\text{dividend per common share}}{\text{earnings per common share}}$$

Investors compare dividend yields to other investment opportunities but sometimes accept a lower yield if management is plowing back earnings into the company with the expectation that reinvestment will lead to increased earnings and dividends in the future. In general, high-growth companies have relatively low dividend yields and payout ratios because they reinvest cash that could otherwise be used for dividends; investors who purchase stock in such companies are not looking for dividends as much as for increases in the market price of the stock. Because these increases may or may not occur, investing in high-growth companies is generally riskier than investing in companies that pay relatively high, stable dividends.

Price Earnings Ratio. Investors expect a return on their investment through dividends and share appreciation. If investors expect that earnings and dividends will increase, they will be willing to pay a higher price for the stock. The *price earnings* (*PE*) *ratio* relates these two factors:

$$\text{price earnings (PE) ratio} = \frac{\text{common stock market price}}{\text{earning per common share}}$$

If the market prices of Lake Company and Brown Company stock are $20 and $16, respectively, and earnings per share are $4 and $2, we might conclude that the Lake Company stock is worth more (sells at a higher price) and the company is doing better (i.e., has higher earnings) than Brown Company. However, the PE ratios are:

$$\text{Lake Company} \quad \frac{\$20}{\$4} = 5 \qquad \text{Brown Company} \quad \frac{\$16}{\$2} = 8$$

Based on the PE ratio, stockholder expectations regarding growth in earnings and dividends will be higher for Brown Company than for Lake Company, and investors will be willing to pay relatively more for a given amount of the earnings of Brown Company than of Lake Company.

Stock ratios are important to analysts. The price earnings ratio helps an analyst decide if the stock is overpriced or underpriced in the marketplace based on the income the company is reporting. The dividend payout ratio helps an analyst determine what management is doing with the earnings produced by operations. Both ratios are important in establishing the price of the company's stock in the market.

ACTIVITY RATIOS

Activity ratios, which measure management's effectiveness in using assets, generally measure the relationship between some asset and some indicator of management's ability to employ the investment in the asset effectively.

The key to understanding activity ratios is to note that the general form of these ratios is an asset divided into the best measure of that asset's activity. The general form is:

$$\text{Activity Ratio} = \frac{\text{Best Measure of Asset Activity}}{\text{Asset}}$$

For the asset accounts receivable, the best measure of asset activity is sales. The less money management is forced to tie up in uncollected accounts for a given volume of sales, the better. Assume, for example, that for annual sales of $1 million, management has $500,000 in accounts receivable at the end of the year. Management's performance would be improved if more sales dollars could be collected and accounts receivable reduced to $100,000.

Activity ratios are usually referred to as turnover ratios. Accounts receivable of $100,000 is said to have turned over ten times if annual sales are $1 million. For a company that does credit business, all sales go through accounts receivable. If sales pass through accounts receivable $100,000 at a time (the average balance), accounts receivable "turn over" ten times. The activity ratio "*accounts receivable (AR) turnover*" is:

$$\text{AR turnover} = \frac{\text{Sales}}{\text{Accounts Receivable}}$$

In this example, the turnover ratio is calculated as $1 million divided by $100,000, or ten. When the turnover of accounts receivable is known, the average collection period (average time funds are tied up in the asset) can be calculated. If accounts receivable turn over 10 times in a 360 day year (a banker's year), the average collection period is 360 divided by ten, or thirty-six days.

$$\text{Average turnover period} = \frac{360}{\text{Asset turnover}}$$

This relationship can also be used to calculate the number of days funds are tied up in any other asset once the asset turnover is known. (The number of days funds are invested in inventory is frequently of interest to financial analysts.)

Other common activity or turnover ratios are these:

$$\text{inventory turnover} = \frac{\text{cost of goods sold}}{\text{inventory}}$$

$$\text{fixed assets turnover} = \frac{\text{sales}}{\text{fixed assets}}$$

$$\text{total asset turnover} = \frac{\text{sales}}{\text{total assets}}$$

The Dupont Method

Frequently the return on sales ratio is combined with the asset turnover ratio so that the components of the return on assets profitability ratio can be studied. The combination of these equations is called the DuPont method of financial analysis.

return on sales × asset turnover = return on assets

$$\frac{\text{net income}}{\text{sales}} \times \frac{\text{sales}}{\text{assets}} = \frac{\text{net income}}{\text{assets}}$$

Depending on the firm and the industry, a company may stress either the return (or margin) on sales or the turnover and still generate the same return on assets. Imagine two car dealerships: a large dealership with high turnover and low prices and a small dealership with low turnover and high prices. Both might generate the same return on total assets:

Return on Sales × Asset Turnover = Return on Assets

large dealership:	.05	×	6	=	.30
small dealership:	.15	×	2	=	.30

LIQUIDITY RATIOS

Liquidity is a measure of a company's ability to pay its short-term debts. High liquidity is evidenced by high current assets relative to current liabilities and by a high proportion of current assets in cash and receivables (as opposed to inventory or prepaid expenses). (Current assets, remember, are short-term assets that either are cash or will become cash in one year. Examples are receivables that will be collected in 90 days or inventory on hand that will be sold in the next quarter. Current liabilities are short-term debts that must be paid in one year or less. Any part of a long-term debt which comes due in the next year is also a current liability. Accounts payable or next year's installment on a forty-year mortgage are examples of current liabilities.)

Working capital—the difference between current assets and current liabilities—is a crude measure of liquidity; a decrease in working capital is not always a sign of decreased liquidity. Working capital is a dollar amount, not a ratio, and is difficult to evaluate in the absence of additional information on the company's activities.

working capital = current assets − current liabilities

Big Company and Little Company, according to the figures below, both have the same dollar amount of working capital, but Big Company obviously has less of a safety buffer available to pay its short-term debts (current liabilities) than does Little Company. The fact that both companies have $5,000 in working capital, by itself, means little.

	Current Assets	Current Liabilities	Working Capital
Big Company	$25,000	$20,000	$5,000
Little Company	$10,000	$ 5,000	$5,000

Because different accounting methods (such as LIFO or FIFO) result in differing inventory amounts on the balance sheet, comparisons of working capital liquidity measures between companies are not valid. The use of different inventory cost flow assumptions also affects intercompany comparisons of the current ratio (discussed below). This changes the focus to trend analysis for individual companies rather than direct comparisons among companies.

There are only two liquidity ratios in common use, the *current ratio* and the *quick ratio*. Both of these ratios are designed to evaluate the company's ability to pay its short-term obligations.

Current Ratio

The current ratio is simply the relationship between current assets and current liabilities.

$$\text{current ratio} = \frac{\text{current assets}}{\text{current liabilities}}$$

The difference in liquidity between Big Company and Little Company (see previous section) is evident when we calculate the current ratios for these two companies. By expressing the relative sizes of current assets and liabilities, the current ratio shows that Big Company clearly has a smaller safety buffer available to pay its short-term debts than does Little Company.

	Current Assets	Current Liabilities	Current Ratio
Big Company	$25,000	$20,000	1.25
Little Company	$10,000	$ 5,000	2

Quick Ratio

One major problem that arises with the quick or acid test ratio (as with any ratio) is composition. The use of broad-based totals (e.g., current assets and current liabilities) masks information about individual account components (e.g., cash and receivables) and fails to disclose vital information, such as how soon the current assets can be converted into cash and used to pay current liabilities or how soon the current liabilities are due for payment. The financial-statement analyst obtains a general idea of the potential magnitude of the composition problem by reviewing the balance sheet to see the extent to which current assets are composed of relatively liquid items.

The quick ratio is current assets minus inventory divided by current liabilities.

$$\text{quick ratio} = \frac{\text{current assets} - \text{inventory}}{\text{current liabilities}}$$

In the quick ratio, inventory is removed from current assets because inventory is usually not directly convertible to cash. Generally, inventory is sold to create an account receivable; the receivable must be collected before cash is available to pay short-term creditors.

The rule of thumb for the current ratio is 2:1 and for the quick ratio is 1:1. These rules of thumb are often cited but are, in fact, quite useless. To have meaning, a ratio must either be compared to that for other companies in the same industry or be viewed as part of a trend for a particular company. An analyst must ask questions: Is the company's liquidity (current ratio) increasing or decreasing? Are any changes appropriate for the economic climate in the company's industry?

OVERALL (DEBT AND EQUITY) RATIOS

Overall (debt and equity) ratios are sometimes called solvency ratios. While liquidity ratios assist analysts in examining a company's short-term debt-paying ability, overall or solvency ratios assist the analyst in determining the relative size of the claims of long-term creditors compared to the claims or property rights of owners.

The existence of too much long-term debt places restrictions on management and increases risk to stockholders, because large amounts of long-term debt increase the fixed charges against income in each reporting period. The times-interest-earned and the fixed-charge-coverage ratios described below assist analysts in evaluating the burden of fixed interest and other periodic charges, such as lease payments. These ratios are similar to the rules of thumb that say a consumer's house payment, or house and car payments, should not exceed a certain percent of the consumer's income. The proportion of company income that should be used to meet interest and other fixed charges, however, varies from industry to industry.

Another effect of high levels of long-term debt is added risk to creditors. As levels of long-term debt rise, creditors are reluctant to continue to loan the company money; eventually, funds will no longer be available or will be available only at very high interest rates.

The more common ratios used to evaluate a company's solvency or overall debt and equity position are these:

$$\text{times-interest-earned} = \frac{\text{earnings before interest and taxes}}{\text{interest expense}}$$

$$\text{fixed-charge-coverage} = \frac{\text{earnings before interest and taxes}}{\text{interest expense} + \text{lease payments}}$$

$$\text{debt-to-total-assets} = \frac{\text{debt}}{\text{total assets}}$$

$$\text{debt-to-total-equity} = \frac{\text{debt}}{\text{total liabilities} + \text{stockholders' equity}}$$

$$\text{debt-to-stockholders'-equity} = \frac{\text{debt}}{\text{stockholders' equity}}$$

How Much Is Too Much Debt?

Because too much long-term debt can be bad because of its claim on a company's earnings, readers of annual reports may have a bias against long-term debt. But companies do not borrow without the desires of stockholders in mind; quite the contrary. Managers use long-term debt to increase returns to common stockholders through financial leverage (see Chapter 12). Long-term debt is not of itself bad, any more than using a mortgage to purchase a home is bad. The danger in both instances is in an excessive level of total indebtedness and the burden imposed by the resulting fixed payments.

CHAPTER PERSPECTIVE

This chapter has discussed ratios, what they are, and how they are used. Ratios express only the relative size of two amounts; from a ratio alone, we cannot tell how large either of the amounts is. A single ratio is of little use; ratios should be used in combinations. The DuPont system of financial analysis is an example of the use of several ratios in combination to analyze the source of a company's return of investment. Wise judgments can be made only when several ratios are used to evaluate relationships.

Ratios are used to examine four different areas of company performance and financial condition: liquidity, profitability, activity, and overall debt to owner's equity. The next chapter continues our discussion and adds to our arsenal of financial statement analysis techniques.

Analyzing Financial Statements

INTRODUCTION AND MAIN POINTS

Chapter 11 introduced the ratios most commonly used in financial-statement analysis. This chapter introduces more tools used in the analysis and interpretation of financial statements.

After studying the material in this chapter:

■ You will know how to analyze financial statements using common size statements.

■ You will know how to analyze financial statements using trend analysis and comparative statements.

■ You will understand how a company can use operating leverage and will know the risks involved.

■ You will understand how a company can use financial leverage and will know the risks involved.

■ You will understand why a calculated ratio is neither good nor bad; its value depends on circumstances.

■ You will see how the information contained in the statement footnotes can help in financial statement analysis.

MAKING JUDGMENTS ABOUT THE FUTURE

The principal purpose of financial analysis is to form judgments about the future: Will the company be able to repay a loan or increase dividends? Will its income grow? Is the debt level likely to rise? To fall? Is the market price of the stock too high or too low? Some amounts listed in financial statements reflect management's expectations; the allowance for doubtful accounts is an example. For the most part, however, the financial statement analyst works with historical information and assumes, unless there is other information to the contrary, that historical trends will continue.

Still, a company may be hurt by some event it cannot control: A competitor may bring out an improved product, a strike may paralyze production, or a major product may become obsolete. Financial analysts watch for developments that indicate that the future will not be like the past. Because good management is critical to success, one of the major questions that the financial analyst seeks to answer is whether the managers are running the company efficiently and effectively.

Financial-statement analysis focuses not only on financial and quantitative information but on nonfinancial and qualitative information as well. Other sources of information that assist in financial-statement analysis are the financial press (for example, *The Wall Street Journal*), reports to the Securities and Exchange Commission, and business service publications such as *Value Line,* and *Dun & Bradstreet.*

COMMON SIZE STATEMENTS

Financial analysts sometimes use a variation of ratio analysis, called *common size statements,* that looks at all the financial statement components. This method presents every item in a statement as a percentage of the largest item in the statement. The procedure may sound confusing but in fact common size statements are quite useful and easy to understand.

Both the income statement and the balance sheet can be converted to common size statements.

Income Statement

The largest item in the income statement is sales; therefore, when the income statement is converted to a common size statement, all items in the income statement are expressed as percentages of sales. For instance, if cost of goods sold is 40 percent of sales, gross profit is then 60 percent of sales. An illustration of a simple income statement converted to a common size statement is shown below.

INCOME STATEMENT

	Dollar Amounts	Common Size
Amounts Sales	$200,000	100
percent Cost of Goods Sold	80,000	40
Gross Profit	120,000	60
Selling Expense	30,000	15
Administrative Expense	50,000	25
Operating Profit	40,000	20
Income Taxes	20,000	10
Net Income	$ 20,000	10

Balance Sheet

The largest item in the balance sheet is total assets or total equities; when a balance sheet is converted to a common size format, all components are expressed as percentages of total assets or total equities. For instance, current assets may be 40 percent of total assets; bonds payable may be 30 percent of total equities. (Remember that total assets and total equities are equal. Either may be used.) An illustration of a simple balance sheet converted to common size is shown below.

BALANCE SHEET

	Assets Dollar Amounts	Common Size Amounts
Current assets:		
Cash	$ 50,000	10 percent
Accounts receivable	75,000	15
Inventories	75,000	15
Total Current Assets	200,000	40
Plant, property and equipment (net of depreciation)	250,000	50
Investment	50,000	10
Total Assets	$500,000	100

	Equities Dollar Amounts	Common Size Amounts
Current liabilities:		
Accounts payable	$ 75,000	15 percent
Notes payable	25,000	5
Total Current Liabilities	100,000	20
Long-term liabilities		
Bonds payable	150,000	30
Mortgage payable	50,000	10
Total Long Term Liabilities	200,000	40
Stockholders' equity		
Common stock	150,000	30
Retained earnings	50,000	10
Total Stockholders' Equity	200,000	40
Total equities	$500,000	100

Side-By-Side Analysis

Common size statements highlight the relationship of all the statement components and are especially useful when comparing the company's performance for two years side by side or when comparing two companies of different size.

When two years' figures for the same company are being examined in common size form, changes in the relative size of the components are readily apparent to the analyst—changes that might have been missed by examining the absolute dollar amounts. For example, if sales have increased, an analyst might not notice that gross profit have decreased by several percentage points or that selling costs have risen sharply as a percent of sales dollars. When the two years are converted to common size statements, both of those changes become obvious.

Analyzing the financial statements of two companies of different size is more confusing than analyzing two years' statements of the same company. Large differences in the dollar amounts for various expense items tend to camouflage differences in the relationship of the income statement components, and large differences in the proportion of the sales dollars spent on administrative expenses or debt service may go unnoticed if the statements are not converted to a common-size format.

HORIZONTAL ANALYSIS

A frequently used variation of common size statements is constructed by using the financial statements of some prior year as the base and expressing the components of a future year as percentages of each component in the base year. This is called *horizontal common size* or *horizontal analysis* because it deals with the changes in financial statements from period to period. This analysis answers questions such as: Are sales, gross profit, expenses, and net income increasing or decreasing over time? What was the change in sales from last year? Has cash increased or decreased over the last two years?

Trend Analysis

Trend analysis is a type of horizontal analysis in which a base year is selected and comparisons are made to the base year by the use of percentages. Sometimes the dollar change from one period to the next period in a particular account is not sufficient by itself to make an informed decision regarding that account;

trend analysis can be useful in comparing financial statements over several time periods because it discloses changes occurring over time and it can provide information as to the direction in which a company is moving.

For instance, suppose advertising in the base year was $10,000 and advertising in the next three years was $11,000, $12,000 and $20,000, respectively. Expressed in horizontal common size as a percentage of the base year amount of $10,000, a trend analysis in advertising appears as:

	Year 4	Year 3	Year 2	Year 1
Dollar Amount	$20,000	$12,000	$11,000	$10,000
Common Size Amount	200%	120%	110%	100%

The jump to 200 percent in year 4 appears significant—something that might warrant additional study. But the large percentage increase may be misleading—what if advertising is a $20,000 expense for a company with total expenses of $800,000? In such case, the small dollar amount involved—while representing a large percentage increase—may be immaterial, and investigation is therefore a waste of time.

Comparative Statements

Developing comparative statements—a form of horizontal analysis using financial statements for two years—shows the dollar and percentage change from year to year. (A two-year analysis of the current assets section of the balance sheets of the Sutter-Felt Company is shown in Figure 12-1.) This analysis requires two steps. First, you must compute the dollar amount of the change from the base year (the year against which you are making the comparison); second, you must divide the dollar amount of the change by the base year amount.

Horizontal analysis allows us to study the changes in accounts year by year, examining both the absolute amount of the change and its relative (percentage) amount. Note in our example that Sutter-Felt's largest percentage increase is for prepaid expenses (100 percent) but that the absolute dollar amount of the change in prepaid expenses is not significant. Percentage changes must be viewed from the perspective of the item's relative dollar value significance.

Increase (Decrease) 1991 over 1990 Assets	1991	1990	Amount	Percent
Current assets:				
Cash	$ 32,000	$ 38,000	$ (6,000)	(15.8)
Accounts receivable, net	123,000	153,000	(30,000)	(19.6)
Inventories	94,000	81,000	13,000	16.0
Prepaid expenses	600	300	300	100.0
Total current assets	249,600	272,300	(22,700)	(8.3)

FIG. 12-1 *Sutter-Felt Company comparative balance sheets December 31, 1990 and 1991*

LEVERAGE

Leverage is frequently a subject for physics courses. When a lever is properly placed across a fulcrum, downward pressure on the handle results in a greatly magnified upward force on the other end; ten pounds of downward pressure may be sufficient to lift a hundred pound weight, enabling a small child to lift a large boulder. When a child lifts a rock with a lever, leverage gives the child a mechanical advantage.

Business managers use leverage to increase the profitability of a business to its owners. Business managers may employ two kinds of leverage: operational leverage and financial leverage. Both are very similar in principle to a child lifting a rock with a lever.

Operating Leverage

A company uses operating leverage to its advantage by balancing the type of costs in its operations. Assume a company manufactures a product that it sells for $10. The labor and raw material costs for each unit of product total $8. (Labor and raw materials are called variable costs because the total amount of these costs varies directly with the number of units produced. Each additional unit produced causes more labor and raw material costs to be incurred.)

Because the company uses a lot of labor, it can manufacture the product with nonvariable or fixed costs (largely related to machinery) of only $20,000 per year. Total fixed costs do not vary when additional units are produced; producing additional units does not, for example, increase the cost of a leased machine. The $20,000 fixed cost remains the same regardless of the number of units produced. With this balance of fixed costs and variable costs, each unit of product contributes $2 to covering the fixed cost of machinery and building profits. For each unit:

Selling price	$10
Labor and Raw Material	8
Contribution per unit	$ 2

Assume now that the company's managers decide to automate several previously manual operations. The annual fixed machinery cost increases to $50,000 and the cost of labor and raw materials per unit decreases to $6. Now each unit contributes $4 to covering fixed charges and building profit.

Selling price	$10
Labor and Raw Material	6
Contribution per unit	$ 4

Leverage increases the impact of a change in sales volume on the company profits. Let us consider the contribution to profits of a 1,000-unit increase in sales.

Manual Operation		Automated Operation	
Selling price	$10	Selling price	$10
Labor and raw material	8	Labor and raw material	6
Contribution per unit	$ 2	Contribution per unit	$ 4
increased units	× 1,000	increased units	× 1,000
Contribution	$ 2,000	Contribution	$ 4,000

Changing the variable labor cost of operations to a fixed machinery cost has increased the contribution of sales of 1,000 units from $2,000 to $4,000. The automation has "leveraged" the effect of a sales increase on company profit.

Increased Risk. Despite its beneficial effect, operating leverage can also have a downside. For instance, assume that instead of a 1,000-unit increase in sales, the company has a 1,000-unit decrease in sales volume. The effect in terms of dollar amount is still the same, but now the $2,000 and $4,000 changes in contribution are decreases rather than increases.

A highly leveraged company has greater fluctuations in profits than a company with low operating leverage. A low leveraged, manual operation does not benefit as much from increases in sales, but neither does it suffer as much from declines. Profits, by and large, remain fairly stable. An automated, highly leveraged company, in contrast, benefits greatly from sales increases and suffers greatly from sales decreases. The contribution lost or gained will be greater, and the pattern of profits less stable.

Higher Breakeven Sales. Another warning about highly leveraged firms: The breakeven sales point for a highly leveraged company is higher than the breakeven point for a less leveraged company. In the example above, for instance, the company has to cover annual fixed charges of $50,000 after automating, but only $20,000 before. Breakeven points for both operating structures are shown below.

Manual operation:

$20,000 fixed cost breakeven point / $2 per unit contribution = 10,000 unit breakeven point

Automated operation:

$50,000 fixed cost breakeven point / $4 per unit contribution = 12,500 unit breakeven point

In summary, operating leverage can improve a company's profits for a given level of sales—but to receive this benefit the company must endure the risk associated with an unstable profit pattern and an increased breakeven sales level.

Financial Leverage

Financial leverage is used to increase the return to owners. The idea is very simple. Assume that investors are forming a company that requires an investment in assets of $100,000. The company is expected to produce earnings of $15,000 per year. If owners supply the entire $100,000, the return on owners' equity will be 15 percent ($15,000/$100,000).

Now assume instead that owners wish to leverage their investment by borrowing half of the $100,000 required to start the business. Funds are available at 12 percent interest. If owners follow this route, investing $50,000 and borrowing $50,000 at 12 percent interest, earnings will be reduced by the $6,000 interest on the borrowed funds ($50,000 × .12) and earnings will be only $9,000. But even these lower earnings will increase the return on owners' equity to 18 percent ($9,000/$50,000).

Increased Risk. All companies use financial leverage to some extent. There is a great body of scholarly thought on what proportion of a company's funding should come from debt and what proportion from owners. Too much debt increases business risk, which in turn leads to higher interest rates on borrowed funds.

When interest rates are high—or returns on assets are low—financial leverage may work against owners. Assume, for instance, that the owners in the illustration above attempt to use financial leverage by borrowing $50,000 but that interest rates rise to 20 percent. If the business does as expected and earns $15,000 before interest, the profit after an interest expense of $10,000 ($50,000 × .20) will be only $5,000 and the return on owners' equity will be only 10 percent ($5,000/$50,000).

Alternatively, assume that owners use financial leverage, borrowing funds as planned at fifteen percent, but conditions change and the company earns only $10,000 before paying the interest charges. After paying the $6,000 interest on the debt, profits will be only $4,000 and the return on owners' equity will be only 8 percent ($4,000/$50,000). If owners had not borrowed at all, the return on owners' equity would have been 10 percent ($10,000/$100,000).

Quite simply, if a firm borrows at an interest rate less than the return on assets, the return on owners' equity will be increased. If a firm borrows at a rate greater than the return on assets, the return on owners' equity is reduced. If the rates are equal, the percent return on owners' equity is not affected.

Firms such as public utilities that have relatively stable revenues and expenses can use considerable financial and operating leverage. Leverage is very risky, however, for companies in cyclical businesses such as automobile manufacturing and construction, in which sales fluctuate greatly from year to year. Several consecutive years of low sales can bring a heavily leveraged firm to bankruptcy.

Measuring Leverage

Both operational and financial leverage can be used to benefit stockholders because they maximize the benefit obtained from growth—but both may also maximize the damage that occurs when business conditions sour.

The extent to which a company uses financial leverage can be determined by examining a company's debt structure and profit pattern. Because companies list their costs by function and not by behavior, it is very difficult to measure operating leverage directly. An understanding of operating leverage may be most useful when analyzing investment or other opportunities in industries that differ in their degree of automation or operating leverage. Machinery manufacturing is, for example, more highly leveraged than the restaurant business. An investor wishing to receive the benefits of operating leverage would invest in machinery manufacturing rather than in a restaurant chain.

THE PARADOX IN INTERPRETING RATIOS

Ratios do not always mean what appears obvious at first glance. For instance, a high accounts-receivable turnover generally means that receivables are collected rapidly. Reducing the sales dollars tied up in accounts receivable results in more dollars available for other purposes. On the other hand, a decrease in accounts-receivable turnover (and an increase in days' sales in accounts receivables) suggests that the firm is becoming less efficient in collecting its accounts. Other things being equal, the faster customers pay, the better. All these are reasonable conclusions an analyst might draw.

However, a high turnover ratio might also indicate that credit policies are too strict. Strict credit policies can drive away customers, reduce sales, and damage profitability. There are tradeoffs: If the firm loses sales because of tight credit policies, the advantage of faster collection may be more than offset by the loss of profits due to lower total sales.

A similar analysis can be used with inventories. Inventory turnover is important because the quicker the inventory is sold, the quicker the company converts its investment back to cash. Slow inventory turnover may result in obsolete goods and excess storage costs. On the other hand, if investment turnover is too high, it may indicate that the company does not carry enough inventory to support its sales—stockouts may occur and customers may be lost. Consequently, a company cannot seek continually to increase its inventory turnover ratio but instead must strive to maintain the most profitable ratio, given its sales level, costs of carying inventory, and risk of experiencing stock-outs.

ADDITIONAL INFORMATION

As we saw in Chapter 2, an annual report contains more than just the financial statements. A thorough understanding of the financial statements requires the analyst to study the information contained in the rest of the annual report. Supplemental schedules and other information are contained in the notes to the financial statements. This section includes disclosures such as the summary of significant accounting policies followed by the company (including inventory and depreciation methods); types of inventory and plant and equipment; information about long-term debt, profit-sharing, and pension plans; litigation involving the company; and research and development project expenditures.

Some annual reports include management's discussion and analysis of financial condition and results of operation. This discussion includes summarized income statement and balance sheet data for the last three years and addresses the company's financial condition and results of operations. It also includes specific information on liquidity, capital resources, and events or uncertainties that might cause future operating results or financial conditions to diverge from those that have prevailed historically.

CHAPTER PERSPECTIVE

This chapter emphasized that judgments can be made only when several ratios are used to evaluate several different relationships and those ratios are compared either to the trend of ratios in prior years or to standard ratios for the industry in which the company operates. It introduced common size statements, which help the analyst examine all the elements of the financial statements as ratios and perform trend and comparative analysis. We have seen that footnotes can contain information affecting the company's future and the analyst's judgment, and that a calculated ratio is neither good nor bad but depends on circumstances.

Finally, the chapter discussed financial and operating leverage and the ways they can increase a company's profitability and return to owners. We have seen how both techniques, while potentially beneficial, can be dangerous because of the risks they carry.

Working With Budgets

INTRODUCTION AND MAIN POINTS

Although they may not realize it, most people budget to some extent in their daily affairs. We make estimates of the income necessary to cover expenditures such as food, clothing, and housing and limit our expenditures to the income earned in a stipulated time period. Our budget serves as both a planning and a control device in that we plan expenditures on the basis of our estimate of income and control spending in accordance with the plan. An intuitive, personal budget performs the same function for the average person as a formal budget does for a large company.

A budget is management's action plan for the future. Budgets may be for short periods of time, perhaps one quarter, or may extend over several years. Companies spend considerable time and resources establishing a budget because, once completed, the budget is one of the most important management tools used to accomplish the company's goals. The budget is management's formal plan outlining the anticipated results of financial transactions for the forthcoming budget period. It both helps management coordinate and plan the various functional activities (such as production and sales) of the company and, during the budget period, acts as a control device by helping management measure actual performance against planned performance. Deviations from plan can be isolated and action taken to improve future performance.

Because many companies are interested in achieving a desired level of profits, budgeting is sometimes called profit planning. Essentially, profit planning is accomplished through the preparation of a number of integrated individual budgets, resulting in what is known as the master budget.

After reading and studying this chapter:
■ You will understand the definition of budgeting.

■■ You will understand the role of the budget as a planning and coordinating device.
■■ You will understand the types of budgets.
■■ You will understand the major components of the master budget.

BUDGETING DEFINED

Budgets are formal, quantitative plans of action. They can be prepared for an organization as a whole or for any element of the organization. Essentially, the budget quantifies management's expectations of future levels of income, financial position, and cash flows after considering not only the direction the company is taking but also the economic environment in which it operates. The *master* or *static budget,* discussed in detail in this chapter, is a summary of all the objectives and goals of all the various subunits of the company. These goals or targets, which include desired levels for items such as sales, production, selling, financing, and administrative expenses, result in a projected income statement, balance sheet, and statement of cash position. The organization's goals for the future and plans for achieving them are captured by the master budget.

THE ROLE OF BUDGETS

The budget serves as a planning device, but it also serves other functions. The budgeting process aids in evaluating performance; since the budget provides objectives and standards that can be used for the evaluation of performance, it focuses on actual results relative to anticipated ones and allows management to assess deviations from the budget and make necessary changes.

By coordinating activities, budgets promote the ideal that the plans and objectives of individual subunits should be consistent with those of the company as a whole. Coordination also means that all subunits work as one cohesive unit so that the company's overall objectives can be met; for example, the purchasing department should integrate its plans with the production department, which in turn then bases its requirements on the sales budget for the period. In practice, however, coordination is difficult to achieve because of "empire building" or simply because people act in their own self-interest. Sometimes this might be unintentional; for example, segment managers may get wrapped up in their own activities. Budgets are helpful, but they depend on the people who implement the plans of the budget by their actions.

As a motivational tool, budgets communicate to managers and employees what is expected of them. For managers, the process provides a way for them to standardize their planning efforts in an attempt to meet the company's goals. It also forces managers to plan. For employees, knowing what is expected helps reduce anxiety.

TYPES OF BUDGETS
Time Frame of Budgets

The normal time frame for a budget is one year, although some budgets, such as those for purchases of plant and equipment, are prepared for up to ten years. The annual budget is usually broken down into quarters; the first quarter is then broken down into months and the next three quarters are carried as quarterly totals. Each quarter is broken down into months as the company moves through the year. The budgeted data are altered if new information indicates that changes are warranted; hence, the budgeting process requires constant scrutiny and modification when conditions change from what was initially expected.

Continuous or *rolling* budgets have gained increased popularity in recent years. This type of budget uses a twelve-month period as its time frame. However, as the year progresses, one month is constantly added so that a twelve-month budget is always prepared. This forces management continually to look into the future in its planning function. The major advantage of this type of budget is that a greater degree of accuracy is achieved because the budget has been recently prepared. However, a disadvantage is that this process requires a substantial commitment of resources in terms of people, time, and money. Management needs to assess whether the benefits of a budget requiring frequent evaluation are greater than the cost.

Categories of Budgets

Among the many forms of budgets are:

■ Flexible budgets that compare actual operations with budgeted operations at the actual level of output. Such budgets are discussed in Chapter 14.

▬ The capital budget, a long-term budget for planning the purchase and retirement of long-lived productive assets, that is used in preparing the master budget.

▬ The master budget, which is divided into two sections: the operating budget and the financial budget. The *operating budget,* which reflects the planned future costs of operating the company, consists of a number of detailed budgets. They are:

    (a) Sales budget
    (b) Production budget
    (c) Direct materials budget
    (d) Direct labor budget
    (e) Factory overhead budget
    (f) Selling and administrative expense budget
    (g) Budgeted income statement

The *financial budget* consists of the cash budget, the capital budget, and the budgeted balance sheet. Figure 13-1 illustrates the relationship between the various budgets that make up the master budget.

PREPARING THE MASTER BUDGET

Preparing a master budget is a complex process that takes into account the goals of the company and the economic environment in which it operates. The steps involved in developing a master budget are:

1. Preparing a sales forecast
2. Calculating the expected production for the period
3. Estimating the costs of direct material, direct labor, factory overhead, and operating expenses
4. Estimating cash flows
5. Preparing the projected income statement and balance sheet

The preparation of the master budget begins with the development of a broad set of assumptions regarding the economy in general, the industry the company operates within, and specific goals that the firm expects to meet. Many times economists are employed in this process. From the assumptions management develops strategies relating to expected sales, production scheduling, anticipated inventory levels, projected expenses, and so on. After analysis of these relevant factors, management quantifies its expectations for the coming budget period.

Basic data are presented in Figure 13-2 for the Hypothetical

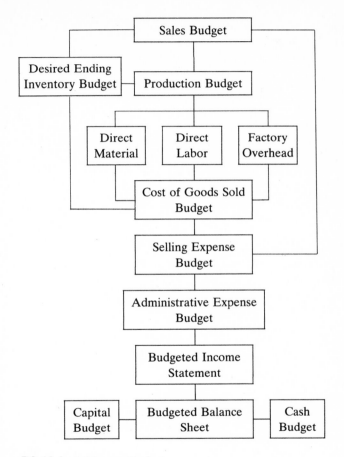

FIG. 13-1 *A Master Budget*

Company, manufacturers of plastic decoy ducks, as it prepares its annual budget. The operating budget is prepared first.

Direct materials	1 pound of plastic raw material cost $3.00
Direct labor	$6.00 per hour
Factory overhead	is applied on the basis of direct labor hours used. That is, for every hour of direct labor used in the manufacturing of a duck, one hour of factory overhead is added to the cost of the unit

Each finished decoy requires:

Direct material	2 pounds of raw material
Direct labor	1 hour
Factory overhead	1 hour (applied on the basis of direct labor)

	Finished Decoys
Anticipated sales for the year	10,000 units
Selling price	$22.00
Beginning inventory	1,000 units $18,000
Desired ending inventory	1,500 units
	Direct Materials
Beginning inventory	3,000 pounds $9,000
Desired ending inventory	5,000 pounds
Factory overhead estimate	$65,100
Selling and distribution expenses	$24,200

FIG. 13-2 *Hypothetical Company Budget Data*

Preparation of the master budget involves a series of interdependent steps, starting with the sales forecast.

THE MASTER BUDGET: THE OPERATING SECTION
Sales Forecasting

The sales budget, which shows expected sales for the coming period in dollars as well as in units, is prepared from the sales forecast, which is affected by such factors as past experience, industry market conditions, economic indicators, and competition. The sales forecast is the starting point for the master budget because production costs and inventory levels are a function of sales volume. Figure 13-3 shows the sales budget for Hypothetical Company; obviously, a company selling multiple products would have a much more detailed sales budget.

Units	Selling Price	Total Sales
10,000	$22.00	$220,000

FIG. 13-3 *Hypothetical Company Sales Budget for the Period Ending December 31, 1990*

Production Budget

After the sales budget is prepared, the production budget can be prepared. The number of units to be produced is a function of anticipated sales and also of the change in inventories from the beginning of the year to the end of the year. Management needs to decide how much inventory it wants remaining at the end of the year. The decision as to anticipated inventory levels takes into consideration the possibility of unexpected high demand and the possibility of a stock-out (not enough units on hand), as well as the costs of carrying excessive amounts of inventory, such as interest. Another input in this decision process is the effective utilization of production personnel and facilities. From Figure 13-1, we see that management wishes to have 1,500 decoys on hand at the end of the year. This figure was determined after consideration of the aforementioned factors. Figure 13-4 presents the production budget.

Budgeted sales in units (from Figure 13-3)
10,000 units
Add: Desired ending inventory of finished decoys
1,500

   Total needed
11,500
Less: Beginning inventory of finished decoys
1,000

   Total units to be produced
10,500

FIG. 13-4 *Hypothetical Company Production Budget for the Period Ending December 31, 1991*

Direct Materials Budget

After the production budget is completed, the company calculates the direct materials to be used. This enables the company to determine its direct materials purchases for the year. Figure 13-5 presents these calculations.

Production (from Figure 13-4)	
units	10,500
Multiplied by 2 pounds per unit	× 2 lbs.
Total pounds of direct material to be used	21,000
Cost per pound	× $3.00
Total cost of direct material to be used	$63,000
Total pounds needed in production	21,000
Add: Desired ending inventory (from Figure 13-2)	5,000
Total direct material needed	26,000
Less: Beginning inventory (from Figure 13-2)	3,000
Direct material to be purchased	23,000
Multiplied by the cost per pound	× $3.00
Cost of purchased direct material	$69,000

FIG. 13-5 *Hypothetical Company Direct Materials Budget for the Period Ending December 31, 1991*

Direct Labor Budget

The direct labor shown in Figure 13-6 is a function of the various labor rates and labor methods used by a company. Hypothetical Company has only one labor rate.

Finished decoy units to be produced	
(from Figure 13-4) 10,500 units	
Multiplied by the direct labor hours needed per unit hour	× 1
Total direct labor hours required	10,500
Multiplied by the cost per direct labor hour	× $6.00
Total cost of direct labor hours	$63,000

FIG. 13-6 *Hypothetical Company Direct Labor Budget for the Period Ending December 31, 1991*

Factory Overhead Budget

Next, the factory overhead budget is prepared. Factory overhead includes all costs of production other than direct materials and direct labor. The costs are broken down by cost behavior pattern. That is, the budget consists of the estimated variable and fixed overhead for the coming period. The budget is necessary in order to apply overhead to the finished decoys. The factory overhead budget for the Hypothetical Company appears in Figure 13-7. Notice that the total estimated factory overhead is $65,100, which is the estimate from Figure 13-2.

Variable Overhead:		
Utilities	$ 6,000	
Fringe benefits	10,500	
Supplies	9,000	
Indirect labor	21,000	
Total variable overhead		$46,500
Fixed Overhead:		
Depreciation	11,300	
Insurance	6,000	
Property taxes	1,300	
Total fixed overhead		18,600
Total factory overhead (from Figure 13-2)		$65,100

FIG. 13-7 *Hypothetical Company Factory Overhead Budget for the Period Ended December 31, 1991*

Factory overhead rate ($65,100/10,500 direct labor hours = $6.20 per direct labor hour)

Ending Inventory Budget

Ending inventory figures were used in Figures 13-4 and 13-5 for the production budget and the direct materials budget. These figures are also needed for the projected income statement and balance sheet as displayed in Figure 13-8.

Finished Goods

	Required	Cost per Unit		
Direct material	2 pounds ×	$3.00	=	$ 6.00
Direct labor	1 hour ×	6.00	=	6.00
Factory overhead	1 hour ×	6.20	=	6.20
Total cost per unit				$18.20

	Units	Cost per Unit
Total Cost		

Desired ending finished goods inventory 1,500 × $18.20 =
$27,300

Direct Materials

Desired ending direct materials inventory 5,000 lbs. × $3.00
= 15,000

Total ending inventory $42,300

FIG. 13-8 *Hypothetical Company Ending Inventory Budget for the Period Ended December 31, 1991*

Cost of Goods Sold Budget

Using the information from Figures 13-5 through 13-8, the cost of goods sold budget can be prepared. This budget is presented in Figure 13-9.

Beginning finished goods inventory (from Figure 13-2)		$18,000
Add: Direct materials used (from Figure 13-5)	$63,000	
Direct labor (from Figure 13-6)	$63,000	
Factory overhead (from Figure 13-7)	65,100	191,100
Cost of goods manufactured		209,100
Less: Ending finished goods inventory (from Figure 13-8)		27,300
Cost of goods sold		$181,800

FIG. 13-9 *Hypothetical Company Cost of Goods Sold Budget for the Period Ending December 31, 1991*

Sales and Distribution Expenses Budget

The sales and distribution expenses budget takes into consideration all selling, general, administrative, and other necessary operating expenses. Some of these expenses, such as sales commissions, are a function of other budgetary items; others are estimated based upon historical patterns taking into consideration anticipated future price changes. The sales and distribution expense budget for Hypothetical Company is shown in Figure 13-10.

Sales commissions and salaries	$ 8,000
Advertising	7,400
Supplies	5,200
Travel	5,200
Total sales and distribution expenses (Figure 13-2)	$24,200

FIG. 13-10 *Hypothetical Company Sales and Distribution Expense Budget for the Period Ending December 31, 1991*

The Budgeted Income Statement

Hypothetical Company's budgeted income statement (presented in Figure 13-11) is simplified compared to what one would expect in the budget of a large manufacturing firm, where greater detail would be provided along with a larger number of supporting schedules. If the number of revenue and/or expense items is very large (as it is with a large manufacturing company), separate budgets might be necessary for each item. That is, expected revenues other than sales, such as interest, and other anticipated expenses would be submitted by the manager or managers responsible for the individual items.

Sales (from Figure 13-3)	$220,000
Cost of goods sold (from Figure 13-9)	181,800
Gross margin	38,200
Selling and distribution expenses (from Figure 13-10)	24,200
Net income	$ 14,000

FIG. 13-11 *Hypothetical Company Budgeted Income Statement for the Period Ending December 31, 1991*

THE MASTER BUDGET: THE FINANCIAL BUDGET

The financial budget is prepared next. For our purposes several key assumptions need to be made in order to demonstrate its preparation. First, assume that Hypothetical Company had the balance sheet at January 1, 1991, shown in Figure 13-12.

ASSETS
Current Assets

Cash	$110,000
Accounts receivable (net)	20,000
Inventory	27,000
Total current assets	157,000

Noncurrent Assets

Property	200,000
Plant & equipment (net)	350,000
Total noncurrent assets	550,000
Total assets	$707,000

LIABILITIES AND STOCKHOLDERS' EQUITY
Liabilities

Accounts payable	26,000
Bonds payable	140,000
Total liabilities	166,000

Stockholders' Equity

Common stock	200,000
Retained earnings	341,000
Total stockholders' equity	541,000
Total liabilities and stockholders' equity	$707,000

FIG. 13-12 *Hypothetical Company Balance Sheet at December 31, 1990*

Further assume that Hypothetical had the capital budget appearing in Figure 13-13 relating to purchases of plant, property, and equipment in the forthcoming year.

	Property	Plant & Equipment	Depreciation Accumulated	Net Amount
Beginning balance	$200,000	$450,000	$100,000	$350,000
Add: Purchase of property	$ 15,000			
Purchase of equipment		$ 20,000		
Less: Depreciation ($11,300 from Figure 13-7)				11,300
Ending balance	$215,000	$470,000	$111,300	$358,700

FIG. 13-13 *Hypothetical Company Capital Budget for the Period Ended December 31, 1991*

Other assumptions are these:
1. The company will collect all of the beginning balance of accounts receivable during the coming year.
2. The company will collect 90 percent of its sales in cash during the coming year.
3. The company will pay for purchases of property, plant, and equipment with the proceeds of a $100,000 bond that it will issue during the year.
4. The balance of accounts payable will be paid during the year.
5. At the end of the year, one-half of the direct materials purchased during the year will still be on account.
6. There will be no changes in the common stock account.
7. All other purchases and expenses will be for cash.

Using the previous information, the cash budget and the budgeted balance sheet (presented in Figures 13-14 and 13-15) can be prepared.

Beginning cash balance (from Figure 13-12)	$110,000
Add: Receipts from sales ($220,000 from Figure 13-13 × .90 assumption #2 above)	$198,000
and accounts receivable (from Figure 13-12 and assumption 1 above)	20,000
	218,000

Proceeds from issuance of bond (from assumption 3 above)	100,000
Total cash inflows	428,000

Less: Disbursements

Purchase of property (from Figure 13-13)	15,000
Purchase of equipment (from Figure 13-13)	20,000
Purchase of direct materials (from Figure 13-5) only 50% paid for in cash	34,500
Payment of direct labor costs (from Figure 13-6)	63,000
Payment of factory overhead costs less $11,300 of depreciation (from Figure 13-7)	53,800
Payment of sales and distribution expenses (from Figure 13-10)	24,200
Payment of beginning balance of accounts payable (from Figure 13-12 and assumption 4 above)	26,000
Total cash outflows	236,500
Ending cash balance (from Figure 13-15)	$191,500

FIG. 13-14 *Hypothetical Company Cash Budget for the Period Ended December 31, 1991*

ASSETS
Current Assets

Cash (from Figure 13-14)	$191,500
Accounts receivable (net) ($20,000 − $20,000 + $220,000 − $198,000)	22,000
Inventory (from Figure 13-8)	42,300
Total current assets	255,800

Noncurrent Assets

Property (from Figure 13-13)	215,000
Plant & equipment (net) (from Figure 13-13)	358,700
Total noncurrent assets	573,700
Total assets	$829,500

LIABILITIES AND STOCKHOLDERS' EQUITY
Liabilities

Accounts payable (50% of direct material purchases from Figure 13-14)	34,500
Bonds payable ($140,000 + $100,000)	240,000
Total liabilities	274,500

Stockholders' Equity

Common stock	200,000
Retained earnings ($341,000 + $14,000 net income from Figure 13-11)	355,000
Total stockholders' equity	555,000
Total liabilities and stockholders' equity	$829,000

FIG. 13-15 *Hypothetical Company Budgeted Balance Sheet at December 31, 1991*

CHAPTER PERSPECTIVE

Our discussion centered on the budget as a formal financial plan. Most companies budget in order to force planning, set a standard for performance evaluation, and provide a means for all functional areas to coordinate their activities.

Budgets can be prepared for any time period; the most common is a single year. Some budgets, particularly capital budgets, may be prepared for extended periods, such as ten years. Companies decide on a time period based on the degree of control they have over operating activities and on the cost/benefit trade-off with the resources that must be committed to the budget process.

The master budget is a collection of budgets, divided into two sections: the operating budget and the financial budget. The operating budget consists of the sales, production, direct materials, direct labor, factory overhead, inventory, cost of goods sold, and the sales and distribution expense budgets; these form the basis of the budgeted income statement. The financial budget consists of a capital budget, a budgeted balance sheet, and a cash budget.

Standard Costs, Variances, and Budgets

INTRODUCTION AND MAIN POINTS

Responsibility Accounting refers to a system of gathering and communicating revenue and expense information to divisions, departments, and individuals by areas of responsibility. An important aspect of responsibility accounting is establishing standard costs in order to assist management in evaluating performance. In a standard cost system, production activities are maintained at both standard and actual costs, and the difference between standard and actual costs assists management in judging performance.

After studying the material in this chapter:

■ You will understand the development, types, and uses of standard costs.

■ You will understand how standard cost variances are computed and reported.

■ You will understand how budget variances are computed and used for budgetary control purposes.

DEVELOPMENT, TYPES, AND USES OF STANDARD COSTS
Development of Standard Costs

Standard costs are predetermined costs, usually expressed on a per unit basis, of what costs should be under normal operating conditions. They are carefully determined, often using engineering and time and motion studies. However, standards are not always based on rigid specifications. Because the primary purpose of standard costing is to aid management in judging performance, a less formal, nonscientific approach to standard-setting can also result in useful standard costs.

Physical standards are developed by analyzing the types and amounts of material, labor, and overhead necessary in the production of a unit. The standard cost of a unit is obtained by multiplying the standard prices of material, labor, and overhead by the physical standards.

Conceptually, responsibility for setting standards lies primarily with the personnel directly involved with the task; those who negotiate with their respective managers regarding the relative tightness of the budget. However, many times management uses a "top-down" approach to the standard-setting process and establishes standards without participation from the personnel involved; this approach can lead to a significant amount of friction between management and the workers and can prove to be counterproductive.

The accountant's primary responsibilities in regard to standards is to convert physical standards, such as pounds or yards, into dollars and to prepare performance reports that compare actual and standard costs.

Types of Standards

Perfect or *ideal* standards reflect the absolute minimum costs attainable under only the best operating conditions. They contain no provision for breakdowns, lost time, or work stoppages. Many managers feel that the use of perfect standards suggests to employees that they must constantly strive to improve their performance and efficiency. However, the use of perfect or ideal standards can be counterproductive; their use tends to discourage workers since it is impossible to meet ideal standards. Furthermore, deviations or *variances* from these standards cannot be interpreted because they contain ordinary or expected inefficiencies as well as abnormal inefficiences. Therefore, it becomes impossible to isolate and bring the abnormal efficiencies to management's attention.

On the other hand, *practical standards* (also called *currently attainable standards*) are those that can be obtained under normal efficient operating conditions. The standards set are "tight" but not unreasonable and include normal allowances for such items as machine breakdowns, lost personnel time, spoilage, and waste.

Practical standards are more useful than ideal standards for motivating personnel, budgetary control, and product costing because they allow for normal inefficiencies. Employees are more highly motivated when they know that the standards being used for evaluative purposes can be attained by a reasonable but still efficient effort. Better budgetary control and product costing can also be achieved with practical standards because, by taking into consideration normal production inefficiencies, realistic budget figures and product costs can be used for planning, forecasting, pricing, and control. Ideal standards should not be used because they result in impractical and unreasonable figures.

Uses of Standards Costs

Basic uses of standard costs include:

1. Motivating employees to improve performance by encouraging a course of corrective action. In many instances, improved employee performance can lead to cost reductions.

2. Monitoring the costs associated with planning and control and by directing attention to situations where conditions or operations are not within the limits or standards set by management. This mechanism of "red-flagging" potential problems is called *management by exception.*

3. Enhancing performance measurement by affixing responsibility to the individual or department responsible for any variations from the standards. Responsibility over cost control can then be evaluated through performance reports.

4. Inventory valuation.

5. Budgetary planning and decision making.

6. Setting selling, transfer prices, and bid prices on contracts. Serving as organizational goals or targets.

7. Transfer prices are necessary when products and/or sevices are exchanged between operating divisions of a firm.

8. Streamlining the accounting system and reducing clerical costs. The accumulation of actual costs takes place over an extended time period, while the use of standard costs allows the costing and pricing of products to be made on a timely basis.

THE GENERAL MODEL FOR VARIANCE ANALYSIS

Our general model for variance analysis separates standards into two categories: price and quantity variances. The general model, representing variable manufacturing costs, is shown in Figure 14-1.

(1)	(2)	(3)
Actual Quantity of Inputs, at Actual Price (AQ × AP)	Actual Quantity of Inputs, at Standard Price (AQ × SP)	Standard Quantity Allowed for Output, at Standard Price (SQ × SP)

Price Variance	Quantity Variance
(1) — (2)	(2) — (3)
Materials price variance	Materials quantity variance
Labor rate variance	Labor efficiency variance
Variable overhead spending variance	Variable overhead efficiency variance

Total Variance

FIG. 14-1 *General Model for Variance Analysis Variable Manufacturing Costs*

A *price variance* is defined as the difference between the actual price of a unit and the standard price of the unit multiplied by the actual quantity of the unit used or purchased. The variance measures the difference between actual unit prices and the standard unit prices for the actual quantity used or purchased.

The *quantity variance* is defined as the difference between the actual quantity of a unit and the standard quantity of a unit multiplied by the standard quantity used. This variance measures the difference between the quantity of units actually used (such as pounds of material) and the quantity of units that should have been used, multiplied by the standard price.

As a general rule, separation or isolation of variances should be done as early as possible. Separation of the total variance into two components gives management the ability to identify the party responsible for control of that variance. For example, the purchasing manager may be responsible for a material price variance, while the production foreman may have responsibility for a quantity (usage) variance.

Material Price and Quantity Variances

In monitoring material price and quantity variances, attention is normally focused on situations in which the cost or quantity of inputs exceeds the standards set. This condition results in unfavorable variances.

What are some of the causes of unfavorable materials price variances? One obvious cause may be improper setting of the standard. Another possible cause is the inability of the purchasing department or manager to seek the lowest price possible. Of course, the unfavorable variance may simply be the result of material prices increases and the unavailability of a suitable replacement material. Inefficient operation of the purchasing department may be another factor causing an unfavorable price variance.

Unfavorable quantity variances can also arise as a result of incorrect standards. In order to conserve cash, a company might buy a lower quality raw material; this, in turn, might cause higher usage of the material, resulting in an unfavorable variance. If workers are not adequately trained or instructed, the result may be excessive material usage or waste and an unfavorable variance. Machinery and equipment need to be properly adjusted and maintained and prescribed production procedures should be followed; failure to do so can also lead to unfavorable material quantity variances because of the use of abnormal quantities of material.

Figure 14-2 demonstrates the calculation of material price and quantity variances. Baker Company uses a standard costing system and has established the following standards for material used in making Product X:

For each unit of Product X, 2.0 pounds of raw material should be used. The standard cost of one pound of raw material is $4.00. During the month, 7,500 pounds of raw material were purchased at a cost of $3.90. All 7,500 pounds were used in the production of 3,000 units of Product X.

(1) Actual Quantity of Inputs, at Actual Price (AQ × AP)	(2) Actual Quantity of Inputs, at Standard Price (AQ × SP)	(3) Standard Quantity Allowed for Output, at Standard Price (SQ × SP)
7,500 lbs. × $3.90 = $29,250	7,500 lbs. × $4.00 = $30,000	2 lbs. per unit × 3,000 units × $4.00 = $24,000

```
                30,000                        24,000
Price           29,250        Quantity        30,000
Variance   =   $750 Favorable  Variance  =   $6,000 Unfavorable
```

Total Variance = 6,000 − 750 = $5,250 Unfavorable

FIG. 14-2 *Baker Company Calculation of Material Price and Quantity Variances*

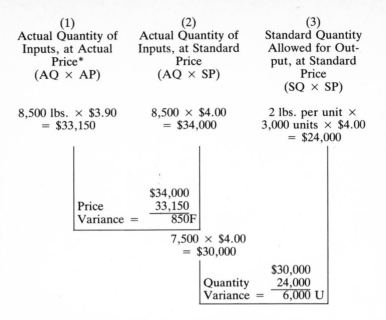

(1) Actual Quantity of Inputs, at Actual Price* (AQ × AP)	(2) Actual Quantity of Inputs, at Standard Price (AQ × SP)	(3) Standard Quantity Allowed for Output, at Standard Price (SQ × SP)
8,500 lbs. × $3.90 = $33,150	8,500 × $4.00 = $34,000	2 lbs. per unit × 3,000 units × $4.00 = $24,000

Price Variance =

$34,000
33,150
 850F

7,500 × $4.00
= $30,000

Quantity Variance =

$30,000
24,000
6,000 U

FIG. 14-3 *Baker Company Calculation of Material Price and Quantity Variances using the Quantity of Materials Purchased*

Note that in our example we assumed that the amount purchased was the same amount put into production. If this were not the case, that is, if the amount put into production were less than the amount purchased, the material price variance would be computed using the amount purchased. In this instance a total variance could be computed because of the difference. (Most firms do compute the price variance when materials are purchased rather than when they are placed into production.)

Labor Rate and Efficiency Variances

Labor variances are measured or isolated when labor is used in the production process. They are computed in the same manner

*The material purchase price variance was computed using the 8,500 pounds purchased while the material quantity variance was computed using the 7,500 pounds used in production. Because of this difference, a total variance cannot be computed.

as the material price and quantity variances, and the three column model can be used. The only difference is that the terms "rate" and "efficiency" are substituted for "price' and "quantity."

Unfavorable rate variances can arise from misallocation of the work force; for example, highly-paid skilled workers being substituted for lower-skilled workers who are paid a lower hourly wage. Favorable rate variances occur when the reverse happens. Overtime pay also results in unfavorable labor rate variances. Finally, an increase in wages without a corresponding change in the standard creates an unfavorable rate variance.

Causes of unfavorable labor rate variances include poor supervision, poorly trained workers, and the use of substandard machinery that leads to breakdowns and work stoppages. Another possible cause is the use of low-grade materials, which can require extra processing time.

Figure 14-4 demonstrates the calculation of labor rate and efficiency variances, assuming the following information for the Baker Company:

Each unit of Product X requires 1.5 hours of direct labor. The standard cost for direct labor is \$12 per direct labor hour. There were 3,000 units produced. The actual direct labor cost was \$13.50 per hour and the actual number of direct labor hours was 4,200.

(1) Actual Hours of Input, at Actual Rate (AH × AR)	(2) Actual Hours of Input, at Standard Rate (AH × SR)	(3) Standard Hours Al- lowed for Output, at Standard Rate (SH × SR)
4,200 hrs. × \$13.50 = \$56,700	4,200 hrs. × \$12.00 = \$50,400	1.5 hrs. per unit × 3,000 units × \$12,000 = \$54,000

$$\begin{array}{ll} & 56,700 \\ \text{Rate} & -\ 50,400 \\ \text{Variance} \quad = & \overline{\$6,300\ U} \end{array}$$
$$\begin{array}{ll} & 54,000 \\ \text{Efficiency} & -\ 50,400 \\ \text{Variance} \quad = & \overline{\$3,600\ F} \end{array}$$

Total Variance = 6,300 − 3,600 = \$2,700 U

FIG. 14-4 *Baker Company Calculation of Labor Rate and Efficiency Variances*

Variable Overhead Spending and Efficiency Variances

Variances arising from deviations from the standard cost of variable overhead items are normally the responsibility of the production department. The calculation of these variances is very similar to that of the labor rate and efficiency variances, with the difference that "spending" is substituted for "rate."

The variable overhead spending variance measures the difference between what was spent for variable overhead items, such as utilities, and what should have been spent as required by the standard, or the actual amount of variable overhead minus the expected amount. The variable overhead efficiency variance is the difference between the actual activity (in hours) and the standard activity (in hours) allowed. Variable overhead normally fluctuates in proportion to some measure of production, such as machine hours or direct labor hours. In this case, we can say that what the efficiency variance really measures is the excess variable overhead incurred or saved because the measure of production (for example, direct labor hours) differed from the standard.

In evaluating variable overhead variances, the two categories of spending and efficiency are different from the material and labor variances. This is due to the fact that variable overhead consists of many types of costs, such as utilities, fringe benefits, and repairs. The best way to evaluate these variances is to observe the difference between the actual cost and the standard cost for each individual item of variable overhead.

Unfavorable variable overhead spending variances can arise because of incorrect setting of standards, waste and carelessness, and increases in the prices of variable overhead items. Since indirect labor is normally a component of variable overhead, increases in the wage rate can also cause an unfavorable spending variance.

Causes of unfavorable variable overhead efficiency variances include poor quality materials and supplies, lack of supervision, and poorly trained workers. Work stoppages and defective machinery and equipment can also lead to unfavorable efficiency variances.

Using the Baker Company example, Figure 14-5 presents the calculation of the variable overhead spending and efficiency variances. We assume that Baker Company applies overhead to Product X on a direct labor hour basis; that is, variable overhead is allocated to Product X on the same basis as direct labor.

Again assume that each unit of Product X requires 1.5 hours

of direct labor and, therefore, 1.5 hours of variable overhead. The standard variable overhead rate is $10 per hour. Actual variable overhead incurred for the production of 3,000 units of Product X amounted to $46,000. The actual number of direct labor hours was 4,200.

(1) Actual Hours of Input, at Actual Rate (AH × AR)	(2) Actual Hours of Input, at Standard Rate (AH × SR)	(3) Standard Hours Allowed for Output, at Standard Rate (SH × SR)
$46,000*	4,200 hrs. × $10.00 = $42,000	1.5 hrs. per unit × 3,000 units × $10.00 = $45,000

Rate Variance = $\begin{array}{r} 46,000 \\ - 42,000 \\ \hline \$4,000\ U \end{array}$ Efficiency Variance = $3,000 F

Total Variance = 4,000 - 3,000 = $1,000 U

FIG. 14-5 *Baker Company Calculation of Variable Overhead Spending and Efficiency Variances*

*The actual variable overhead rate could be computed by dividing the actual cost by the actual direct labor hours since variable overhead is applied on the same basis ($46,000/4,200 = $10.952).

Notice that the variable overhead efficiency variance and the labor efficiency variance (Fig. 14-4) are both favorable. Again, this is because variable overhead has been allocated on the basis of direct labor hours. Because we were efficient in our usage of direct labor, we used less variable overhead. This relationship always occurs when variable overhead is allocated based upon some production measure such as labor hours. The key is to pick the best production measure; that is, the one that has the closest relationship to the incurrence of variable overhead. This measure of activity is sometimes referred to as a cost driver and may not be labor cost since in recent years many companies have moved from being labor intensive to machine intensive. Computer time or machine hours might be a more appropriate cost driver for use in applying variable overhead.

Variances for Fixed Overhead

Unlike materials, labor, and variable overhead costs, fixed variable overhead costs do not vary with production. Standard costs for fixed overhead are set at the beginning of the period and are then spread over the units of production during the period. Variances arise because the actual amount of fixed overhead differs from that which was anticipated at the beginning of the period. Unlike materials, labor, and variable overhead costs, fixed overhead costs are beyond the control of production personnel. They normally cannot be changed quickly; as a result, analysis of these variances is of dubious value to the production department manager. Therefore, we forgo any further discussion of the fixed overhead variance.

Reporting of Variances

We said earlier that one of the keys to variance analysis is to isolate the variance as soon as possible. Computer-integrated manufacturing systems allow immediate feedback regarding variances and allow management to take corrective actions that minimize the variances and assist in controlling costs. A decisive advantage is that the corrective action can take place during production rather than after production ceases.

Variances can be formally integrated into the accounting system and separately isolated and accounted for. In such cases, variances are accumulated in accounts on a daily, weekly, or monthly basis. Variance reports are prepared accordingly and distributed to the appropriate level of management for action. There is no prescribed form of report for variance analysis; each report is tailored to meet the needs of the intended user.

VARIANCE ANALYSIS AND BUDGETARY CONTROL: FLEXIBLE BUDGETING

We introduced the master budget in Chapter 13, discussing how the budget is prepared as the first step in the planning and control process. In this chapter, we presented standard costing and ways the system can be used to plan and control the costs of materials, labor, and variable overhead. We now turn to the concept of *flexible budgeting*, which also assists management in the planning and control phase of the budgeting process.

Budgeted Costs and Standard Costs

Budgeted costs and standard costs are not necessarily the same. Budgeted costs usually refers to total costs; for example, we budget for $100,000 of total variable cost for a particular fiscal period. Normally, standard cost relates to *unit* cost rather than *total* cost. In our previous discussion we referred to the standard cost per unit of material; you might view standard cost as the budgeted *cost per unit*. Standard costs do not differ from budgeted costs if the standards are reasonably attainable; in such cases they can be used in the preparation of budgets.

Static Budgets

The master budget, the budgetary technique discussed in Chapter 13, was essentially based upon past expenditures. The process also took into account existing asset and liability levels, possible changes in costs to the firm, and changes in economic environment. This type of budget is sometimes referred to as a *static* budget, since each item in the budget is a single figure which is not adjusted for alternate levels of activity. A static budget is prepared prior to the beginning of the period and is necessary for management to plan future operations and to set predetermined overhead rates for product costing purposes. Such a budget appears in Figure 14-6 for the Baker Company for 1991. (The comparison of actual and budgeted results is an example of a *performance report,* discussed in Chapter 16.)

	Actual Results	Static Budget	Variance
Number of Units	80,000	100,000	20,000 U
Sales	$280,000	$300,000	$20,000 U
Variable Expenses:			
Direct materials	22,000	36,000	14,000 F
Direct labor	43,000	42,000	1,000 U
Overhead	21,400	20,000	1,400 U
Selling	57,600	72,000	14,400 F
Total Variable Expenses	144,000	170,000	26,000 F
Fixed Expenses:			
Overhead	63,000	60,000	3,000 U
Selling	15,000	10,000	5,000 U
Total Fixed Expenses	78,000	70,000	8,000 U
Operating Income	$ 58,000	$ 60,000	$ 2,000 U

FIG. 14-6 *Baker Company Performance Report for the Period Ending December 31, 1991*

One problem in analyzing this report is that the number of units sold is not equal to the number initially budgeted. It is therefore difficult to determine whether the $2,000 unfavorable variance in operating income is the result of increased fixed expenses, a decrease in the sales volume, or a combination of these. This is especially puzzling because total variable expenses were lower than expected. That is, in Figure 14-6, total fixed expenses were in excess of the amount budgeted. Also, actual sales were lower than budgeted sales and could have contributed to the unfavorable variance. On the other hand, total variable expenses were less than the amount budgeted. What caused the $2,000 unfavorable budget variance? We cannot make this determination by comparing the actual costs at 80,000 units with the budgeted costs at 100,000 units.

Flexible Budgets

To permit a more detailed and helpful analysis, companies prepare *flexible* or *variable* budgets for various activity levels. Figure 14-7 shows a flexible budget for three different activity levels. Note that the amounts for 100,000 units are those from the static budget in Figure 14-6.

Number of Units	Amount Per Unit	70,000	100,000	130,000
Sales	$3.00	$210,000	$300,000	$390,000
Variable Expenses:				
Direct materials	.36	25,200	36,000	46,800
Direct labor	.42	29,400	42,000	54,600
Overhead	.20	14,000	20,000	26,000
Selling	.72	50,400	72,000	93,600
Total Variable Expenses	$1.70	119,000	170,000	221,000
Fixed Expenses:				
Overhead		60,000	60,000	60,000
Selling		10,000	10,000	10,000
Total Fixed Expenses		70,000	70,000	70,000
Operating Income		$ 21,000	$ 60,000	$ 99,000

FIG. 14-7 *Baker Company Flexible Budget 1991*

In reviewing Figure 14-7, note two things. First, the cost per unit is calculated by taking the amount of a particular budget item and dividing that amount by the activity level from the static budget level. For example, the static budget amount for direct materials is $36,000. Dividing this amount by 100,000 units results in a cost per unit of $0.36. At an activity level of 70,000 units, total direct material cost would be $25,200 (70,000 units × $0.36). Also note that since fixed costs do not fluctuate with volume changes, they are expressed as total amounts rather than on a per unit basis.

Flexible Budget Formula

Using the data from Figure 14-7, we can construct a *flexible budget formula*, which will allow us to compute a budget at any level of activity.

Revenues	−	Variable Expenses	−	Fixed Expenses	=	Operating Income (or Loss)

Units Sold × Selling Price Per Unit	−	Units Sold × Variable Costs Per Unit	−	Fixed Expenses	=	Operating Income (or Loss)

Using this formula, Baker Company's flexible budget formula is:

$$\$3.00\ X\ +\ \$1.70\ X\ +\ \$70,000$$

where X is the chosen activity level. You can confirm the amounts of operating income from Figure 14-6 by substituting 70,000, 100,000, and 130,000 units for "X" in Baker Company's flexible budget formula.

Analysis of Baker Company's Actual Results

Using the static budget, the flexible budget, and the actual results, we can isolate the variances from planned results for Baker Company. Figure 14-8 presents this analysis.

	(A) Actual Results (Based on Actual Activity Level)	(B) Flexible Budget Variances	(C) Flexible Budget (Based on Actual Activity Level)	(D) Sales Volume Variance	(E) Static Budget
Units	80,000	-0-	80,000	20,000	100,000
Sales	$280,000	$40,000 F	$240,000	$60,000 U	$300,000
Variable Expenses:					
Direct materials	22,000	6,800 F	28,800	7,200 F	36,000
Direct labor	43,000	9,400 U	33,600	8,400 F	42,000
Overhead	21,400	5,400 U	16,000	4,000 F	20,000
Selling	57,600	-0-	57,600	14,400 F	72,000
Total Variable Exp.	144,000	8,000 U	136,000	34,000 F	170,000
Fixed Expenses:					
Overhead	63,000	3,000 U	60,000	-0-	60,000
Selling	15,000	5,000	10,000	-0-	10,000
Total Fixed Exp.	78,000	8,000 U	70,000	-0-	70,000
Operating Income	$ 58,000	$24,000 F	$ 34,000	$26,000 U	$ 60,000

Flex. Budget Var.
= $24,000 F

Sales Volume
Var. = $26,000 U

Total Variance from Static Budget = $2,000 U

FIG. 14-8 *Baker Company Report on Actual vs. Budgeted Performance For the Period Ended December 31, 1991*

The actual results for 1991 in Column A are from Figure 14-6. Column C is the flexible budget based upon the activity level used in Column A. Column E is the static budget from Figure 14-6 prepared prior to the beginning of the fiscal year.

The *sales volume variance* is isolated in Column D. This variance results from the differences between the static and flexible budget amounts for revenues, expenses, and operating income. In our example, the targeted amount of sales of 100,000 units was not achieved. This might have been caused by environmental factors outside the control of Baker Company, an overly optimistic sales forecast, or inefficiencies of the sales staff. Obviously, detailed analysis would have to be conducted to determine the cause and to plan any necessary corrective action. As you might expect, operating at an activity level lower than anticipated lowers total variable expenses. The sales volume variance for 1991 for Baker Company is $26,000 and is unfavorable.

The *flexible budget variance* for Baker is a favorable $24,000 (see Column B in Figure 14-8). This result was caused by selling 80,000 units at a price greater than that initially budgeted and incurring $16,000 more in variable and fixed expenses than budgeted for at an activity level of 80,000 units. Each unit was sold at an average selling price of $3.50 (total sales of $280,000 divided by 80,000 units). Market forces, such as a lack of competition, may have indicated to management that an increase in selling price was warranted. (It may also have been a contributing factor in failing to reach the desired sales level of 100,000 units.) Management will certainly want to know why variable expenses were higher than budgeted. Examining the components of variable expenses, similar to our previous discussion concerning standard costs (price and efficiency variances), might answer these questions. Fixed expenses exceeded the budget by $8,000; this variance also needs to be investigated on an item-by-item basis. (That is, the components of fixed overhead and selling expenses have to be reviewed individually.) The favorable flexible budget variance of $24,000 subtracted from the unfavorable sales volume variance of 26,000 equals the total unfavorable budget variance of $2,000 presented in Figures 14-6 and 14-8.

Cost control is important if a company is to be profitable. The flexible budget approach is one way to control costs by providing management with a signal when actual amounts differ from budgeted amounts at a given activity level.

CHAPTER PERSPECTIVE

According to our discussion of standard costs, standard costs are predetermined costs that management believes should be attainable under normal but efficient operations. Standard costing systems monitor and isolate differences between standard and actual costs.

The price variance for direct materials measures the difference between what was actually paid for materials and what was called for by the standard. The efficiency variance indicates how well the production manager utilizes materials. Similarly, the labor rate variance measures the effect of changing actual labor rates from standard rates. The labor efficiency variance can be a signal indicating the inefficient use of labor.

Variances arising from the application of variable overhead items are categorized as spending and efficiency variances. Their isolation and calculation is similar to that of the labor variances; however, their interpretation is more difficult because of the many items included in variable overhead.

Static budgets are prepared prior to the beginning of the fiscal year and relate to only one level of activity. The interpretation of operating results can be difficult when actual operations differ from the activity level used in the preparation of the static budget. Flexible budgets are used to present budgetary figures at any activity level. The flexible budget formula allows management to make meaningful comparisons of actual and budgeted amounts at the same activity level, as well as to take corrective action when actual amounts exceed budgeted amounts.

Business Plans and Loan Applications

INTRODUCTION AND MAIN POINTS

Companies that seek credit are frequently required to prepare a business plan as part of a loan application; but managers often file the plan away once the loan is secured. However, the business plan has potentially much wider use than just satisfying lender requirements. The business plan contains projected financial statements and resource requirements that managers can use in several ways to help control the business. This chapter discusses the importance of the business plan as part of the loan application package and the uses managers may make of the business plan; it also presents a detailed outline of its composition. The chapter ends with a brief discussion of personal loan applications, also frequently part of the loan application of a small, privately owned company.

After studying the material in this chapter:

— You will understand the importance of a good business plan in securing business loans.

— You will see how managers can use a business plan to monitor and control operations, examine the feasibility of proposed projects, and choose between alternative projects.

— You will know the components that make up a comprehensive business plan.

— You will understand how a business plan is used as part of a business loan application.

— You will know the items requested on most personal loan applications and how such applications are used as a component of a business loan application for a small, privately-held company.

THE ROLE OF A BUSINESS PLAN

A business plan is a comprehensive document that describes a company's past, current, and projected operations and operating results and includes a statement of the strategy, tactics, and resources that will be used to achieve the projected results. Business plans are often required by lenders as part of a loan application, but they are also useful—perhaps essential—in managing and directing a business.

A business plan is an invaluable working guide and reference tool. The plan requires a company's goals to be formally and quantitatively stated and allows managers to measure performance, evaluate alternative courses of action, and coordinate the activities necessary to carry out the plan. A carefully thought-out business plan is a repository of information useful to both lenders and owners. Owners use it internally to provide consistent policy, establish operating control, and assure that activities are goal-directed. The plan is used externally by a lender to examine a company's history, status, and potential in order to make a lending decision; lenders want to know precisely a company's strengths and strategy before risking funds in a loan commitment.

Facing the Hard Questions

Preparation of a business plan forces managers to answer hard questions in precise ways. Cash flows, sales, income, and other activity measures must be forecast; financial statements must be prepared and projected for future years; and strategies must be expressed in writing. Enthusiastic managers who only have a "gut feel" and "great optimism" for a new project may find it difficult to justify their beliefs in a formal document. As a result, a major achievement of business plans (as with any budgeting process) is to force managers to plan and evaluate effectively.

Who? What? When?

A business plan forces managers to answer the following basic questions:[1] Who? What? Where? When? Why? How?

WHO will be involved in the activities?

WHAT goals does the company expect to achieve?

WHAT resources (financial and otherwise) will be required to achieve these goals?

WHERE will the goal-directed activities take place?

---

[1]Taken, with modification, from "Your Business Plan," a pamphlet distributed by the Economic Development/Small Business Development Center, Louisiana State University, Baton Rouge, LA.

WHEN will each of the goals be accomplished?

WHY is the company pursuing new goals (or continuing to pursue the old)?

HOW will the goals be achieved?

THE MANAGER'S USE FOR A BUSINESS PLAN

A business plan may be prepared by a manager or an accountant. For a small mom-and-pop business, a business plan prepared by an accountant will cost from a few hundred to several thousand dollars; Small Business Development Centers in many cities will assist small businesses (or prospective entrepreneurs) in preparing a business plan as part of a loan application. Either way, however, the manager must set the goals, make the strategic decisions, and compile the data to be used by the accountant. The accountant can prepare a schedule of cash collections, for instance, but the manager must first decide "credit sales of the new product will be $40,000 next April and we expect customers to pay in 30 days, with an estimated 2% bad debt loss."

A company benefits from the preparation of a business plan even when no additional financing is needed. Once the plan is prepared, managers of a company will find it invaluable as both a reference and a guide. A business plan is the road map the company can follow to success (it hopes). No prudent person would take a trip without an intended destination and a map showing the route to be followed and the terrain to be encountered. Similarly, no prudent manager should direct a company without a well-thought-out business plan that establishes goals to be reached and the route for reaching them. A business plan, like a road map, helps:

1. identify and locate a desired destination or goal
2. evaluate alternative routes to the goal
3. plan progress toward the goal
4. compare actual progress toward the goal to planned progress
5. communicate the goal, the planned route, and the actual progress to others

The data accumulated and the decisions made while preparing a business plan help managers evaluate the feasibility of a new business venture, evaluate alternative ventures, and deal responsibly with lenders by selecting appropriate financing and supporting assertions of creditworthiness.

Evaluating Feasibility

A business plan forces a manager to forecast financial and non-financial operating needs for the life of a proposed project (or at least three to five years). The manager must not only be certain that a project will be profitable and return positive cash flows but must also must demonstrate that it is reasonable to believe that the cash will be available when the debt and other payments are due. The business plan should state exactly how personnel needs will be met; personnel with adequate skills must be available when needed without depriving other operations. The business plan should also state exactly which facilities will be used and at what cost. It is not enough to say "we will use present employees and existing facilities"; the business plan should state which employees and what portion of existing facilities would be used.

If a suitable, detailed business plan cannot be made, it may signal that the new venture may not be feasible. If management believes, despite the contents of the plan, that the venture is still feasible, at least they make that decision with full knowledge of existing facts. In such a case, managers should decide exactly what factors are encouraging a favorable outlook and reconstruct the plan to reflect those factors. If a convincing business plan cannot be completed for a new venture, it is doubtful that the new venture will be successful.

Evaluating Alternatives

A business plan provides the format not only for evaluating the feasibility of a venture but for preparing cash flow, income, and other projections for two or more alternative projects for comparison. If managers have no other formal method of evaluating alternatives, they can use the business plan format discussed later in the chapter simply by preparing business plans for all alternatives and selecting the proposal that accomplishes management's goals with the least risk.

Projected financial statements can be analyzed using the ratio analysis techniques discussed in Chapters 11 and 12 to determine which alternative yields the most attractive financial results or provides the greatest return on investment to stockholders. Cash flows can be compared to see which alternative requires the least financing or best provides for debt repayment.

Dealing with Lenders

Many lenders require a business plan as part of a company's loan application. The plan assures the lender that company management has carefully studied the activity to be financed and the impact it may have on the company's cash flows, operating results, and financial position. (Continuous monitoring of cash needs also impresses lenders and is discussed in the section that follows.) A well-prepared business plan may enhance the company's prospects of securing financing, casting the application in a much more favorable light than a similar application not so well documented.

In addition to convincing the lender to provide financing, a carefully prepared business plan can help management select the most appropriate souce of financing. A business plan provides a format for analyzing the effect of different forms of debt, with different restrictions and repayment schedules (a note versus a mortgage, for instance) and different proportions of owner- and creditor-supplied capital. Financial leverage, discussed in Chapter 12, changes as the interest rate changes; often a larger proportion of debt to owner financing leads to higher interest rates as lenders see more and more risk of default.

Monitoring Operations and Cash Flows

A business plan can be updated monthly or quarterly to keep managers alert to potential problems. Projections of cash flows and operating results can be revised as conditions change; projected financial statements can be updated; variables that interact can be watched closely (inventory needs might cause cash shortages, for example). As each succeeding month or quarter approaches, cash needs and the results of operations become less and less uncertain and projections more and more certain. Managers can take steps to avoid problems before they occur.

Monitoring cash flows is particularly useful in relations with lenders. Lenders react much more favorably to managers who detect a cash shortage several periods in advance and make arrangements to borrow than to managers who rush in frantically to solve an immediate, unanticipated crisis. Lenders are much more likely to believe projected repayment schedules when the company's cash position is continuously monitored. How much faith, a lender might ask, should be placed in a projection of cash to be available on a proposed loan repayment date if the same managers were not able to anticipate the need for financing?

THE CONTENTS OF A BUSINESS PLAN

There is no set format for preparing a business plan because each company must tell its own story. Companies in different industries must present their plans in the unique context of their environment; a chemical company might need to install special pollution controls on a new building, for example, while an apparel manufacturer might not. Different companies in the same industry may have different goals—growth versus diversification, perhaps; the same company may pursue different goals at start-up than when it is mature and expanding.

Still, all business plans possess some common elements. The following major sections appear in any business plan:

- Business description
- Products and services
- Sales and marketing plan
- Operating plan
- Financial information (past, present and projected)

Each of these major sections can be expanded to include additional areas (an analysis of financial data, for instance), and other major sections can be added (a personnel or management development plan might be necessary if a large expansion is intended). The detailed business plan format that follows is based, with modifications, on a client loan package used by the Small Business Development Center at Clemson University.

BUILDING A BUSINESS PLAN

There are three main sections to a business plan. First is an executive summary that contains a brief description of the company, its product, and requirements for additional resources. The second section is the detailed business plan that includes economic, marketing, social, and strategic factors that will impact the plan. This section, which also includes the financial data, is the most comprehensive of this part of the business plan. Preparation of the financial data stresses the importance of making and documenting careful assumptions about the objectives of the business plan. The third section of the business plan includes supporting documentation, such as contracts and personal resumes.

I. Executive Summary (not to exceed two typewritten pages)
    A. Company name, address, and phone number
    B. Name(s), address(es), and phone number(s) of all key personnel
    C. Brief description of the business

    D. Brief overview of the market for your product

    E. Brief overview of the strategic actions you plan to take to make your firm a success

    F. Brief description of the managerial and technical experience of key personnel

    G. Brief statement of what the financial needs are and what lender's money would be used for

II. Detailed Business Plan

    A. Background of the type of business you are in

        1. Brief history of the business

        2. Current situation

    B. Your business

        1. What makes your business unique?

        2. How does it create value for others?

        3. Describe the key factors that will dictate the success of your business (i.e., price competitiveness, quality, durability, dependability, technical features)

    C. Market analysis

        1. Who are the potential buyers for your products? (be specific)

        2. What is their motivation to buy from you?

        3. How many customers does the market contain? (How large is the total market?)

        4. What is the potential annual sales volume?

        5. What is the nature of the buying cycle?

            a. Is the product a durable good that lasts for years or a product that is repurchased on a regular basis?

            b. Is the product likely to be purchased only during certain seasons of the year?

        6. Specify the target market—what do you know about the potential customers in your geographic area?

            c. If yours is a consumer product:

        i. What are the product features you feel influence the consumer's buying decision?

        ii. What, if any, research supports your feeling?

        iii. Does the consumer have a preference as to where he/she purchases products? How strong is the preference?

        7. Break-even analysis

            d. What volume of inventory do you need to sell at what price to break even?

            e. How did you set prices?

        8. External market influences: How might each of the following affect the sale or profitability of your product?

Economic Factors
Recession
Inflation
High/low unemployment
Social Factors
Age of customers
Location demographics
Income levels
Size of household
Societal attitudes

D. Competitor analysis
1. Describe each of the following factors and discuss how they will influence your success:
a. Existing competitors: Who are they? List major known competitors. Why do you believe the potential customers in your target market buy from them now?
b. Potential firms that might enter the market: Who are they? When and why might they enter the market? What would be the impact in your target market segment if they enter?
c. List the strengths and weaknesses of each competitor's business.

E. Strategic plan for your business
1. How do you plan to market your products to the target market you identified above? Identify your specific marketing strategy on key factors such as pricing, product promotion and advertising, and customer service.
2. How will your products compare to those presently in the market? Compare on a competitor-by-competitor basis.

F. Specifics of your organization and management
1. How is your business organized?
a. Legally (corporation, S corporation, partnership, sole proprietorship)
b. Functionally
2. Who are the key people in your business? What are their backgrounds, and what do they bring to the business that will enhance the chance of success?

G. Financial Plans (tie the response to this question to your production and marketing plan.)
1. How much money do you need to make this product and your business a long-term success?

2. What sources (loans, owner investment, etc.) can be used to finance proposed projects?

3. How will debt be repaid? Include a schedule of projected cash receipts and disbursements by month for the first year and by quarter for the second and third years.

4. Does your past performance indicate that your future activities will be successful? Include current and prior year financial statements. Balance sheets and income statements, as well as tax returns for the past three years, should be included.

5. Do you have assets that can be pledged as collateral for the loan? Include a list of market values for assets (including assets to be purchased).

6. How will proposed projects or expansion affect your financial statements? Include projected income statements and balance sheets for the life of the loan or at least three years, if the term of the loan is shorter. A ratio analysis of current and projected financial statements as discussed in Chapters 11 and 12 may assist a lender in making credit decisions (and demonstrate that you are controlling the business and are aware of its financial condition). Figure 15-1 shows part of a sample business plan for a hypothetical firm.

III. Supporting Documents

A. Supporting documents include personal resumes, personal balance sheets, cost of living budget, credit reports, job descriptions, letters of reference, copies of leases, contract obligations, legal documents, and any other items relevant to the plan.

BUSINESS LOAN APPLICATIONS

The business plan is generally an integral part of a commercial loan application package. If you are preparing a first-time loan application for a financial institution that does not know you or your business, the plan should be much more detailed than if it is being submitted to a lender to whom you are already known. If you know the lender or lenders you wish to approach, it is much more efficient to visit and ask for the necessary application requirements and forms; the business plan can then be tailored to each specific lender's requirements and prepared with sufficient detail to meet all requirements.

The specific requirements of a loan application package vary from lender to lender. Still, some requirements are common to

FIG. 15-1

SAMPLE BUSINESS PLAN

Name and Address of Business: Stop and Shop Market
Grand Avenue East #1000
Apex, N.C. 27502

History of Business: The business was established in 1960 by the current owner, Glenn Jones, who is retiring. Mr. Jones will remain with the business for a period of one year to assure smooth transfer of ownership and continued customer support. Sales of the business have been growing slowly and steadily in the past 5 years (at a rate of 10 percent per year), gross profit margins have remained stable, and suppliers are strong.

Plan of Operation: Mr. and Mrs. King have observed the operation of Stop and Shop for the past six months and believe that no major changes in the current operation are warranted.

Sales Plan:
1. Current hours of 7 AM thru 10 PM will be maintained seven (7) days a week.
2. Product line will be extended slowly to include fresh coffee and lunch sandwiches, more quick-stop items, and larger bread and milk selections.
3. Advertising will be increased, with the help of co-op advertisers.
4. Interior and exterior remodeling will be postponed until ownership transfer is complete and the customers are comfortable with the new ownership.

Cost Reductions:
1. Mr. and Mrs. King will manage the store, thus eliminating the position of store manager for the current time.
2. Gross profit margins will be increased with quantity purchases and special incentive product purchases.
3. Close watch will be maintained on inventory to assure that no stale inventory occurs.

Market Potential: The population growth potential of the five-mile radius surrounding Stop and Shop has been estimated by the local council of governments at 38 percent per year for the next five years. The highway upgrade of the major thoroughfare will enhance Stop and Shop's accessibility. The targeted sales growth of 15 percent per year can be obtained by the projected growth rate in households in the surrounding area.

The two major competitors of Stop and Shop are located in a less desirable location in the Apex area, one in a deteriorating neighborhood and one whose accessibility will be limited by new highway construction to take place in the next eighteen months. Clearly, Stop and Shop will be able to draw some market from these two stores.

Managerial Capacity: Mr. and Mrs. King have previous managerial experience in operating the Hot Spot Convenience Store in Morganton, N.C. for ten (10) years. They served as co-managers for the business, employing a total of seven other employees, handling all facets of this business operation. This included personnel hiring and management; bookkeeping and financial statements; inventory control; and purchasing.

nearly all loan application packages. The components below appear in most loan application packages:[2]

Business Loan Application Components

1. Introductory statement or cover letter including the amount, purpose, and repayment schedule for the financing needed.
2. Summary of application, containing essentially the Executive Summary from the business plan, plus the security or collateral to be provided.
3. Personal information, including resumes, personal financial statements (see Chapter 19), credit references, and tax returns for all officers, directors, and major stockholders or owners.
4. Company information, consisting primarily of the company's business plan, as outlined above.
5. Projections of profits, cash flows and balance sheets, as described in Section II, Part G of the business plan.

PERSONAL LOAN APPLICATIONS

The owner's personal loan application is required as part of many small-business loan applications. The lender depends on the creditworthiness of the company's owner and expects repayment from the owner if the business is unable to repay the loan. If the company is a corporation, legally limiting the owner's liability, the lender will require the owner to co-sign with the company and accept legal liability for the debt. (The owners of unincorporated businesses are liable for the debts of their companies without co-signing.)

A personal loan application generally requires a personal balance sheet and a personal income and expense sheet. A personal balance sheet asks for all personal assets and liabilities so that the lender can determine the applicant's net worth. (Chapter 19 discusses personal financial statements in great detail and includes a comprehensive example of the preparation of personal financial statements for a hypothetical loan applicant.) An example of a bank loan application form requiring a personal balance sheet and personal income and expenses is shown in Figure 15-2.

---

[2]These components are taken from the sample loan package outline on page 29 of *Small Business Reporter (Business Financing),* published by the Bank of America, San Francisco, CA, in 1988.

FIG. 15-2 *Bank loan application form requesting personal balance sheet and income/expense data.*

Generally, when the borrower has collateral to back up the loan application, the following loan-to-value guidelines establish the upper limits on the amounts lent to both individuals and companies.

Asset	Loan to Value Ratio (upper limit)
Developed real estate	75 - 80%
Undeveloped real estate	50 - 80%
Inventory (of real property)	35 - 50%
New equipment	70 - 90%
Used equipment	- 50%
Accounts receivable	70 - 75%

CHAPTER PERSPECTIVE

The general contents of a comprehensive business plan include a business description, a discussion of products and services, a sales and marketing plan, an operating plan, and detailed financial information, including past, present, and projected financial statements. Each of these sections can be expanded to include additional areas, and other sections such as a personnel or management development plan, can be added. This chapter has discussed the business plan both as a vital element in a business loan application and as a tool that allows management to monitor and control operations, examine the feasibility of proposed projects, and choose between alternative projects. The chapter ended with a brief discussion of personal loan applications, often required of the owner as part of the loan application for a small, privately held business. A personal loan application generally requires a personal balance sheet and an itemized statement of personal income and expenses.

Performance Reports: Evaluation and Analysis

INTRODUCTION AND MAIN POINTS

In Chapters 13 and 14 we covered budgeting and standard costing, two managerial tools used for profit planning and control. Chapter 13 dealt with the preparation of a master budget detailing a company's plans and goals for the future; Chapter 14 discussed the use of standard costing and flexible budgeting in evaluating and controlling actual costs incurred during the period and introduced the performance report in the context of comparing actual and budgeted costs.

However, as companies become more decentralized, it becomes essential for management to be able to evaluate performance on a departmental or divisional level. In this chapter we discuss some of the methods and guidelines used to evaluate the performance of a company's departments or divisions.

After reading and studying this chapter:

▬ You will understand the purpose and structure of performance reports.

▬ You will understand the definition and advantages of responsibility accounting and be able to identify responsibility centers.

▬ You will understand how segments of an organization are evaluated using the contribution approach, return on investment, and residual income.

PURPOSE AND STRUCTURE OF PERFORMANCE REPORTS

In Chapter 13 we introduced the master budget, management's quantitative plan of action to achieve company objectives. *Performance reports* present the assessment of performance of a company's operational activities. Many times these reports consist of comparisons of budgeted and actual results. In Chapter 14 we presented the *flexible budget,* a comparison of budgeted to actual results, as an example of a performance report. We noted at that time that the comparison of budgeted goals to actual results was an important factor in evaluating performance and identifying the need for corrective action. A simplified flexible budget performance report comparing budgeted amounts to actual results appears in Figure 16-1.

	Actual	Budgeted	Variance
Sales	$100,000	$150,000	($50,000) U
Variable Expenses	60,000	97,500	37,500 F
Fixed Expenses	18,000	16,000	(2,000) U
Total Expenses	78,000	113,500	35,500) U
Operating Income	$ 22,000	$ 36,500	($14,500) U

FIG 16-1 *Income Statement Performance Report for the Period Ended September 30, 1991*

Variances, described as favorable or unfavorable, are highlighted when actual activities differ from initial expectations. Since actual sales were $50,000 less than budgeted sales (an unfavorable variance), there was a decrease in net income, about which management should be concerned. The marketing department needs to be concerned as to whether the budget figure was unrealistic or whether sales personnel did an inadequate job of selling the company's products. Actual variable expenses were less than budgeted, resulting in a favorable variance. This variance might have been caused by reduced sales; if this is the case, the variance is really not favorable. Fixed expenses exceeded the budget by $2,000; management needs to examine the elements of both fixed and variable expenses to decide what action, if any, needs to be taken.

This simplified example demonstrates how management uses performance reports to monitor operations and identify areas requiring corrective action. The performance report on budget to actual results is used as a planning and control device to guide the company in its efforts to improve profitability. Other forms of performance reports used in the evaluation of the operating processes of a company will be discussed in this chapter.

Some employees have negative feelings towards the budgetary process because they fear performance evaluations. Employees, as well as managers, should be made aware of the purpose of performance evaluations; that is, their preparation is designed to identify areas needing management's attention. They are not designed to assess blame or fault. The central idea is to identify problem areas and turn unfavorable variances into favorable ones.

To be of any use, performance reports must be prepared and disseminated in a timely fashion. If too long a time elapses before issuance of the report, corrective action may not be feasible and unfavorable variances will not be eliminated in the future.

Characteristically, a performance report focuses on *management by exception,* a strategy in which attention is directed only to activities that deviate from expectations on the assumption that managers have little time to waste examining operations that are running smoothly. Therefore, attention is directed only to those areas not performing according to plan.

Performance reports involve layers of summary data; a manager receives detailed information on performance below his level, but summarized data for higher management levels. Figure 16-2 presents a performance report showing the effects of this summarization process. As we move up the chain of command there is a greater summarization of the results of operations.

Refer to the report for the Chicago store manager in the bottom third of the exhibit. A basic question regarding this report is "What items should the store manager be held accountable for?" Should the manager be held responsible for noncontrollable costs such as depreciation, insurance, and property taxes? Many management authorities believe that if a manager cannot influence these types of costs in the short run, then he or she should not be held accountable for these costs. These experts advocate including in the performance report only those costs that are controllable by the manager in the short run. Others favor a more inclusive approach to the preparation of performance reports; they feel that by including all costs in the preparation of performance report managers are made more aware of the fact that in the final analysis both controllable and noncontrollable costs need to be recovered in order for the company to be profitable. Both formats are used in practice, and one is not necessarily better than the other. The choice is one of personal preference and should be made on the basis of which format is consistent with the goals and objectives of the company's responsibility accounting system.

Soft Hackle Company

Operating Income of Branches and District Direct Expenses:	Midwest District Manager Performance Report		
	Budget	Actual	Variance
Illinois Branch	$110,000	$111,000	$ 1,000 F
Iowa Branch	97,000	84,600	12,400 U
Nebraska Branch	103,400	105,500	2,100 F
District Office Expenses	(67,600)	(69,000)	1,400 U
Operating Income	$242,800	$232,100	$10,700 U

Operating Income of Stores and Branch	Illinois Branch Manager Performance Report		
Direct Expenses:	Budget	Actual	Variance
Chicago Store	$ 16,600	$ 14,800	$ 1,700 U
Moline Store	46,200	48,000	1,800 F
Springfield Store	67,300	69,700	2,400 F
Branch Office Expenses	(20,000)	(21,500)	1,000 U
Operating Income	$110,000	$111,000	$ 1,000 F

Operating Income of Chicago Store:	Chicago Store Manager Performance Report		
Revenue	$ 30,000	$ 28,000	$ 2,300 U
Selling Expenses	4,700	5,600	900 U
Repairs Expense	500	200	300 F
General Expense	1,600	1,300	300 F
Property Taxes and Insurance Expense	2,000	2,000	-0-
Depreciation Expense	3,000	3,000	-0-
Wages Expense	2,000	1,100	900 F
Operating Income	$ 16,500	$ 14,800	$ 1,700 U

FIG. 16-2 *Performance report for the period ended July 31, 1991*

RESPONSIBILITY ACCOUNTING

Responsibility accounting refers to a system of gathering and revenue and expense information and communicating it to divisions, departments, and individuals by areas of responsibility. Using the responsibility accounting system that incorporates budgeting, standard costs, and variance analysis, top management can delegate decision-making authority to lower management levels and then evaluate performance based on projections.

Benefits of Responsibility Accounting

Perhaps first and foremost, responsibility accounting allows managers to apply the management by exception principle (see Chapter 14), focusing attention only on those activities not proceeding according to plan and spending more time on other broader issues affecting the organization. Responsibility accounting allows managers to delegate authority because it provides management with a method for guiding performance as well as evaluating that performance. Managers are better able to set objectives when they know that the objectives will be used as the yardstick by which their performance will be measured.

Responsibility Centers

Companies that use responsibility accounting develop budgets and performance reports for every component of the company, each of which is called a *responsibility center.* Each responsibility center is a unit that management has decided needs control over its costs, revenues, and/or investment and has its own individual budget. Responsibility centers can be *cost centers, profit centers,* or *investment centers.*

A *cost center* is a unit that is responsible for and reports only costs. Examples include accounting and purchasing departments. These units are not responsible for generating revenue; thus the focus is on control of costs. Performance reports for cost centers report only costs; normally, variance analysis, using standard costs and flexible budgets, are used to measure performance. For example, an accounting department might be evaluated on the cost of processing a certain number of transactions.

Units that are responsible for selling a product can be either profit or investment centers. A *profit center* is responsible for, and reports, revenues, expenses, and income. Examples include the men's or jewelry departments of a large department store. The unit reports revenues less expenses and is normally evaluated using the contribution margin approach (revenues–controllable expenses). (The contribution margin approach is discussed later in this chapter.)

An *investment center* is responsible for, and reports, revenues, expenses, and income, as well as the investment in assets required to support its operations. The Chevrolet division of General Motors and the corporate headquarters division of IBM Corporation are examples of investment centers. In addition to revenues and expense, investment is reported so that a return on investment can be computed. Return on investment and residual income, discussed in the following sections, are the two most popular methods of measuring the performance of an investment center.

SEGMENT ANALYSIS

Most companies measure performance of major segments, which can be divisions, categories of customer, sales territories, or product lines. Decentralization within companies results in the delegation of decision-making to units and individuals at lower levels of the organization. Particular segment managers have varying degrees of autonomy. If a manager has control over only revenue and expenses, the profit center concept is used; on the other hand, if the manager has control over revenues, expenses, and the assets of the segment, the investment center concept is used.

Evaluation Criteria of a Profit Center

Figure 16-3 presents the segment income statement for the Corvis Company, maker of custom fly fishing rods. Corvis makes both bamboo and graphite fly fishing rods and also repairs damaged rods.

	Bamboo Division	Graphite Division	Repair Division	Total for Company
Sales	$230,000	$190,000	$80,000	$500,000
Less: Variable Expenses	168,000	140,000	62,000	360,000
Contribution Margin	62,000	50,000	18,000	130,000
Less: Direct Fixed Expenses	30,000	20,000	10,000	60,000
Segment Margin	$ 32,000	$ 30,000	$ 8,000	70,000
Less: Unallocated Common Fixed Expenses				45,000
Net Income				$ 25,000

FIG. 16-3 *Corvis Company Segment Income Statement for the Period Ended May 31, 1991*

Profit centers such as the Bamboo Division are best evaluated using the *contribution margin approach,* which focuses on the behavior patterns of variable or fixed costs and their controllability by the division. Variable and fixed expenses are separated in Figure 16-3. This is done because fixed expenses generally do not fluctuate with changes in volume and are much less controllable in the short run than variable expenses. *Direct fixed expenses* are those expenses that can be specifically identified with a segment; *common fixed expenses*—those that cannot be specifically associated with a segment—are expenses that would continue to be incurred even if a division were to be closed or eliminated, such as the salary of the president of the Corvis Company. In Figure 16-3, these common fixed expenses are identified as unallocated. Any allocation of these costs could significantly change the operating net income of each of the divisions, and most allocation schemes are arbitrary. However, some companies do attempt to allocate common fixed expenses even though division managers do not have any control over these allocated costs.

There are two methods for allocating common fixed expenses: benefit received or responsibility of incurrence. If neither approach is appropriate, some other reasonable, but arbitrary, basis (such as sales) is used. Assume the following information for Corvis Company:

Item		Basis for Allocation
General Expense	$10,000	Sales
Insurance Expense	20,000	Cost of Segment Assets
Maintenance Expense	15,000	Square Footage
Total Common Fixed Expenses	$45,000	

	Bamboo Division	Graphite Division	Repair Division	Total
Sales	$230,000	$190,000	$80,000	$500,000
Cost of Segment Plant Assets	50,000	30,000	20,000	100,000
Square Footage per Segment	8,000	10,000	12,000	30,000

The allocation of common fixed expenses would be as follows:

	Bamboo Division	Graphite Division	Repair Division	Total
General Expense	(a) $ 4,600	(b) $3,800	(c) $1,600	$10,000
Insurance Expense	(d) 10,000	(e) 6,000	(f) 4,000	20,000

Maintenance
Expense   (g)   4,000   (h)   5,000   (i)   6,000   15,000

Total Common Fixed Expenses $45,000

(a) $230,000/$500,000 × $10,000 = $4,600
(b) $190,000/$500,000 × $10,000 = $3,800
(c) $80,000/$500,000 × $10,000 = $1,600
(d) $50,000/$100,000 × $20,000 = $10,000
(e) $30,000/$100,000 × $20,000 = $6,000
(f) $20,000/$100,000 × $20,000 = $4,000
(g) 8,000/30,000 × $15,000 = $4,000
(h) 10,000/30,000 × $15,000 = $5,000
(i) 12,000/30,000 × $15,000 = $6,000

Summarizing our discussion, the contribution approach for segment reporting and analysis includes the following information:

▬ *Contribution Margin:* sales minus variable costs
▬ *Segment Margin:* contribution margin minus direct fixed expenses. Direct fixed expenses are specifically traceable to a segment and include discretionary fixed expenses such as advertising and research development that would normally be eliminated if the segment were eliminated.
▬ *Net Income:* segment margin minus unallocated common fixed expenses. Unallocated common fixed expenses are those that are not directly traceable to a segment and include depreciation, property taxes, and insurance.

Evaluation Criteria for an Investment Center

Two evaluative criteria used with the investment center concept are *return on investment* and *residual income.*

Return on investment (ROI) calculates return (income) as a percentage of the assets utilized (investment) by a segment. The formula for ROI is:

$$\text{ROI} = \frac{\text{Income}}{\text{Investment}}$$

ROI, rather than absolute amounts of income, is used because a segment with a large amount of assets usually has a greater amount of income than a segment with a small amount of assets. ROI is a more useful measure of performance when the investment bases of segments differ.

The calculation of ROI is relatively simple. However, there

is some disagreement as to the definition of *income* and *investment*. Possible definitions for income include net income, operating income, and segment income, while investment can be defined as total assets, operating assets, or controllable assets. After investment is defined, a choice needs to be whether to use cost, cost less accumulated depreciation, or replacement cost for the investment in assets. Whichever definitions and valuation bases are chosen must be used consistently for comparative purposes.

The ROI formula can be broken down into two components as follows:

$$ROI = \frac{Income}{Sales} \times \frac{Sales}{Investment}$$

This model was developed by financial analysts at E.I. DuPont de Nemours & Co. (hence its name, the DuPont model) in the late 1930s and was introduced briefly in our discussion of ratio analysis in Chapter 11. The basic premise is that both profitability from sales and the efficient employment of assets in generating sales are factors that should be weighed in evaluating the profitability of a company.

The first factor, income/sales, or *margin*, is a measure of the percentage of each sales dollar resulting in income. The second factor, sales/investment, is called *turnover* and represents the efficiency with which a company uses its investment in assets to generate sales.

The point of separating the formula into two components is to emphasize the importance of efficient employment of a company's investment in assets as well as of earning a profit from sales. This can be underscored by an example. In 1990 the average ROI for American companies was approximately 15 percent. Suppose this ROI was achieved by a heavy equipment manufacturer and a grocery chain in the following manner:

	Margin	×	Turnover	=	ROI
Grocery Chain	1%	×	15 times	=	15%
Heavy Equipment Manufacturer	15%	×	1 time	=	15%

By focusing on either margin or turnover or both, management can create a plan to bolster ROI. Assume a company wants to increase ROI to 20 percent from the current 15 percent, computed as follows:

$$ROI = \frac{\$15,000}{\$200,000} \times \frac{\$200,000}{\$100,000} = 15\%$$

ROI can be increased by reducing expenses while holding turnover constant:

$$ROI = \frac{\$20,000}{\$200,000} \times \frac{\$200,000}{\$100,000} = 20\%$$

ROI can also be increased by increasing turnover by decreasing the company's investment in assets and holding margin constant.

$$ROI = \frac{\$15,000}{\$200,000} \times \frac{\$200,000}{\$75,000} = 20\%$$

ROI can be increased by actions that have the effect of increasing both margin and turnover. This can be accomplished by disposing of nonproductive assets. The investment in assets is reduced and income is increased through a reduction of depreciation expense.

$$ROI = \frac{\$19,000}{\$200,000} \times \frac{\$200,000}{\$95,000} = 20\%$$

This third example illustrates the point that excessive investments can have the same effect in terms of reducing ROI as excessive expenses.

If there is a problem with using ROI as a performance measure, it is the tendency of division managers who are evaluated on that basis to accept only those additional investments for which the rate of return exceeds that of the division's ROI. For example, assume a division is earning $20,000 per year on an investment in assets of $100,000. The division ROI is therefore 20 percent ($20,000/$100,000). This 20 percent ROI is above the company's minimum rate of return of 14 percent. If the division manager were presented with a project that would yield 17 percent on a $10,000 investment, the manager would not accept the proposal because it would reduce the division's ROI to 19.7 percent.

	Status Quo	Proposed Project	If Accepted
Income	$ 20,000	$ 1,700	$ 21,700
Investment	100,000	10,000	110,000
ROI ($20,000/$100,000)	20%		
ROI ($21,700/$110,000)			19.7%

In this instance, the division manager has taken an action that is in the manager's own best interest, but the action is not in the best interest of the company as a whole, because the 17 percent return on the project is above the company's minimum rate of return of 14 percent. This situation, called *suboptimization*, can occur when a company uses ROI as its sole criterion for evaluating the performance of a division.

To overcome suboptimization, companies sometimes use *residual income* to measure performance. Residual income is the amount of income that a segment earns on its investment in assets over a desired minimum ROI. Unlike ROI, RI is an absolute dollar amount, calculated as follows:

RI = Income − (Minimum ROI × Investment in Assets)

The division's residual income from our previous example is:

$20,000 − (14% × $100,000) = $6,000

Using RI, a division manager accepts investment proposals as long as the rate earned exceeds the division's minimum ROI, increasing the division's RI. Returning to our previous example, the proposed project provides a higher rate of return (17 percent) than the division's minimum rate of return (14 percent). Acceptance of the project increases RI by $300.

	Status Quo	Proposed Project	If Accepted
Investment in Assets	$100,000	$10,000	$110,000
Minimum Rate of Return 14%	(14,000)	(1,400)	(15,400)
Rate of Return 20%	20,000		20,000
Rate of Return 17%		1,700	1,700
Residual Income	$ 6,000	$ 300	$ 6,300

In conclusion, the use of RI focuses on the maximization of RI, not ROI. Some authorities consider RI to be a better measure of performance than ROI; They believe that the use of RI encourages division managers to accept investment projects that would be rejected if ROI were used. A disadvantage of RI is that it does favor larger divisions with larger investments in assets, making the comparison of segments or divisions of varying sizes very difficult.

CHAPTER PERSPECTIVE

Management's plans are implemented through the budgeting process. Monitoring the difference between actual results and budgeted amounts results in variances. Using the concept of management by exception, performance reports highlight these deviations from expectations, and managers deal only with situations in which a problem exists. Performance reports should be prepared on a timely basis so corrective action can be taken when necessary; employees should not be antagonistic toward performance reports, since they are prepared in an attempt to identify areas needing attention and not to assess blame. Finally, the performance report should focus on items under direct control of the department or individual being reported on.

Responsibility accounting seeks to provide information to evaluate a manager based upon the revenue, expense, or investment items over which he or she has control. Management establishes responsibility centers as part of a responsibility accounting system. Analysis of the performance of a responsibility center depends on the classification of the responsibility center. A center that produces no revenue and only incurs expenses is reported as a cost center and is evaluated on the basis of cost reduction or in relation to a budgeted amount. A profit center earns both revenues and expenses and is therefore evaluated on the basis of income, essentially the difference between the revenues and expenses under the control of the profit center manager. An investment center has revenues, expenses, and an investment base. Two different criteria exist for evaluating an investment center: ROI compares an income figure to an investment base, and RI evaluates performance in terms of how much of investment center income exceeds income based on a minimum rate of return.

INTERNAL AUDIT REPORTS

INTRODUCTION AND MAIN POINTS

Auditors have traditionally examined records or accounts to check their accuracy. Today, auditors are responsible not only for checking the accuracy of accounting records but for checking and reporting on the results of business activities in all areas. We have seen (in Chapter 2) that external auditors express opinions on financial statements included in company annual reports. Internal auditors examine and report on efficiency, effectiveness, and goal attainment in all areas of operation.

In this chapter, we examine the role of internal auditors, the steps involved in an internal audit, and the reports issued by the internal auditor.

After studying the material in this chapter:

▬ You will know the difference between internal and external auditors.

▬ You will know the five aspects of company operations that concern internal auditors.

▬ You will understand the seven steps in the audit process and how the auditor relies on internal control in making the examination.

▬ You will understand the format of the report of the internal auditor and how it is used.

▬ You will see that the internal auditor tries to remain independent and objective even though an employee of the company being audited.

KINDS OF AUDITORS

The original definition of *auditor* was one who listens; an audit in ancient Rome was called a "hearing of the accounts." While traditionally the role of the auditor has been to examine accounting records and check their accuracy, the role of the auditor is currently expanding; auditors are responsible not only for checking accounting records but for checking the results of business operating activities in all areas. Auditors issue two types of reports: external audit reports, discussed in Chapter 2, and internal audit reports.

External Auditors and Financial Statement Audits

The external auditor's audit opinion of published financial statements tells stockholders, creditors, and others outside a company how much they can rely on its financial statements as a basis for making business decisions, such as whether to buy or sell shares of a company's stock, make commercial loans, or extend trade credit necessary to do business with a company. To make these decisions, financial-statement readers need the auditor's assurance of fairness and compliance with generally accepted accounting standards. The external audit report is addressed not to company management but to the stockholders of the company and is publicly circulated; the external auditor is responsible to third parties outside the firm who use the audited financial statements as a basis for making business decisions. External auditors are always Certified Public Accountants (CPAs) and their function is much better known by the public than is that of internal auditors.

Internal Auditors and Operational Audits

If an external auditor acts as the agent of stockholders and creditors, internal auditors are the eyes and ears of a company's management inside the company. In fact, internal auditing is sometimes called *management auditing* or *operational auditing* because, in addition to accounting records, internal auditors check, monitor, and examine the operating activities that managers would check, monitor, and examine if they had the time (and audit skills). In an operational audit, the internal auditor examines business activities and creates reports on those activities to assist management in achieving efficient, effective, goal-directed operations.

External auditors are concerned only with the accuracy of the accounting records. Internal auditors are concerned with the same operating areas—efficiency, effectiveness, and goal attainment—that concern company managers. For example, an internal auditor might examine the operation of the purchasing department to see if bid procedures are being followed and if material is being purchased only from approved buyers and only in grades that meet engineering specifications. A credit department might be audited to see if it has established standards for granting credit and if controls are in place to help assure that those standards are being followed by employees. Sometimes internal auditors give opinions on what they observe, but frequently they report only what they see and express no opinion.

Unlike the CPA, the internal auditor is an employee of the company responsible to management and the board of directors and not to third party financial-statement users. Internal auditors are not required to be licenced, but many are certified as Certified Internal Auditors (CIAs) by the Institute of Internal Auditors (IIA). Internal auditors may also be CPAs or have other credentials as evidence of competence, particularly in data processing. Internal and external auditors are compared in Figure 17-1.

	Internal Auditor	External Auditor
Certification required?	no (CIA optional)	yes (CPA required)
Responsible to third parties?	no	yes
Reports to:	top management and the board	stockholders*
Report contains audit opinion?	sometimes	yes
Reports on fairness of financial statements?	no	yes
Reports on compliance with accounting rules and policies?	yes	yes
Reports on compliance with administrative rules and policies?	yes	no
Reports on efficiency and effectiveness of operations?	yes	no

*The firm's external auditor is selected and retained by the audit committee of the board of directors. The audit committee is composed of outside directors who are not managers of the company.

FIG. 17-1 *Internal Versus External Auditors*

CONDUCTING AN INTERNAL AUDIT

Internal auditors are concerned with five aspects of business operation. (Hereafter, internal auditors and internal audits will

be referred to simply as "auditors" and "audits.") Auditors may
seek to determine:

1. the reliability and integrity of information
2. the extent of management's compliance with company
   policies, plans, and procedures and government laws and
   regulations
3. how well assets are safeguarded
4. the effectiveness and efficiency of operations
5. the extent to which established objectives and goals are
   accomplished.

As a rule, a particular audit is concerned with only one or
two of these aspects, rather than all five. A branch bank might
be audited to determine if assets are safeguarded and if bank
policies and government regulations are being followed, while
a manufacturing plant might be audited to see if operations are
effective and efficient and if company goals are being accomplished. Each audit seeks to address specific management con-
cerns and has specific audit objectives.

An audit generally proceeds in seven steps, in the following
general order:[1]

1. A preliminary survey is performed.
2. An audit program is developed.
3. Field work is performed.
4. Working papers are prepared to document the audit
   findings.
5. Deficiency findings (if any) are prepared.
6. The audit report is written and presented.
7. Any deficiencies found are monitored by the auditor
   until they are resolved.

Preliminary Survey

The internal auditor frequently begins the audit by making a
preliminary survey of the operation to be audited, visiting the
site, interviewing managers and operating personnel, inspecting
operations, and attempting to become familiar with the activity
to be audited. In this stage of the audit, the auditor generally
tries to alleviate any fears the auditees might have by explaining
the scope of the audit—what will be examined and what will

---

[1]The reference book perhaps most used by internal auditors is *Sawyer's
Internal Auditing,* written by Lawrence B. Sawyer and Glenn E. Sumners,
and published in 1988 by the Institute of Internal Auditors. Our discussion
of the internal audit report follows the discussion in the Sawyer text.

not—and explaining that in most cases the auditor is trying to help, rather than to police.

Overall, the internal audit profession is trying to enhance its image by focusing attention on the good that is done, rather than the culprits who are caught. The auditor's goal is to help managers do a better job; as a result, most auditors want to see operations improved, not employees disciplined. Usually, an auditor explains that if a problem is discovered, the manager of the problem area will be told immediately and will have the opportunity to correct or at least to begin correcting the problem before the audit report is issued. In that way, both the problem and the manager's action to correct it can be included in the audit report.

Objectives and Standards. An auditor, whether internal or external, must audit against some standard; when an auditor examines an account balance or an operating activity, the examination is meaningless if there is no standard with which to compare.

Financial-statement data are audited using generally accepted accounting principles as the standard for correct presentation; regulated activities in a bank are audited using federal and state requirements. These standards are readily available for auditors to use in examining financial statements and regulated activities. But what does the auditor do when no standards exist? In such cases, the auditor and the manager of the operation to be audited must establish and agree on standards to be used in the audit.

Sometimes the standards used in an audit are the policies and procedures already in existence for the operation. If there are no policies and procedures, or if they are outdated or incorrect, standards must be established before the audit can be performed. To develop standards against which to audit, the auditor looks first at the goals of the operation and then at the activities that should take place if the goals are to be achieved.

Suppose, for example, that an auditor has been asked to audit a personnel department that has no written policies and procedures (or has them but the auditor desires, as part of the audit, to confirm the adequacy of the policies and procedures followed). In either case, the auditor must determine what standards the personnel department should follow. First, the auditor considers what should be the goals of a personnel department. The auditor may decide (in discussion with the personnel department manager) that one goal is to hire qualified people; another goal may be to maintain employee files; still another may be to provide adequate training.

Limiting our discussion to the first of these goals, we can illustrate how the auditor might determine what procedures would result in hiring qualified people and hence serve as standards against which to audit. After consideration and discussion, the auditor may decide that, to hire qualified people, the personnel department must require applicants to complete application forms listing their qualifications and then must somehow verify that the qualifications are legitimate. Even before that, there must be a job description for each position to be filled; the qualifications necessary to perform the job must be determined. Once those determinations have been made, the auditor has operating standards that can be used to audit the performance of the personnel department in hiring qualified people:

▬ Each position should have a job description that includes the qualifications required for the job.

▬ Each applicant must complete an application form that includes a request for the applicant's qualifications.

▬ The qualifications of each potential new hire must be checked by the personnel department.

▬ The qualifications of each new hire must meet or exceed the qualifications listed in the job description.

Documents supporting the personnel department actions that satisfy each of these operating standards should be in the department files. The auditor does not determine what qualifications are required for a job or whether an applicant is qualified for a job (that is the responsibility of the personnel department), but the auditor *can* decide if the personnel department is following operating procedures that can reasonably be expected to accomplish department goals.

Internal Control. One goal of the preliminary survey is to examine the system of internal control, that is, any policy, procedure, or management action that provides assurance that company objectives will be met. In the example of the personnel department, files must be maintained on each new hire and their content reviewed by a supervisor to be sure that policies are followed. If no files are kept, the auditor cannot evaluate hiring activities; if files are not reviewed, the auditor cannot be certain that all files are complete unless he or she checks each file. Both the maintenance of the files and their regular review are internal control measures.

Some internal controls are designed to provide assurance that policies are followed; others are meant to safeguard assets. We discuss below several internal control measures and explain why they are important.

1. Prenumbered documents:

Many documents are used either to record important information or to authorize certain activities. All documents that management wishes to control should be prenumbered. When documents are prenumbered, management can control their use by requiring employees to account for all documents in their possession. Employees are reluctant to misuse prenumbered documents—by giving a special parking permit to a friend, for example—if they know they must account for all documents in their possession.

2. Separation of incompatible duties:

An error or an intentional fraud is less likely to occur if people must conspire to conceal it than if it can be committed by one person acting alone. To reduce the likelihood of such incidents, an asset such as cash or supplies should be held by one person and the accounting records maintained by another. When such related functions are separated, intentional misstatement of the accounts, either to commit theft or to conceal an error, requires collusion and is less likely to occur.

When incompatible duties are not separated, auditors must do much more checking to be sure that the operating results or account balances are not materially misstated. An auditor examining inventory records maintained by the person who also has custody of the inventory has to examine a bigger sample of the records—perhaps all of them—to be certain that fraud or errors have not caused the inventory account to be misstated. If these functions are separated, less checking is necessary.

Other incompatible functions include ordering and receiving materials, and issuing checks and reconciling the bank balance. In the first instance, the employee can create a bogus order, indicate receipt when no goods were received, and cause a payment to be made to a fictitious supplier. In the second, an employee might issue a check to a fictitious payee and conceal the check when it is returned with the bank statement.

3. Mandatory vacations:

Many fraudulent schemes require constant attention if they are to be concealed. Often, managers are shocked when a fraud is uncovered. "Why, Jane was so devoted to her job! She had not missed a day's work in ten years. She never took vacations and came in sick many times!" Why would Jane miss work? She could not miss work and let someone else do her job without risking exposure of her schemes. Mandatory vacations allow someone new to do each job, making it more difficult to conceal fraudulent activities. If employees must take a periodic vacation, the auditor can be more confident about the accuracy of account balances.

4. Limited access:

Many companies require cards or badges for access to the plant or offices on a "need to know" or "need to go" basis. Access may be limited by:

1. something you know, such as a password
2. something you have, such as a key or a "smart card" (as used in a bank machine) imprinted with an access code
3. something you are, such as a body part (a retina, finger, or hand print)

When preliminary surveys are not needed. When a company has many essentially identical operations, such as branches of a bank or stores in a chain, a single audit program may be used for all operations and no preliminary survey is needed. Also, an audit may be begun without a preliminary visit when the auditor wishes the audit to be a surprise. Surprise counts of cash or audits of some types of records (especially records of cash receipts) are common.

Developing and Performing the Audit Program

The auditor develops a program for the audit based on the observations made and standards developed during the preliminary survey. The audit program includes a list of all tests the auditor wishes to perform; as each test is completed, the auditor documents the results in audit work papers.

An auditor seeking to determine the reliability of accounting information or the extent to which an operation meets certain standards could check every transaction or operating activity. Between audits, however, companies may accumulate millions of separate transactions or operating activities; checking each one is not feasible. Instead, the auditor looks for ways to report on a large volume of activities without checking each individual activity. This is accomplished by examining only a sample of the activities on which the auditor must report. The size of the sample is determined by judgment or statistics based on several factors, among them the kind of internal controls management has placed on the activity. For example, if the files of the personnel department discussed previously are reviewed by a supervisor after each new hire is processed and any errors or omissions are corrected, the auditor can be confident about the operation of the department after checking fewer files than if no supervisory review is made.

Deficiency Findings

A deficiency is anything that is not as it should be. Generally, deficiencies are required actions not taken, required actions taken improperly, or prohibited actions taken. Auditors classify deficiencies in three categories:

1. A *major deficiency* is one that can prevent the company from attaining a major goal. Failing to perform background checks of workers hired to work in sensitive areas is a major deficiency; a dishonest employee might steal information (or cash or whatever is sensitive).

2. A *minor deficiency* is one that is more than a random error but which would not prevent the company from attaining a major goal. Failing to file all the references of workers is a minor deficiency.

3. *Insignificant deviations* are random errors of the sort all people make occasionally. Filing a worker's references in the wrong file is an insignificant deviation.

For each deficiency discovered, the auditor completes a deficiency finding report that includes the following items:
- The *standard* the operation was supposed to meet
- The actual *condition* of the operation (what was actually accomplished)
- The *procedures* that should have been followed
- The *cause* of the departure from standard
- The *effect* of the departure from standard
- A *conclusion* as to what needs to be corrected
- A *recommendation* as to how the correction might be made

Auditors are careful to document deficiency findings because major and minor (but never insignificant) findings are probably included in the auditor's report and the person responsible for the problem frequently challenges the auditor's observation. When challenged, the auditor can then produce documentation in the deficiency finding report. The deficiency finding reports are not given to the auditee, but all major and minor findings are normally included in the final audit report.

The Audit Report

Internal auditors do not submit their reports to people outside the company; as a result, there is no standard report form as there is for a CPA report on published financial statements. The primary purpose of an internal auditor's report is to communicate the auditor's findings to the auditee and the auditee's manager and to make recommendations. The Institute of Internal Auditors recommend that an audit report contain the elements shown in Figure 17-2.

---

1. *Purpose.* The audit report should include the reason the audit was performed, such as "to determine the effectiveness of company policies on hiring new employees."

2. *Scope.* The auditor should explain what was covered by the audit and what was not. The auditor might explain, for instance, that the audit examined compliance with company policies for hiring factory workers but did not include an examination of the hiring policies for engineers.

3. *Audit results.* The report should tell what was found. "Job descriptions specify the qualifications necessary for each position, but those qualifications were not met by 40 percent of the new hires during the last six months."

4. *Recommendations.* The report of a problem should be accompanied by a recommended course of action to correct any problem reported. Perhaps the auditor would recommend that "personnel department employees receive additional training and that supervisors monitor compliance with company policy and document their monitoring activity in the file of each new hire."

5. *Opinions and conclusions (where appropriate).* Audit opinions are the auditor's evaluation of the effects of any deficiencies found, such as: "Compliance with position qualification requirements is inadequate. Failure to hire qualified workers might result in significant cost the company in excess scrap." Although many internal auditors avoid drawing a conclusion or stating their opinion on the activity they audit, managers are frequently curious.

FIG. 17-2 *Contents of an Internal Audit Report*

Generally, the auditor reviews a draft of the audit report with the manager of the activity audited. Since there is no standard language in an internal audit report (as there is in the audit report of a CPA), the auditor can often change any language in the report that offends the auditee, so long as the original meaning of the report is not altered. Responses of the auditee may be included in the audit report if there is disagreement over its content.

Copies of the final report are sent to the auditee, the auditee's superior, and any other person in the company responsible for seeing that the deficiencies found are corrected. Summaries of audit reports and audit findings are increasingly provided to the audit committee of the board of directors. (The audit committee of the board is composed of outside directors, not directors who are also company managers.)

After the audit report is submitted, the auditor monitors deficiencies until either the deficiency is corrected or upper management decides that no correction is necessary because it has decided to accept the risk of the deficiency. A decision to accept the risk of a continuing deficiency is usually based on a cost/benefit analysis that determines that the cost of correcting the problem is greater than the expected benefit from correcting the problem. Management, for instance, might decide not to place a guard at the plant entrance because the expected theft loss is less than the cost of a guard.

INDEPENDENCE

If people are to rely on the auditor's work, the auditor must be independent. Because auditors are employees of the company they audit, they cannot be independent in the same way that an external auditor is independent. An auditor who reports, for example, on the effectiveness of the person who controls the audit department salaries would not be seen as free of bias.

While the auditor cannot be independent of the company as a whole, the auditor can be made independent of the activities audited by having the internal audit department report directly to top management or to the board of directors. Frequently, auditors are protected from pressures because only the audit committee of the board of directors has the authority to dismiss the director of the internal audit department.

CHAPTER PERSPECTIVE

This chapter has discussed internal audit reports. Internal auditors are responsible not only for checking the accuracy of accounting records but for checking the results of business activities in all areas. Internal auditors perform operational audits and report on the efficiency and effectiveness of operations. An internal audit consists of seven steps: the preliminary survey, the audit plan, field work, work paper preparation, deficiency findings, audit reports, and follow-up. This chapter discussed the role of internal auditors in management audits and the format of the report the internal auditor issues. Internal auditors are kept independent of the activities on which they report by having the internal audit department report to a high management level or to the audit committee of the board of directors.

Reports of Governmental and Not-For-Profit Organizations

INTRODUCTION AND MAIN POINTS

While many people may have an interest in the accounting reports discussed in the preceding chapters, all people should be interested in the accounting reports of governmental and not-for-profit organizations. Churches, schools, charities, and federal, state, and local governments all use accounting reports based on the principles discussed in this chapter. We introduce the goals of governmental and not-for-profit accounting and reporting and explain how the methods used meet those goals. The chapter discusses all forms of not-for-profit accounting but concentrates on accounting and reporting for governmental units, using as its model the material published by the Government Finance Officers Association. Once you understand the accounting used by governmental units, you will be able to understand the accounting and reporting methods unique to each type of not-for-profit accounting.

After you have studied the material in this chapter:

■ You will understand how and why governmental and not-for-profit accounting is different from that used by for-profit organizations.

■ You will see how funds are structured and why they are used.

■ You will know the different types of funds used and how each is accounted for.

■ You will understand the special nature of budgeting for governmental and not-for-profit organizations.

■ You will see how budgets for governmental and not-for-profit organizations are recorded in the accounts.

■ You will understand the special nature of encumbrances and how they are used.

■ You will know the parts of the comprehensive annual financial report and how they fit in the financial reporting pyramid.

NOT-FOR-PROFIT ACCOUNTING

Not-for-profit accounting is a separate form of accounting used by governmental units and other entities that do not seek to create a profit from their operations. Organizations of this type include the following:

1. Governmental units, including federal, state, and local governments
2. Schools, colleges, and universities, both public and private
3. Health and welfare organizations, including hospitals and nursing homes
4. Charitable organizations, including such organizations as the United Way and the Red Cross that have restricted service objectives
5. Religious organizations, including churches and church related organizations
6. Private trusts and foundations

Governmental units and other not-for-profit organizations differ from profit-seeking organizations in ways that affect their accounting reports: They do not seek to generate profits and they do not have customers or stockholders to provide financial resources.

The Lack of a Profit Motive

When an organization is formed to create a profit, an annual measure of net income is a good measure of the success of the organization's success in meeting its goals. But what of a not-for-profit organization? Consider these examples. The National Guard is a governmental unit. The National Guard meets, flies planes, drives tanks, and does other things, but it creates no profit. The United Way seeks to help children, battered women, and other people in need of assistance—but it creates no profit. How can an accounting report demonstrate that the National Guard or the United Way is meeting its goals?

Absence of Customers or Stockholders

A profit-oriented company such as Exxon or JC Penney obtains its operating funds ultimately from the investments of its owners and the revenues received from its customers; capital obtained from creditors must be repaid from these two sources. A governmental unit or a not-for-profit organization has no owners or customers in the traditional sense and obtain their resources instead from either taxes (paid involuntarily) or contributions (made voluntarily). In both cases (taxes and contributions), the resource provider does not receive, or expect to receive, a benefit in proportion to the amount of resource provided, paying more taxes brings no more benefit than paying less (or no) taxes. An individual person cannot obtain more or less national defense by increasing or decreasing a personal tax payment; a contributor to the United Way does not expect to receive a dividend from profits (of which there are none).

FOCUS ON GOVERNMENT ACCOUNTING REPORTS

All government and not-for-profit organizations have similar characteristics, but they are also all different in the manner in which their accounting reports are prepared. Our discussion focuses on the similarities of accounting reports for all government and not-for-profit organizations and will address in specifics only the accounting and reporting requirements of governmental units. Once you understand governmental accounting reports, you will be able to understand reports of the various other not-for-profit organizations.

FISCAL RESPONSIBILITY

To understand the accounting reports of governmental units, you must first understand the fiscal responsibilities of governmental administrators. To accomplish this, let us pretend we are back in the days when Marshal Dillon was walking the streets of Dodge City. Let us pretend that the town council has just passed a law against wearing a gun in the saloon. If a cowboy wears a gun in the saloon, Marshal Dillon will fine him $10. All fines collected from gun-wearers are to be used to bury outlaws that Marshal Dillon is forced to shoot. Marshal Dillon carries his own money in his vest. To keep track of the money collected from fining gun-wearers and to avoid mingling it with his own, Marshal Dillon decides to keep the fine money in a cigar box in the bottom drawer of his desk.

Now suppose the town passes another law: Cowboys racing horses down Main Street in a reckless manner will be fined $20. The fines collected from reckless horseracers is to be used to pay the town drunk to remove the horse manure from Main Street. To keep track of the monies collected from fining horseracers, Marshal Dillon keeps that money in a second cigar box in the bottom drawer of his desk. He writes "Gun Fines" on one box and "Horse Fines" on the other and writes all amounts collected or spent on the top of each box.

Marshal Dillon now has fiscal responsibility like that of modern city governments: He receives money from specific sources that is designated for specific purposes. By law, he cannot spend the money received from horseracers to bury dead outlaws, nor can he use the money from gun-wearers to clean the streets. Marshal Dillon has established two cigar box *funds* to assist in keeping the monies from the two sources separate. By putting all fines in the appropriate box rather than mingling finds with his own money and by spending from the appropriate box when he cleans the street or buries an outlaw, Marshal Dillon is able to demonstrate two aspects of fiscal responsibility: He is able to account for all money entrusted to him, and he is able to demonstrate that money collected from each source is spent for the purpose intended by the town council.

These same responsibilities are thrust upon modern-day administrators. They must account for all money entrusted them and assure that money collected for specific purposes is, in fact, spent for those purposes. A gasoline tax may be intended for road maintenance; a sales tax may be levied to fund education; an assessment may be collected to pay for sewer construction. Money from each source is kept in a separate fund to assure that it is spent for its intended purpose and no other.

The Governmental Accounting Standards Board (GASB) Statement 1 says:

A governmental accounting system must make it possible both: (a) to present fairly with full disclosure the financial position and results of financial operations . . . of the governmental unit in conformity with generally accepted accounting principles, and (b) to determine and demonstrate compliance with finance-related legal and contractual provisions.

Marshall Dillon's cigar boxes would enable him to accomplish the GASB Statement 1 goals.

FUND ACCOUNTING

The method of accounting used by Marshal Dillon in our hypothetical situation is called *fund accounting*. Fund accounting, like the accounting used in for-profit operations, is based on the different types of accounts and the way events are recorded. Try thinking of a government entity in terms of properties and property rights: All the economic resources of a governmental unit are owned by someone. The dollar amount of properties must equal the dollar amount of property rights. The basic accounting relationship (called, as in Chapter 2, the accounting equation) can be stated as:

$$\text{Properties} = \text{Property rights}$$

The accounting term for properties owned by the government is *assets*. The two types of claims against the assets of a governmental unit are *liabilities* (to the government's creditors) and any excess of funds over liabilities (which technically belongs to the taxpayers). The excess of assets over liabilities is called *fund balance*. The dollar amount of assets must equal the dollar amount of liabilities plus fund balance, as follows.

$$\text{Property Rights} = \text{Liabilities} + \text{Fund Balance}$$
$$\text{or}$$
$$\text{Assets} = \text{Liabilities} + \text{Fund Balance}$$

This equation shows the relationship of balance sheet accounts in each fund. Just as Marshal Dillon might have had two (or more) cigar boxes to keep separate monies from specific sources intended for specific expenditures, a governmental unit has a number of separate funds, each with a balance sheet structured as shown in the governmental accounting balance sheet equation. Understanding the governmental fund balance sheet equation is fundamental to understanding governmental fund accounting.

The construction of the fund balance sheet provides a system of checks on the accuracy of the fund accounting system for governments, just as accounting does in for-profit organizations. This system of checks is called the *double-entry system* (just as in for-profit accounting in Chapters 1–3), because each economic event must affect the fund balance sheet in two ways to keep the equation in balance. For instance, if a fund is formed with cash of $500,000, two components of the equation, the asset cash and fund balance, must be increased to show the effect of this transaction. If either assets or fund balance is not increased, the equation will not balance.

$$\begin{array}{ccccc} \text{Assets} & = & \text{Liabilities} & + & \text{Fund Balance} \\ +\$500{,}000 & = & 0 & + & \$500{,}000 \end{array}$$

If the fund then borrows another $1,500,000, two more effects must be recorded: Assets are increased by the cash received and the property rights of the bank are recorded.

Assets	=	Liabilities	+	Fund Balance
+$500,000	=	0	+	$500,000
+1,500,000	=		+	1,500,000 + 0

Total $2,000,000 = $1,500,000 + $500,000

If supplies are purchased for $4,000, cash must be decreased and the asset "supplies" increased. One asset is traded for another of equal value, and the equation still balances. When a loan is repaid, cash is decreased and a liability is decreased. Whenever one account is increased, another must be decreased to keep the equation in balance.

"Due From" and "Due To"

Fund balance sheets often have "Due from" and "Due to" accounts. These accounts are asset and liability accounts that designate receivables from and liabilities to other funds within the government or not-for-profit entity. Suppose a government fund established to receive and spend monies collected from a city transportation system temporarily lends money to the city's general revenue fund. "Due from the General Fund" in the transportation fund balance sheet is a receivable from the general fund. If instead the transportation fund borrows from the general revenue fund, the liability is shown in the transportation fund balance sheet as "Due to the General Fund." "Due from" and "Due to" amounts are different from other assets and liabilities because they do not represent claims from or obligations to entities outside the government. An amount due to the general fund from the transportation fund, for example, does not remove cash from the government; payment of this liability simply transfers cash from one fund to another.

Figure 18-1 shows a balance sheet for a Transportation Special Revenue Fund that contains a "Due to" liability to the general fund. This figure and all others which follow are taken from the 1988 edition of *Governmental Accounting, Auditing and Financial Reporting,* published by the Government Finance Officers Association, 180 N. Michigan Avenue, Suite 800, Chicago, Illinois 60601. This book, referred to as the *GAAFR,* is the authority on the proper form for state and local government accounting reports.

Revenues and Expenditures

The fees, taxes, and other charges collected by a government fund are called revenues, the same name used for similar items

Name of Government
Transportation Special Revenue Fund
Comparative Balance Sheets
December 31, 19X8 and 19X7
(amounts expressed in thousands)

	19X8	19X7
Assets		
Cash	$ 65	$ 70
Investments	1,174	706
Interest receivable	1	6
Total assets	$1,240	$782
Liabilities and fund balances		
Liabilities:		
Vouchers payable	$ 332	—
Due to other funds—general fund	—	38
Total liabilities	332	38
Fund balances:		
Reserved for encumbrances	353	—
Unreserved, undesignated	555	$744
Total fund balances	908	744
Total liabilities and fund balances	$1,240	$782

Transportation Special Revenue Fund
Comparative Statements of Revenues, Expenditures and
Changes in Fund Balances
For the fiscal years ended December 31, 19X8 and 19X7
(amounts expressed in thousands)

	19X8	19X7
Revenues:		
Motor fuel tax	$729	$355
Intergovernmental	100	—
Interest	77	44
Total revenues	906	399
Expenditures:		
Current:		
Highways and streets	742	—
Excess of revenues over expenditures	164	399
Fund balances, January 1	744	345
Fund balances, December 31	$908	$744

The notes to the financial statements are an integral part of this statement.

FIG. 18-1 *Governmental fund*

Source: Government Finance Officers Association

in a for-profit organization, but the outflows are called expenditures, rather than expenses. The expanded governmental balance sheet equation, including revenues and expenditures, is shown below.

$$\text{Assets} =$$
$$\text{Liabilities} + \text{Fund Balance} + \text{Revenues} -$$
$$\text{Expenditures}$$

Since government funds do not create net income, there is no income statement. Still, the relationship between resources received and expended is useful to both taxpayers and government administrators. As a result, instead of an income statement, funds publish a Statement of Revenues, Expenditures, and Changes in Fund Balance, as shown in Figure 18-1.

APPROPRIATIONS AND BUDGETARY ACCOUNTS
Another way administrators fulfill their fiduciary responsibilities is through a system of budgetary accounts unique to government and not-for-profit organizations. We saw in Chapters 13 to 15 that the budget and the budgeting process for profit-oriented organizations is an elaborate planning and controlling process. For a profit-oriented organization, budgets are only guidelines and are not recorded in the accounts. In governmental and not-for-profit accounting, budgets are not only guidelines; they are both an authorization to spend for some purpose and a legal maximum that can be spent. The budget amounts are recorded in the accounting system of government and not-for-profit organizations.

At the first of each year, both the estimated revenues to be received and the amounts appropriated to be spent are recorded in the accounting system. Estimated revenues are not assets, but they are recorded in the accounting system as though they are; appropriations are not liabilities, but they are recorded as though they are. Estimated revenues and appropriations are recorded in a self-balancing system of accounts separate from the actual assets and liabilities (shown previously in the governmental balance sheet equation).

If a governmental unit expects to receive estimated revenues greater than its appropriated expenditures, fund balance will increase; if estimated revenues are less than appropriated expenditures, fund balance will decrease. The self-balancing budgetary accounts interact as shown below (the governmental balance sheet equation is shown for contrast). The budgetary accounts show what inflows and outflows are authorized and expected. The balance sheet shows what assets, liabilities, and fund balance actually are.

Budgetary Account Equation
Estimated Revenues =
Appropriations + Change in Fund Balance
Governmental Balance Sheet Equation
Assets = Liabilities + Fund Balance

Just as each fund is a separate balance sheet, each fund has separate self-balancing budgetary accounts showing the estimated revenues to be collected, appropriations to be spent, and the effect on fund balance. If a fund is expected to collect revenues of $100,000 and to have authorized appropriations of $80,000, the budgetary account equation appears as:

Estimated Revenues =
Appropriations + Change in Fund Balance
$100,000 = $80,000 + $20,000

Figure 18-2 shows a Comparative Statement of Revenues, Expenditures and Changes in Fund Balance—Budget and Actual for the Transportation Special Revenue Fund shown in Figure 18-1. This figure is also taken from the Government Finance Officers Association's *GAAFR*.

ENCUMBRANCES

Because the $80,000 appropriation above is both an authorization to spend and a maximum that can be legally spent, government administrators will likely want to spend the entire $80,000 but will be fearful of spending more than is authorized and violating their fiduciary responsibilities. As a result, many funds use a system of encumbrances to help assure that they do not overspend.

We illustrate the operation of an encumbrance system for the hypothetical fund above. Let us assume $55,000 is spent on operating activities and an order for $6,000 of supplies is placed, but the supplies are not yet received. How much more can the fund spend? An administrator examining the books sees only the appropriation of $80,000 and expenditures of $55,000 and may well assume that $25,000 of the budget is still available.

But this is not true: $6,000 has been committed for the supplies ordered but not received.

To prevent the $6,000 order from being overlooked or forgotten, the amount of the order is "encumbered," that is, it is recorded in the *budgetary* accounts and acts like an expenditure in that it reduces the balance of appropriations available to be spent. Accountants periodically provide a report to administrations on the unencumbered balance of each appropriation. Such a report for the hypothetical fund in our illustration follows.

Hypothetical Fund
Schedule of Unencumbered
Appropriation
Balance
As of March 31, 19XX

Appropriations	$80,000
Expenditures	55,000
Unexpended Balance	$25,000
Encumbrances	6,000
Unencumbered Balance	$19,000

Reserve for Encumbrances

Unlike expenditures, encumbrances are not shown as a deduction from revenues in a fund Statement of Revenues, Expenditures, and Changes in Fund Balance. Financial-statement readers are alerted to the presence of encumbrances by a Reserve for Encumbrances set aside in the fund balance sheet. The logic here is that fund balance is equal to assets minus liabilities and represents the unexpended, unrestricted funds available to be used. Since, in fact, a portion of the fund balance does not represent assets available to be expended, the amount of the fund balance needed to cover the encumbrance is shown in the Reserve for Encumbrances account. When the purchase order that caused the obligation to be created is processed and the purchased items are received, an expenditure is created, reducing fund balance, and the encumbrance removed. Our hypothetical fund balance sheet would show fund balance reduced by a $6,000 Reserve for Encumbrance because of the supply order not yet received and paid for.

Other Reserves of Fund Balance

In addition to the reserve for encumbrances, fund balance is reserved in several other cases in which the fund balance does not represent expendable resources. One example of this is the Reserve for Inventories, which designates the portion of fund balance not available to be expended because a portion of the assets are invested in inventories of supplies that will be consumed rather than converted to cash and expended in support of fund activities.

TYPES OF FUNDS

The funds we have discussed thus far focus on the collection and spending of financial resources and are unique to governmental and not-for-profit organizations. There are, in fact, three broad categories of fund types: governmental, proprietary, and fiduciary funds. Two of these—governmental and fiduciary funds—are *spending-focus* funds, which function as we have explained in this chapter. The third broad category of funds, proprietary funds, is used to account for profit activities of governments (such as utility companies) and are accounted for just as profit-oriented companies account for their activities, as explained in Chapters 1 to 8.

Within each broad category of funds, there are different fund types.

Governmental Funds

Governmental funds are spending-focus funds that are concerned with the flow of current financial resources. There are four types of governmental funds:

1. *The general fund:* Used to account for all financial resources not accounted for in other funds.
2. *Special revenue funds:* Used to account for revenues received from specific sources and legally designated to be spent on specific purposes.
3. *Capital projects funds:* Used to account for monies to be spent on acquiring or constructing major capital projects, such as a civic center or new courthouse.
4. *Debt-service funds:* Used to account for the accumulation of resources to be used for the payment of general long-term debt.

18-1, which shows a special revenue fund for transportation, is an example of a governmental fund. All governmental funds have a statement showing revenues, expenditures, and change in fund balance and a balance sheet showing the resources (assets), obligations (liabilities), and fund balance.

Proprietary Funds

Proprietary funds are profit-focused funds that are concerned with the flow of economic resources, not just the spending of money. There are two types of proprietary funds:

1. *Enterprise funds:* Used to account for operations with operating goals similar to private, for-profit organizations. In these funds, unlike the governmental funds just discussed, a measure of profit (revenues versus expenses) is necessary for control.

2. *Internal service funds:* Used to account for a department that provides goods or services to another department on a cost or cost-plus-reimbursement basis such that the relationship between revenues and expenses is so important that for-profit accounting methods are used. A university, for example, may establish a motor pool with the idea that the motor pool will furnish cars and vans for faculty and students to use on university business and that the charges for vehicles will cover the cost of the motor pool. After an initial investment, the motor pool will operate as if it is a for-profit operation: user departments will be charged for vehicle use and these charges will cover the cost of motor pool operations. Because the motor pool must operate as if it is a for-profit operation, governmental accounting procedures that focus on spending and fiscal responsibility are not enough. Financial statements like those used by for-profit operations are necessary.

An example of a proprietary fund is contained in Figure 18-2, which shows operating statements for an internal service fund for a department supplying management information systems to other departments.

Fiduciary Funds

Fiduciary funds are both spending-focus and profit-focused funds that are concerned with the flow of current financial resources and economic resources. There is only one type of fiduciary fund, called a *trust and agency fund,* used to account for assets they hold as a trustee. An example of a trust and agency fund for a fund acting as trustee for funds intended to provide perpetual care is shown in Figure 18-3.

Name of Government
Management Information Systems Internal Service Fund
Comparative Statements of Revenues, Expenses and Changes
in Retained Earnings
For the fiscal years ended December 31, 19X8 and 19X7
(amounts expressed in thousands)

	19X8	19X7
Revenues:		
Charges for services	$593	$452
Operating expenses:		
Costs of services	374	341
Administration	64	58
Depreciation	92	83
Total operating expenses	530	482
Operating income (loss)	63	(30)
Nonoperating revenues:		
Interest	2	1
Net income (loss)	65	(29)
Retained earnings, January 1	296	325
Retained earnings, December 31	$361	$296

Name of Government
Management Information Systems Internal Service Fund
Comparative Statement of Changes in Financial Position
For the fiscal years ended December 31, 19X8 and 19X7
(amounts expressed in thousands)

	19X8	19X7
Cash flows from operating activities:		
Cash received from users	$643	$452
Cash paid to suppliers and employees	(506)	(385)
Interest received	2	1
Net cash provided by operating activities	139	68
Cash flows from investing activities:		
Purchase of investments	(33)	—
Purchase of fixed assets	(67)	(90)
Net cash used in investing activities	(100)	(90)
Cash flows from financing activities:		
Advance from other funds—general fund	20	—
Net cash provided by financing activities	20	—
Net increase (decrease) in cash	59	(22)
Cash, January 1	5	27
Cash, December 31	$ 64	$ 5

Reconciliation of Net Income to Net Cash Provided by
Operating Activities

	19X8	19X7
Net income (loss)	$ 65	$(29)
Adjustments to reconcile net income to		
net cash provided by operating activities:		
Depreciation expense	92	83
Decrease in due from general fund	41	—
Decrease in due from water and sewer fund	9	—
Increase in compensated absences	5	2
Increase (decrease) in accounts payable	(73)	12
Total adjustments	74	97
Net cash provided by operating activities	$139	$ 68

The notes to the financial statements are an integral part of this statement.

FIG. 18-2 *Proprietary fund*

Source: Government Finance Officers Association

Name of Government
Perpetual Care Nonexpendable Trust Fund
Comparative Balance Sheets
December 31, 19X8 and 19X7
(amounts expressed in thousands)

	19X8	19X7
Assets		
Cash	$ 231	$ 16
Investments	1,753	1,848
Interest receivable	82	41
Total assets	$2,066	$1,905
Liabilities and fund balances		
Liabilities:		
Accounts payable	$ 13	$ 18
Fund balances:		
Reserved for perpetual care	1,193	1,102
Unreserved, undesignated	860	785
Total fund balances	2,053	1,887
Total liabilities and fund balances	$2,066	$1,905

Name of Government
Perpetual Care Nonexpendable Trust Fund
Comparative Statements of Revenues, Expenses and
Changes in Fund Balances
For the fiscal years ended December 31, 19X8 and 19X7
(amounts expressed in thousands)

	19X8	19X7
Operating revenues:		
Interest	$ 41	$ 141
Operating expenses:		
Costs of sales and services	13	144
Operating income (loss)	28	(3)
Nonoperating revenues:		
Gain on the sale of investments	138	57
Net income	166	54
Fund balances, January 1	1,887	1,833
Fund balances, December 31	$2,053	$1,887

The notes to the financial statements are an integral part of this statement.

FIG. 18-3 *Fiduciary fund*

Source: Government Finance Officers Association

Name of Government
Comparative Schedules of General Fixed Assets
By Source
December 31, 19X8 and 19X7
(amounts expressed in thousands)

	19X8	19X7
General fixed assets:		
Land	$39,333	$38,775
Buildings	8,291	7,875
Improvements other than buildings	4,604	4,604
Machinery and equipment	4,376	7,401
Construction in progress	2,308	722
Total general fixed assets	$58,912	$59,377
Investment in general fixed assets by source:		
General fund	$ 8,801	$11,744
Special revenue funds	3,873	3,497
Capital projects funds	44,531	42,442
Donations	1,707	1,694
Total investment in general fixed assets	$58,912	$59,377

FIG. 18-4 *Fixed asset account group*

Source: Government Finance Officers Association

THE
COMPREHENSIVE
ANNUAL
FINANCIAL
REPORT

CONDENSED
SUMMARY
DATA

GENERAL PURPOSE
FINANCIAL STATEMENTS
(COMBINED
STATEMENTS -
OVERVIEW)

GENERAL
PURPOSE
FINANCIAL
STATEMENTS

COMBINING STATEMENTS -
BY FUND TYPE

INDIVIDUAL FUND AND ACCOUNT GROUP
STATEMENTS

SCHEDULES

TRANSACTION DATA
(THE ACCOUNTING SYSTEM)

— Required
- - May be necessary

FIG. 18-5 *The financial reporting "pyramid"*

Source: Government Finance Officers Association

Fixed Assets and Long-Term Debt

Long-term debt and fixed assets are accounted for in the financial statements of proprietary (for-profit) funds just as they are in for-profit organizations. But spending-focus governmental funds concentrate solely on expendable resources and do not include either long-term debt or fixed assets in their financial statements. Instead, these items are disclosed in two self-balancing account groups not considered to be funds: the *General Fixed Asset Account Group* and the *General Long Term Debt Account Group*. An example of the General Fixed Asset Account Group is shown in Figure 18-4.

COMPREHENSIVE ANNUAL FINANCIAL REPORT

Every government is required to prepare a comprehensive annual financial report, identified by the acronym CAFR in the Government Finance Officers Association's *GAAFR*. The CAFR contains three sections:

1. Introduction
2. Financial
3. Statistical

This report is intended to provide the comprehensive information that might be needed by the most demanding reader of governmental financial reports. The CAFR contains the general purpose financial statements, in addition to other data. The financial reporting pyramid in Figure 18-5 is reproduced from the Government Finance Officers Association *GAAFR*.

CHAPTER PERSPECTIVE

This chapter introduced the goals of governmental and not-for-profit accounting and reporting and explained how the methods used meet those goals. The chapter discussed all forms of not-for-profit accounting but concentrated on accounting and reporting for governmental units, using as its model the material published by the Government Finance Officers Association. Once you understand the accounting sytsem used by governmental units, you are able to understand the accounting and reporting methods unique to each type of not-for-profit accounting. The chapter explained how funds are structured and used, including the special nature of budgeting and budgetary accounts and encumbrances. Finally, the comprehensive annual financial report and the financial reporting pyramid was introduced.

Personal Financial Statements

CHAPTER

19

INTRODUCTION AND MAIN POINTS

Personal financial statements may be prepared for an individual, a married couple, or a family and are used for financial planning, tax planning, obtaining credit, or complying with the disclosure requirements of a regulatory body (as many public officials must do).

Prior to 1968 many political candidates prepared their personal financial statements on either a cost or current value basis; there were no generally accepted accounting principles governing the preparation of those statements. Then, in 1968, the American Institute of Certified Public Accountants (AICPA) issued *Industry Audit Guide, Audits of Personal Financial Statements,* which required that these statements be prepared on a cost basis with supplementary disclosure of current values.[1] In 1982, the AICPA revised its position, asserting that because current values provide more relevant information than cost values, personal financial statements should be prepared on an estimated current value basis, with historical cost presented as supplementary information.

After studying the material in this chapter:
- You will know where to find the sources of information used to prepare personal financial statements.
- You will understand the composition of personal financial statements.
- You will know the techniques that can be used to obtain the current values of the assets and liabilities included in personal financial statements.
- You will understand how personal financial statements are prepared.

---

[1]*Industry Audit Guide, Audits of Personal Financial Statements* (New York: American Institute of Certified Public Accounts, 1968)

━ You will know what additional information should be disclosed in personal financial statements.

SOURCES OF INFORMATION FOR PERSONAL FINANCIAL STATEMENTS

The sources of information necessary to prepare personal financial statements include bank, brokerage, and property tax statements; tax returns; insurance policies; wills; prenuptial agreements; and decrees of divorce. If an individual has an ownership interest (investment in stocks or bonds) in a closely-held entity (the stock of which is not actively traded), the financial statements and tax return of that entity may be a source of information. Other documents, such as titles to assets, may be found in an individual's safe deposit box. The individual, couple, or family is also a source of information for use in preparing the financial statements.

COMPOSITION OF PERSONAL FINANCIAL STATEMENTS

The focus of personal financial statements is on personal assets and liabilities at current value, not on the individual's net income. Personal financial statements consist of a statement of financial condition or a balance sheet at a point in time and an optional statement of net worth that presents the changes in net worth for a period of time. An income statement is not prepared because of the combination of business and personal revenue and expense items.

Statement of Financial Condition

The statement of financial condition presents the estimated current values of assets, the estimated current amounts of liabilities, the estimated income taxes on the differences between the estimated current values of assets and the estimated current amounts of liabilities and their tax bases, and net worth at a specified date. "Net worth" is the difference between total assets and total liabilities, including estimated income taxes on the differences between the estimated current values of assets and the estimated current amounts of liabilities and their tax bases. Generally, assets and liabilities are based on the accrual basis of accounting and are listed in order of liquidity and maturity, without classification as to current or noncurrent.

A statement of financial condition is shown in Figure 19-3 as part of the comprehensive illustration given later in this chapter.

Statement of Changes in Net Worth

The statement of changes in net worth, which is optional, presents the major sources of increases and decreases in net worth, such as income, expenses, changes in the estimated current value of assets, changes in liabilities, and changes in estimated income taxes on the differences between these amounts and their tax bases.

When the statement of changes is included in personal financial statements, it should be broken down into realized and unrealized sections. Realized increases in net worth are the tangible, liquid revenue and income items of the individual for whom the statement is being prepared. These sources include salaries, wages, interest, dividend revenue, rental income, and income from outside business interests. Realized decreases are expenses such as income taxes, interest, and personal expenditures.

Unrealized increases, which are potential, changeable amounts, arise from the increase in current values of assets, decreases in the current value of liabilities, and decreases in the estimated income taxes on the difference between the estimated current value of the assets and the current amounts of the liabilities and their tax bases. Unrealized decreases are caused by decreases in the estimated current values of assets, increases in the estimated current amounts of liabilities, and increases in the estimated income taxes on the differences in current value of assets and the amounts of liabilities and their tax bases.

Assume, for example, that an individual has a parcel of land originally purchased for $100,000. If the market value of the land today is $160,000, the statement of changes in net worth prepared today would include an unrealized increase in net worth of $60,000 relating to the land. If the tax rate is 30 percent, an unrealized decrease in net worth of $18,000 ($60,000 gain × 30 percent) would be included in the estimated income taxes on the difference between the estimated current value of the assets and their tax bases.

A statement of changes in net worth is shown in Figure 19-4 as part of the comprehensive illustration given later in this chapter.

Comparative Financial Statements.

The presentation of comparative financial statements of the current period and one or more prior periods is optional; however, such a presentation is much more informative than financial statements for only a single period.

For instance, a stock investment may represent a significant portion of an individual's assets. If an external event such as the Iraqi invasion of Kuwait has an adverse effect on the stock market and the individual's investment, personal financial statements presented on that date might be misleading because in this case, the statements provide only a picture at one point in time. Comparative financial statements would be more useful because the reader would be able to view each item separately and determine whether the item were growing or decreasing over time, as well as determining the proportion of the change to other items in the statement.

CALCULATING CURRENT VALUES

Theoretically, current value is the agreed-upon price at which an item would be exchanged between a willing buyer and a willing seller. However, when assets do not have a ready market value, determining a current value can be difficult. For instance, stock in a closely-held corporation may not have a market value because the stock, which is owned by a small number of owners, such as a family, is not actively traded. This is why an assortment of techniques is necessary to estimate the current values of assets and liabilities.

The primary techniques for valuing assets and liabilities are based on available current market values, appraisals and valuations by specialists, and discounted (present value) future cash flows. Other, less frequently used, methods include the use of liquidation values, price indexing using the historical cost of assets, and capitalization of past or prospective earnings.

The three primary evaluation techniques can be illustrated by considering a piece of land owned by an individual. Assume the individual paid $10,000 for the land, which is now appraised at $20,000. If developed and rented, the land is expected to create cash inflows of $3,000 for the next ten years. Assume also that the individual has been offered $21,000 for the land by a large industrial company. Assuming an 8 percent annual rate of interest, Figure 19-1 displays values that might be used in the preparation of the statement of financial condition.

Historical Cost	$10,000
Appraisal Value	20,000
Discounted (Present Value) Value of Future Cash Flows ($3,000 per Year for 10 years @ 8 percent)	20,130
Current Resale Value	21,000

FIG. 19-1 *Illustration of Valuation of Possible Current Values for Land in the Statement of Financial Condition*

Discounted Future Cash Flows

We touched on the concept of present value in Chapter 4 in our discussion of bonds. Recall that the present value of a bond is its cash value at a point in time. Discounted cash flow refers to the present value, at a point in time, of a stream of receipts or payments to be received or paid in the future. The receipts or payments pattern is called an *annuity*. The concept of present value is related to the application of compound interest. Earning interest on interest is referred to as compounding. For example, assume that we invest $1,000 in a savings account at a rate of 10 percent compounded annually. The balance in the account after five years would be $1,611 computed as follows

Year	Principal at Beginning of Year (a)	Interest at 10% (b)	Principal at End of Year (a + b)
1	$1,000	$1,000 × 10% = $100	$1,100
2	$1,100	$1,100 × 10% = $110	$1,210
3	$1,210	$1,210 × 10% = $121	$1,331
4	$1,331	$1,331 × 10% = $133	$1,464
5	$1,464	$1,464 × 10% = $147	$1,611

The future value of a $1,000 deposit made today would grow to $1,611 at the end of five years. We can depict this sequence of deposits in the form of a time line as such:

Today	Year 1	Year 2	Year 3	Year 4	Year 5

$1,000 ⟶ invested at an annual rate of ⟶ $1,611
10% grows to

The present value of an amount views the compound interest concept in reverse. That is, the present value of $1,611 to be received in five periods is $1,000.

There are formulas for calculating future and present values. From these formulas factors can be derived and tables prepared. An example of a present value table is presented in Figure 19-2 for ten periods at various interest rates. Many calculators and computer programs include future and present value functions. From the table we can see that the present value factor for 5 periods at 10 percent is .621. Multiplying $1,611 by this factor results in a present value of $1,000 (rounded).

Interest Rate

No. of rate	1%	4%	5%	6%	8%	10%	12%	15%
1	.990	.962	.952	.943	.926	.909	.893	.870
2	.980	.925	.907	.890	.857	.826	.797	.756
3	.971	.890	.864	.840	.794	.751	.712	.658
4	.961	.855	.823	.792	.735	.683	.636	.572
5	.951	.822	.784	.747	.681	.621	.567	.497

FIG. 19-2 *Present Value of $1 Due in N Periods*

The present value of an annuity is simply the combined present values of the individual payments or receipts discounted back to today. Extending our previous example, suppose we wish to know whether we should accept a lump sum of $3,500 today, or five receipts of $1,000 each to be received at the end of each of the periods. The appropriate interest rate is 8 percent. Using the present value factors from Figure 19-2 we can calculate the present value of this annuity to be:

Payments	1	2	3	4	5

Present
Value
$ 926 = ←——— $1,000 × .926

857 = ←————— $1,000 × .857

794 = ←————————— $1,000 × .794

735 = ←——————————————— $1,000 × .735

681 = ←————————————————————— $1,000 × .681

$3,993

Because the present value of the receipts is greater than the lump sum, we would opt to receive the annuity rather than the lump sum.

There are also formulas for calculating the present value of annuities. These formulas can be used to derive factors for an annuity table. Such a table appears in Figure 19-3.

Interest Rate

No. of Rate	1%	4%	5%	6%	8%	10%	12%	15%
1	.990	.962	.952	.943	.926	.909	.893	.870
2	1.970	1.886	1.859	1.833	1.783	1.736	1.690	1.626
3	2.941	2.775	2.723	2.673	2.577	2.487	2.402	2.283
4	3.902	3.630	3.546	3.465	3.312	3.170	3.037	2.855
5	4.853	4.452	4.329	4.212	3.993	3.791	3.605	3.352
6	5.795	5.242	5.076	4.917	4.623	4.355	4.111	3.784
7	6.728	6.002	5.786	5.582	5.206	4.868	4.564	4.160
8	7.652	6.733	6.463	6.210	5.747	5.335	4.968	4.487
9	8.566	7.435	7.108	6.802	6.247	5.759	5.328	4.772
10	9.471	8.111	7.722	7.360	6.710	6.145	5.650	5.019

FIG. 19-3 *Present Value of $1 To Be Received Periodically For N Periods*

Remember we stated earlier that the present value of an annuity was the combined present values of the individual payments or receipts discounted back to today. If we sum the individual present value factors for five periods at 8 percent from the present value table in Figure 19-2, we get 3.993 (.926 + .857 + .794 + .735 + .681). This is the present value factor from the annuity table in Figure 19-3 for five periods at 8 percent.

Referring back to our illustration relating to the land in Figure 19-1, we can calculate the present value of the receipts to be received from renting the property. The rental amount is $3,000 for 10 years and the rate of interest is 8 percent. The present value is $20,130 ($3,000 × 6.710 factor, from Figure 19-3).

Determining Current Market Values

Marketable securities and stock options of publicly traded companies are reported at their market price on the date of the financial statement. If a stock is not actively traded in the open market, the bid price is used. (The bid is the price at which a securities dealer is willing to pay for the stock.) Investments in life insurance are shown at their cash surrender value less any outstanding loans. Intangible assets are shown at appraisal value, anticipated selling price, or the discounted value of future cash flows. If a current value cannot be objectively determinable, historical cost can be used. Real estate can be reported by using either appraisal value or, in some cases, discounted future cash flows. Accounts receivable are normally reported at the discounted value of future cash receipts (flows) using the current rate of interest at the statement date. Accounts receivable of $20,000 due in three months would be discounted as follows if the interest rate were 1 percent per month:

Accounts Receivable Balance × (factor for 1% interest for 3 months) = Discounted Cash Flow
$20,000 × .971 = $19,420

Nonforfeitable rights such as vested pension and profit-sharing benefits, payables and other liabilities (excluding income taxes), and noncancellable commitments such as lease payments are also reported at their discounted future cash flows. Liabilities are presented at the discharge amount (amount needed to pay off or settle the debt) if this amount is lower than the discounted amount. Figure 19-4 summarizes how the values of sample personal financial statement items might be obtained.

Receivables	Discounted cash flow
Marketable securities, bonds, and stock options	Quoted market prices
Life insurance	Cash surrender value minus any outstanding loans
Investment in closely-held companies	Liquidation value, earnings multiple, appraisal value, discounted value of future cash flow, replacement cost, or adjustment to the book value or cost
Investment in land or real estate	Current resale value based on sales of similar property, appraisal value, or discounted value of future cash flow
Intangible assets	Discounted value of future cash flow
Future interests (nonforfeitable rights)	Discounted value of future cash flow
Payables and other liabilities, including noncancelable commitments	Discounted value of future cash flow or discharge amount that amount is less than the discounted amount
Income taxes payable	Unpaid taxes from prior periods and the estimated taxes payable for the current period based on year-to-date taxable income reduced by withholdings and estimated tax payments to date

FIG. 19-4 *Determining the Current Values of Assets and Current Amounts of Liabilities*

"Income taxes payable" is the most complicated of the reported liabilities. In fact, three types of income taxes payable are possible in personal financial statements: income taxes payable for prior years (unpaid income taxes for completed tax years); income taxes estimated to be payable for the current year (estimated income tax for the expired portion of current tax year to the date of the financial statements); and an estimate of income taxes to be paid in the future based on the difference between (a) the estimated current value of an asset or the estimated current amount of a liability and (b) the tax base of the asset or liability at the statement date. The first two types of income taxes payable are reported as a single sum in the liability section of the statement; the third type is computed and reported as if the current value of the assets and liabilities had been realized or liquidated, taking into consideration current tax laws and regulations. The calculation of this component of income taxes payable will be demonstrated later.

Investments in closely-held businesses are difficult to value because normally they lack a ready market value. Consequently, liquidation values, multiples of earnings, and replacement values are used. It is likely that the use of different estimating techniques will result in different estimated current values; the problem lies in determining which of the values is the best estimate of current value, which requires a subjective assessment.

PERSONAL FINANCIAL STATEMENTS: AN ILLUSTRATION

The following information was furnished by Joe and Ann Walka, who own Walkas' Bookstore, as of September 30, 1991:

Assets

1. Mr. and Mrs. Walka's personal checking account had a balance of $26,000.
2. The Walkas held marketable securities of the Zee Company. The 100 shares had cost the Walkas $1,000 and currently had a market value of $55 a share.
3. Dividends receivable from the Zee Company totaled $1,000.
4. Mr. Walka had an IRA with contributions totaling $2,000. The current market value of the account was $2,500.
5. The value of vested pension benefits from Mr. Walka's previous employer was $25,000.
6. Based on several recent sales in their town, the Walkas estimate that the current value of their bookstore business was $75,000. The couple's initial investment in the bookstore was $45,000.
7. The couple purchased their home for $100,000. A recent appraisal valued the residence at $155,000.

8. Personal property had been insured for a replacement cost of $45,000. An estimate of selling price was $35,000. The personal property was purchased for $42,000.

9. The cash surrender value of life insurance was $75,000. Mrs. Walka had borrowed $20,000 against the policy.

10. Real estate had been purchased 2 years ago for $20,000. The market value of similar property was $30,000 on September 30, 1991.

Liabilities

1. Personal debts (including credit cards) totaled $11,000.

2. A personal loan for $5,000 could be extinguished for $4,400 on September 30, 1991. This means the Walkas could pay off the loan early for $4,400 and not have to incur additional interest.

3. The mortgage on the Walkas' home totaled $75,000. The discounted future cash flow of the mortgage is $68,000 based on a 10 percent interest rate.

4. Income taxes payable amounted to $14,000.

Based on this information, the statement of financial condition for Mr. and Mrs. Walka would be as shown in Figure 19-5. Each entry is based on the information items above; cash, for example, is from item 1, marketable securities are from item 2, and so on. Net worth is determined by subtracting the liabilities of $97,400 from the assets of $410,000. You should study this exhibit until you understand how each value was determined.

Assets	
Cash	$ 26,000
Marketable Securities (at market value $55 × 100 shares)	5,500
Dividends Receivable	1,000
Individual Retirement Account (at market value)	2,500
Vested Pension Benefits	25,000
Investment in Closely-held Business, bookstore (at resale value)	75,000
Home (at appraisal value)	155,000
Personal Property (at market value)	35,000
Cash Surrender Value of Life Insurance (less loan of $20,000)	55,000
Real Estate (at market value)	30,000
Total Assets	$410,000

Liabilities and Net Worth

Personal Debts (including credit cards)	$ 11,000
Personal Loan (at cash necessary to extinguish the loan)	4,400
Mortgage payable (at discounted cash flow)	68,000
Income Taxes Payable	14,000
Total Liabilities	97,400
Estimated Income Taxes on the Difference Between the Estimated Current Values of Assets and the Estimated Current Amounts of Liabilities and Their Tax Bases	37,680
Net Worth	274,920
Total Liabilities and Net Worth	$410,000

FIG. 19-5 *Mr. and Mrs. J. Walka Statement of Financial Condition At September 30, 1991*

The estimated current value of the Walkas' total assets is $410,000. Some items are not taxable income nor are they deductible. Gains on the sale of a personal residence are only taxable to the extent that they exceed $125,000 for individuals over 55. If we assume that the Walkas are over age 55, the $55,000 increase in value is not taxable. Decreases in value in personal property such as automobiles and household items are not deductible for income tax purposes. Therefore, the decrease in value of the Walkas' personal property ($7,000) is not deductible. The total amount not subject to tax is $48,000 ($55,000 − $7,000).

The couple can pay off their debts for a total of $97,400. This is the current amount of their liabilities.

The tax bases and cost of the Walkas' assets are as follows:

Assets		Liabilities	
Checking account	$ 26,000	Personal debts	$ 14,000
IRA	-0-	Personal loan	5,000
Marketable securities	1,000	Mortgage payable	75,000
Dividends	-0-	Income taxes payable	14,000
Pension benefits	-0-		$108,000
Bookstore	45,000		
Home	100,000		

Cash surrender value of life insurance	55,000
Real estate	20,000
	$247,000

The calculation of the estimated income taxes on the difference between the estimated current values of assets and the estimated current amounts of liabilities and their tax bases would be as follows:

Assets:

Current value of assets	$410,000
Less: Tax base and cost	247,000
Unrealized increase in value	163,000
Less: Net amounts not subject to tax	48,000
Unrealized increase subject to tax	115,000

Liabilities:

Tax bases of liabilities	108,000
Current amounts	97,400
Unrealized increase in value	10,600
Total appreciation from increase in assets and decrease in liabilities	125,600
Estimated effective tax rate	30%

Estimated income taxes on the difference between the estimated current values of assets and the estimated current amounts of liabilities and their tax bases	$ 37,680

The optional statement of changes in net worth for Mr. and Mrs. Walka is shown in Figure 19-6 and is constructed from the information items in the Statement of Financial Condition.

Realized Increases in Net Worth from:	
Bookstore Net Income	$ 30,000
Dividends	1,000
Total Realized Increases in Net Worth	31,000
Realized Decreases in Net Worth from:	
Personal Expenses	3,400
Interest Expense	9,750
Income Tax Expense	9,700
Property Tax Expense	3,250
Total Realized Decreases in Net Worth	26,100
Net Realized Increase in Net Worth	4,900

Unrealized Increases in Net Worth from:	
Mortgage Payable	7,000
Loan Payable	600
Bookstore	10,000
Home	23,100
Cash Surrender Value of Life Insurance	5,000
Property	12,350
Total Unrealized Increases in Net Worth	58,050
Unrealized Decreases in Net Worth from:	
Personal Property	3,000
Estimated Income Taxes on the Difference Between the Estimated Current Values of Assets and the Estimated Current Amounts of Liabilities Over Their Tax Bases	17,400
Total Unrealized Decreases in Net Worth	20,400
Net Unrealized Increase in Net Worth	37,650
Net Increase in Net Worth	42,550
Beginning of Year Net Worth	232,370
End of Year Net Worth	$274,920

FIG. 19-6 *Mr. and Mrs. J. Walka Statement of Changes in Net Worth For the Year Ended September 30, 1991*

ADDITIONAL DISCLOSURES IN PERSONAL FINANCIAL STATEMENTS

Personal financial statements may require disclosure to augment and amplify other information contained in those statements, just as do corporate financial statements. The disclosures may be made in the body of the financial statements or in the notes and include:

■ the names and relationships of the individuals covered by the statement.

■ the methods and assumptions used to determine the current values of assets and liabilities.

■ any changes in methods and assumptions from those used in a prior year.

■ maturities, interest rates, and other details of any receivables and debt.

■ identification of all intangible assets, along with their useful lives.

■ the names and nature of companies in which the individual has major investments.

■ material investments in closely held businesses, along with the percentage owned, nature of the business, basis of accounting, and summarized financial data for the most recent year.

▬ jointly owned assets, along with the nature of the joint ownership.

▬ the face amount of the life insurance policies owned by the individual.

▬ methods and assumptions employed in computing estimated income taxes.

▬ details as to vested rights in pension and stock ownership plans.

▬ commitments of a noncancelable nature, such as long-term leases.

CHAPTER PERSPECTIVE

Financial statements are prepared for individuals, couples, or family groups at a point in time (perhaps at year-end) on an accrual basis. Unlike those prepared for corporations, however, the statements are prepared using estimated current values for assets and liabilities.

Sources of information used to identify all of the assets and liabilities of the individual include bank statements, brokerage statements, life insurance policies, tax returns, and other documents. After identifying the individual's assets and liabilities, the estimated current values of the assets and amounts of the liabilities are determined based on recent transactions involving similar assets, appraisals, discounted cash flows, price indexing of historical cost, and liquidation values.

The resulting values for assets and liabilities are used to construct the personal financial statements. These statements consist of a statement of financial condition (not including an income statement) and an optional statement of changes in net worth. The statement of financial condition presents the estimated current value amounts of assets and liabilities in their order of liquidity and maturity. The cost or tax basis of the assets and liabilities may be presented as supplemental information; the presentation of comparative financial statements of the current period and one or more prior periods is optional but desirable.

To be complete, personal financial statements must include certain footnote disclosures. These disclosures may be made in

the body of the financial statements or in notes accompanying
the statements and include the individuals covered by the statements, methods used to determine estimated current values including estimated income taxes on unrealized gains and losses,
identification of intangibles, and maturities, interest rates, and
collateral for all receivables and debt.

Glossary

Activity ratios a measure of management's effectiveness at using assets.

Administrative expenses costs associated with managing a company.

Audit report prepared by an accountant that attests to the accuracy and fairness of the presentation of data in the financial statements of a company in accordance with generally accepted accounting principles.

Balance sheet a report of resources owned and debts owed by a company at a particular point in time; includes assets, liabilities, and owners' equity.

Bonds a form of long-term debt, usually repaid in ten to twenty years.

Budget a formal, quantitative statement of management's expectations of future income, financial position, and cash flows. The master budget summarizes goals and objectives for all subunits of a company.

Business plan a comprehensive document that describes a company's past, current, and projected operatings and operating results.

Business resources those items of value that the business possesses and that can be used to produce a profit.

Common size statements a variation of ratio analysis that converts items in a financial statement to percentages of the largest item in the statement.

Compilation a report by an accountant issued after checking a company's financial statements for proper form, appropriate disclosures, and accurate mathematics.

Consolidated statement the combined financial statements of a parent company and its subsidiaries.

Contingency a situation in which the company stands to gain or lose as the result of a past transaction or event.

Depreciation the assignment of historical cost of a long-lived productive asset to production periods. Land cannot be depreciated.

Earnings per share (EPS) company earnings divided by the number of shares of stock outstanding.

Encumbrance a budgeted amount of money that has been committed but not yet actually paid out.

Equity property rights.

Expenses decreases in owners' equity produced by outflows of assets.

Factory overhead total of all indirect costs of production, such as costs of supervisor labor, maintenance, equipment and factory depreciation, manufacturing supplies, energy, and insurance.

FIFO a method of recording inventory flow by listing First-In-First-Out; assumes the oldest units are sold first.

Fully diluted EPS   includes in the denominator all items that could reasonably be converted to common stock.

Historical cost   original cost of an asset.

Horizontal common size analysis   a variation of common size statements that uses the statements of a prior year as a base and expresses each component of a future year as a percentage of the corresponding component in the base year.

Income statement   a report of the results of business activities for a period of time, typically one year. Includes revenues and expenses.

Intangible assets   long-lived productive assets that do not have a physical existence. These include patents, copyrights, trademarks, franchises, organizational costs, purchased goodwill, and research-and-development costs.

Inventory   current assets, carried in the balance sheet at historical cost or at the lower of cost or market value.

Liabilities   accounting term for debts. Current liabilities are those expected to be paid within one year of the date on the balance sheet. Noncurrent liabilities are not expected to be paid within one year of the date on the balance sheet.

LIFO   Last-In-Last-Out method of inventory flow.

Liquidity ratios   measure a company's ability to pay its short-term debt.

Matching principle   requires that costs directly associated with producing a certain revenue be expected in the same period that the revenue is recorded.

Obligations   amounts owed to nonowners.

Overall (debt and equity) ratios   measure the relative size of claims of long-term creditors compared to the claims or property rights of owners.

Owners' equity   accounting term for owners' investment; includes both owners' initial investment and reinvestment of company earnings not distributed to owners.

Period costs   nonmanufacturing costs, such as selling and administration.

Periodicity   the assumption that a company's life must be divided into periods of time in order to measure profit or loss.

Product costs   manufacturing costs.

Profitability ratios   measure of either management's operating efficiency or stock performance.

Receivables   all claims expected to be settled in cash, primarily as a result of the company's trade or business.

Responsibility center   a company unit that has control over its costs, revenues, and/or investment and has its own budget. May be a cost center, a profit center, or an investment center.

Retained earnings   profits earned by the business and not paid out as dividends to the owners.

Revenue   increases in owners' equity produced by inflows of assets as a result of doing business.

Revenue recognition principle requires that revenue be recorded when the activities necessary to sell a good or provide a service have been completed, regardless of whether cash has been collected or a receivable created.

Review report issued by an accountant after reviewing a company's financial statements, but without performing the tests done for a full audit that guarantee compliance with generally accepted accounting principles.

Segment analysis assessment of performance of divisions, categories, sales territories, or product lines of a company.

Selling expenses costs associated with producing sales, including sales personnel salaries and commissions, office staff salaries, payroll taxes and pension expenses related to the sales staff, advertising, delivery and shipping costs, and telephone expense.

Short term one year or one company operating cycle, whichever is greater.

Statement of cash flows describes all of the changes that have occurred in the balance sheet during the fiscal year in terms of their effect on cash.

Stock a share in the company's ownership. May be preferred or common.

Stock option stock right issued to corporate employees and officers entitling them to acquire common stock at a preset price within a specified period of time.

Stock warrant an entitlement that allows the holder to acquire shares of stock at a fixed price within a specified period of time.

Treasury stock stock issued by a company and later reacquired but neither canceled nor retired.

Trend analysis type of horizontal analysis that presents the current year's performance as a percent of the performance of a prior year.

Uncollectible account bad debt or doubtful account.

Weighted-average inventory inventory flow measure that charges both ending inventory and cost of goods sold with the weighted-average cost of all units available for sale.

Index

BARRON'S BUSINESS KEYS Each "key" explains 50 important concepts and contains a glossary and index. Each book: Paperback, 160 pp., 4³/₁₆″ × 7″, $4.95, Can. $6.50. ISBN Prefix: 0-8120

Titles include:

Books may be purchased at your bookstore, or by mail from Barron's. Enclose check or money order for total amount plus sales tax where applicable and 10% for postage and handling (minimum charge $1.75, Canada $2.00). Prices subject to change without notice.

Barron's Educational Series, Inc.
250 Wireless Blvd., Hauppauge, NY 11788
Call toll-free: 1-800-645-3476, in NY: 1-800-257-5729
In Canada: Georgetown Book Warehouse
34 Armstrong Ave., Georgetown, Ont. L7G 4R9
Call toll-free: 1-800-247-7160